I0127519

ECONOMIC INTEGRATION

OTHER BOOKS FROM
THE CENTER OF INTERNATIONAL STUDIES
PRINCETON UNIVERSITY

Gabriel A. Almond, *The Appeals of Communism*

Bernard C. Cohen, *The Political Process and Foreign Policy: The Making of the Japanese Peace Settlement*

Percy E. Corbett, *Law in Diplomacy*

W. W. Kaufmann, editor, *Military Policy and National Security*

Klaus Knorr, *The War Potential of Nations*

Lucian W. Pye, *Guerrilla Communism in Malaya*

Charles De Visscher, *Theory and Reality in Public International Law*, translated by P. E. Corbett

Myron Weiner, *Party Politics in India*

Economic Integration

Theoretical Assumptions and Consequences of European Unification

BY ROLF SANNWALD AND
JACQUES STOHLER

TRANSLATED BY HERMAN F. KARREMAN

FOREWORD BY ALBERT COPPÉ

PRINCETON, NEW JERSEY
PRINCETON UNIVERSITY PRESS
1959

Copyright © 1959, by Princeton University Press
ALL RIGHTS RESERVED
L.C. Card No. 59-11125

❖

This book is a translation of
Wirtschaftliche Integration:
Theoretische Voraussetzungen und Folgen eines
europäischen Zusammenschlusses
by Rolf Sannwald and Jacques Stohler, 1958
Kyklos-Verlag Basel
J.C.B. Mohr (Paul Siebeck) Tübingen

❖

Printed in the United States of America
by Princeton University Press
at Princeton, New Jersey

FOREWORD

The High Authority of the European Coal and Steel Community has often sponsored the scholarly study of problems which lie beyond the more limited scope of its own activities. In doing so, it is pursuing two ends. First, theoretical research, in abstracting from the confusing complexity of day-to-day problems, is particularly well adapted to shed light on the inner logic of the idea of integration. Second, the systematic application of the results obtained by scientific research is of great importance to the High Authority.

The authors of the present book, selected and supported by the research department of the List Gesellschaft, have succeeded in achieving both ends. Therefore, it is a pleasure for the High Authority to have the opportunity to write the foreword to a study which demonstrates the fruitfulness of cooperation between men of theory and men of practice.

ALBERT COPPÉ

Luxembourg   Vice-President of the High Authority,
January 1958   European Coal and Steel Community

PREFACE TO THE SWISS EDITION

"So FAR there has been no international, or at least inter-European, organ to bring together, in a common effort, the experts of science, economics, administration, and politics. It therefore seems indispensable, in the era of the Coal and Steel Community and similar European attempts at integration, to set up a research institute in which experts from different countries could first examine and then discuss international and particularly inter-European economic problems. . . ." To meet this requirement has been one of the main tasks of the List Gesellschaft since 1955.

With the appearance of this eighth volume of the publications of its research department, the List Gesellschaft has definitely come closer to the goal that it set for itself and has in some ways surpassed it. The combination of research and subsequent discussion with men of affairs has proved very fruitful in the writing of the present volume.

This publication by two Swiss collaborators, Dr. Rolf Sannwald and Dr. Jacques Stohler, deals with a theme whose aspects were developed in a continuous exchange of opinion with the experts of the High Authority of the European Coal and Steel Community. This close cooperation, which has been stressed in the foreword by Professor Albert Coppé, the Vice-President of the Community, as an essential feature of the study, took two forms. First, the division chiefs and senior officers of the High Authority placed at the disposal of the authors all the documents and other materials accumulated by them in the course of five years. In addition, at various phases of the research, the work of the authors was discussed in carefully prepared meetings held at intervals of about two months. Besides Franz Etzel, also a Vice-President of the Coal and Steel Community, to whom we are greatly indebted for his sympathetic encouragement, the regular and leading participants in the discussions were Dr. Rudolf Regul and Prof. Dr. Rolf Wagenfuehr, and usually Dr. Hans Michaelis as well as other experts. Regular participants from the List Gesellschaft included members of the advisory committee on research—in particular, its secretary, Prof. Dr. Erwin von Beckerath—and the undersigned director of the research department. These conferences, usually attended by a great number of additional participants from the High Authority, contributed substantially to the direction and substance of the research. The presence of men experienced in practice prevented an unrealistic theoretical approach. On the other hand, the theses of theoreticians may have stimulated the responsible officers of the High Authority to think through formally matters which they have to administer in day-to-day work.

What emerged from this interchange of theoretical and practical ideas was further enriched by personal contact of the authors with leading persons in the coal and steel sectors of Germany and France. In this way, they succeeded in matching opinions and experiences collected from the viewpoint of supranational management with information on the economic goals that the countries set for themselves. The result is a well-balanced study.

The authors have endeavored to analyze the material they gathered with a rigorous application of modern economic theory. That in such a procedure Lord Keynes has been advanced as a chief witness need hardly be said. Others in the field of international economics—such as Haberler, Kindleberger, Samuelson, Stolper, Tinbergen, and Viner—whose contributions the authors drew on for the development of their theory, must be mentioned here with appreciation. Moreover, the authors want to stress that they owe a good deal to James Edward Meade, whose fundamental studies in the field of economic integration have guided their research at essential points.

It is hardly possible for the List Gesellschaft to single out all those who, by advice or financial contributions, have supported this study. We are indebted to all of them.

While the present volume has come into existence with the

help of successful cooperation by many, the authors, as objective scholars, have written with the sole purpose of contributing to the knowledge of economic unification.* The result of their work is—with the exception of two fields, agriculture and transport, which have been excluded and reserved for subsequent treatment—a theory of economic integration which has not, to our knowledge, hitherto been presented in such completeness anywhere in the economic literature.

Because of the basic character of this research, the book does not contain recommendations or prescriptions for the politician. What economic theory can achieve, and what Dr. Sannwald and Dr. Stohler have achieved, lies on a different level. It consists, as every economic analysis does, of the selection and classification of problems, and their presentation in a logical structure, in order to work out "solutions" for the selected problems with the help of economic theory. These "solutions" consist essentially of proof that certain goals, regarded as desirable from the point of view of economic policy, can be achieved only under certain specific conditions—and under no others—and also in the discovery and analysis of economically possible alternatives. Such theory will be of interest not only to scholars but also to responsible policymakers. To the latter, such theory makes clear what the economic consequences and conditions are of the decisions which they must make under the influence of extra-economic objectives. Finally, the book should also prove useful to the student of economics and institutions.

HARRY W. ZIMMERMANN

Basel
January 1958

---

* Naturally, only the authors are therefore responsible for the volume; neither the Coal and Steel Community nor the List Gesellschaft shares this responsibility, although Professor Salin wishes to emphasize that he personally shares fully the views of the authors.

PREFACE TO THE AMERICAN EDITION

COMPARED with prewar practice, the postwar attempts at integration in Western Europe have been one of the most unusual developments on the international scene. The pioneers and zealots of this unification movement may feel frustrated with the slow pace and the as yet uncertain measure of their achievement. To the outside observer, however, the record seems remarkable as an experiment in breaking out of the traditional confines of nationalist institutions and seeking the satisfaction of a variety of needs—economic and technological, political and military—within a wider and perhaps more effective framework for decision-making than the small nation-state can afford.

This experiment in institutional innovation has aroused substantial interest in the United States. However, the main justification for a translation of this book—which is, after all, concerned with economic theory rather than the politics of integration—lies in its excellence as a treatise on the theory of economic integration. To be sure, most of the theory presented in the volume is not new to the specialist, and the book indeed owes a great deal to the previous studies of Meade, Viner, Haberler, and other economists. But its excellence is threefold. First, it summarizes in one volume a fairly large and widely scattered literature. Second, building on the existing literature, it presents further additional refinements and, moreover, covers the subject more comprehensively than has been the case thus far. Finally, the book is painstakingly precise in taking the reader through the study of numerous models.

Some portions of the original edition, thought to be much less interesting to American than European readers, have been left out of the English edition. It would have been possible to delete more, but this would have deprived the volume of its third claim to excellence.

The translation was undertaken by Herman F. Karreman of the Econometric Research Program, Princeton University.

PREFACE TO AMERICAN EDITION

The English version was edited by Jean MacLachlan and myself. The List Gesellschaft and the Center of International Studies, Princeton University, jointly provided the financial means to make the publication of the American edition possible.

KLAUS KNORR

Princeton, New Jersey
Center of International Studies
August 1958

CONTENTS

ment revenue – The structure of the tariff systems – The structure of demand – Increasing marginal costs – Primary, secondary, and tertiary effects of a tariff change – Divergences inside a country – Advantages of mass production – International distribution of income – The case of quantitative restrictions – Discrimination by commodities

CONTENTS

CONTENTS

ECONOMIC INTEGRATION

INTRODUCTION:

The Relative Economic Stagnation of Europe

SINCE WORLD WAR I the United States of America has ranked economically first among all nations. The moment of the beginning of the "American Era" is significant: it coincided with the beginning of the process of disintegration in the world economy. While the American economy has been able since then to develop on the basis of a single market spanning a whole continent, the multilateral equilibrium of trade among the nations in Europe has been disturbed by the rise of economic nationalism.

The European economy was at least functionally integrated before World War I—i.e., interference by borders and customs regions was reduced to a minimum. And the currencies of the most important economies stood in a constant relationship to gold and thereby to each other. The mobility of goods and productive factors—in particular, of capital—was increased by these favorable conditions to an extent that has not been attained since then. In that era, there was an almost absolute security of property and person throughout Europe. "These factors of order, security and uniformity, which Europe had never before enjoyed over so wide and populous a territory or for so long a period, prepared the way for the organization of that vast mechanism of transport, coal distribution and foreign trade, which made possible an industrial order of life in the dense urban centers of new population."[1]

This well-organized and therefore also delicate economic system was profoundly disturbed by World War I and completely destroyed by the conditions of peace. The result was not only a splitting-up of the European Continent into a multitude of sovereign states, some of them new, but also the

[1] J. M. Keynes, *The Economic Consequences of the Peace*, London, 1920, pp. 13ff.

3

destruction of the intra-Continental amalgamation of national economies. Political borders are not economically unimportant; on the contrary, they are full of meaning, particularly when they are multiplied.

One of the major factors which in part caused and in part accompanied the disintegration of Europe was the antagonism between Germany and France. Economic nationalism flourished in the interwar period, but the new power constellation which emerged during World War II made the most progressive European minds realize that the future of West Europe between the two great power blocs could be saved only by a reduction of national sovereignties on behalf of Continental unification. The French declaration of May 9, 1950, which led to the formation of the European Coal and Steel Community, manifested for the first time the willingness of a government to overcome old antagonisms and to adopt in their stead a program of European integration. As Robert Schuman wrote: "The peace of the world cannot be safeguarded without creative efforts of the same magnitude as the dangers that threaten it. The contribution which an organized and vigorous Europe can make to civilization is indispensable for the preservation of peace. In declaring itself the champion of a unified Europe for more than twenty years, France has always taken as its main object the service of peace. Europe was not founded, we have had war instead. Europe will be built neither overnight, nor in one fell swoop: it will be built by concrete developments, by creating true solidarity first. The collectivity of European nations requires the elimination of the centuries-old opposition of France and Germany: the move has to be inaugurated by France and Germany. To that end, the French government proposes to proceed immediately to action on a modest but decisive scale."[2]

The extent to which Europe can organize itself as a power depends on its economic potential. It can maintain itself stra-

[2] P. Reuter, *La communauté européenne du charbon et de l'acier*, Paris, 1953, Preface by Robert Schuman, pp. 3f.

tegically, politically, and ideologically only when it is saved from the status of an underdeveloped area. "Only those countries which can actually hold their own militarily without foreign support are able to determine their political course by themselves and not only to put up with history, but also to shape it."[3] Historical experience supports this thesis.[4]

Since the middle of the eighteenth century, competition for the largest productive capacity has always been related to the struggle for military and political leadership in the world. Indeed, the advocates of European economic integration take the increase of production as the main objective of their efforts, because the Continent has fallen behind industrially in the course of the last century—at least so far as the comparison between the heavy industry of Western Europe and that of the Eastern bloc is concerned.

The parallel that can be drawn between the aspiration for political power and the productive capacity of a nation can best be traced in the strategic sector of the iron and steel industry; and this correlation remains significant in the present day for several reasons. First, it is probable that iron and steel still represent the foundation of military strength, despite the newest developments of arms technology. During the last few years, steel amounted quantitatively to 95 per cent of world metal production and, in American aircraft production in World War II, more steel was used than any other metal. Second, the steel industry is enjoying a clear priority in the Soviet Union during the Cold War period.

If one traces this parallel from the beginning of the Industrial Revolution, one observes at once how remarkably the equilibrium of pig iron production was maintained among the various West European states in the eighteenth century, before the advent of imperialism. Though France enjoyed a cer-

[3] Carlo Schmid, "Europa zwischen Ost und West," *Aussenpolitik* (1957), page 219.
[4] Cf. John B. Parrish, "Iron and Steel in the Balance of World Power," *The Journal of Political Economy* (1956), pp. 369ff.

tain lead in 1790, no country was then in the position, on the basis of productive capacity, to bring a constant military pressure to bear upon its neighbors. After 1800 this equilibrium was destroyed by the English Industrial Revolution, which set in with the force of an explosion. British iron production increased about 3000 per cent between 1800 and 1870 and, at the end of this period of growth lasting for seven decades, England contributed half of the world's iron production. The era of England's lead in the concert of Great Powers had started; her Victorian hegemony rested on the solid foundation of the largest iron output in the world.

After 1870, the industrialization of three new candidates for world hegemony, the United States, Germany, and Russia, expanded rapidly. The growth of American iron and steel production temporarily exceeded even the earlier British rate and the share of the United States in total output went up to 40 per cent. American isolationism explains the phenomenon that for a long time the political predominance of the United States existed only potentially and that an industrial straggler, Germany, could gradually claim a leading political position. German iron and steel capacity expanded after 1870 at a higher rate than that of any other European country. Moreover, the Russian process of growth came to a standstill around the turn of the century, so that by 1913, one year before the German declaration of war, Germany was producing more iron than England and France together.

At the outbreak of World War I steel capacity was about equally distributed between the Central Powers (21.5 million tons annually) and the European Allied Powers (22.5 million tons). The scales went down on the side of the Central Powers when the United States, with an annual capacity of 40 million tons, entered the war in 1917.

Through the Treaty of Versailles, German steel capacity was reduced from 19 to 12 million tons as a consequence of the return of Lorraine to France and, by and large, the distribution of capacity which had prevailed at the turn of the century was restored. After 1920 the United States finally reached the stage of industrial supremacy that Great Britain had occupied in the nineteenth century. But, behind the Treaty of Versailles and the "equilibrium" of Continental iron and steel that it brought about, a new constellation shaped up which, as later years proved, was unstable and explosive. The political borders that were newly established by the Allies impeded the free exchange of iron ore and coal and consequently the economic development of the Continent. The European share in world iron and steel production declined slowly but persistently.

Two factors contributed to the change in the global structure of steel capacity in the 1930's. While the Western democracies suffered from economic stagnation, two countries with planned economies—the Soviet Union and, to a lesser extent, Japan—started to increase their production forcefully. The Soviet Union attained the highest rate of growth of all countries; its output increased from 5 million tons in 1929 to 10 million in 1937. Consequently, it became more and more clear that within a measurable span of time Russia would become a steel power ranking only after the United States, and that Germany, which had reoccupied this position in 1937, would descend to third place. The total mobilization of the factors of production in the Third Reich therefore made sense, viewed from the angle of pure power politics and the race for the greatest steel capacity.

Germany entered World War II with about the same capacity as in World War I. With its 20 million ton capacity, it matched the 20 million tons of France and England together, which were later increased by an annual 18 million tons of Russian steel. The early military success of the *Blitzkrieg* soon shifted the weight considerably. Germany's army occupied an area with a steel production of 25 million tons and, on top of that, at the culmination of the Russian campaign it controlled 4.5 million tons of Soviet capacity. The Axis had for a time in Europe a capacity of 60 million tons of steel at its command: the British-Russian alliance, however, had only 26.5 million tons. As in World War I, it was the military intervention of the United States that shifted the balance of steel production and at the same time decided the outcome of the struggle by increasing the capacity of the "United Nations" to 110 million tons.

The German defeat in World War I had resulted in a restoration of the equilibrium among the steel powers of the Continent as well as Anglo-American supremacy. The old Continental equilibrium could not be established again after World War II. The Soviet Union emerged with a considerable headstart as the second most important steel producer of the world, and the center of European steel production had shifted definitely eastward (see Table 1).

TABLE 1

Principal Producers of Basic Steel in 1913, 1954, and 1956
(millions of tons)

1913 Production		1954 Production		1956 Production	
1. U.S.A.	31.8	1. U.S.A.	80.1*	1. U.S.A.	104.5
2. Germany	18.9	2. Soviet Union	41.0	2. Soviet Union	48.6
3. Great Britain	7.8	3. Great Britain	18.8	3. West Germany	23.2
4. France	7.0	4. West Germany	17.4	4. Great Britain	21.0
5. Russia	4.8	5. France	10.6	5. France	13.4

* The recession in the United States obscured the figures for 1954; US capacity amounted to 114 million tons in this year. (Derived from statements of John B. Parrish, *op.cit.*)

This shift in the order of the top-ranking industrial countries indicates a basic change. This development was accelerated in the 1940's when the Soviet Union added to its capacity by territorial annexations. The strategic importance of Soviet capacity is, moreover, greater than is indicated by the number of tons because a larger share of Russian steel production, compared with that of the West, is reserved for military purposes.

Before World War II, three-quarters of Europe's steel was produced west of Poland. The share of West Europe had fallen to about half by 1954 (56 per cent in 1956). In addition, while three separate states (Great Britain, West Germany, and France) have the main share of the West European capacity, the Eastern share is controlled by only one power.

The necessity for cooperation among the former European rivals follows not only from a newly discovered feeling of solidarity, but particularly from their recognition of an inferior potential. The strategic position of the Continent has been strengthened materially by placing national industries under one administration—the High Authority of the Coal and Steel Community. Nevertheless, the Community will not be able to stand comparison with the Eastern bloc in the near future. A steel output in the Eastern bloc (Soviet Union, Czechoslovakia, German Democratic Republic, Poland, Hungary, and Rumania) of 59 million tons in 1955 confronts an output by the ECSC countries of 52 million tons. The production target of the Eastern bloc is 89 million tons in 1960, while the ECSC hopes to produce about 70 million tons by then.[5]

Apart from its strategic significance, the integration of the coal and steel sectors represents no more than a start. Problems raised by the present stage of the industrial revolution can no longer be solved within the narrow framework of the individual economies of Europe[6]—and this the *less* so because

[5] Cf. *Statistical Information of the European Coal and Steel Community*, Luxembourg, November-December 1956, page 3.

[6] Cf. E. Salin, "Industrielle Revolution," *Kyklos* (1956), pp. 299ff. The leaders of the delegations in their report to the government-appointed committee at the Conference of Messina gave, in all frankness, this opinion about the facts resulting from the compartmentation of the European market: "There is in Europe no automobile factory large enough to stand competition with the productive American machines. None of the countries on the Continent is in the position to build large commercial aircraft without help from outside. The knowledge, obtained with great sacrifices in a few European countries, in the field of atomic energy, is negligible compared with what the United States makes available to its industry and to other countries. . . . None of our countries is in a position to afford the extremely high costs of research and basic investment needed for exploitation of the technological revolution in the atomic age. On the other hand, the exploitation of the productive possibilities presented by this new source of energy, and the new processes based upon

9

the American economy, even by utilizing a traditional technology, was able to advance strikingly in the period between the wars—an advance which has not yet been matched by Europe despite the accelerated growth since the war. This is clearly indicated by a comparison of the per capita real income of the United States and the European Coal and Steel Community (see Table 2). Real income per capita of the

TABLE 2

Per Capita Gross National Product of the ECS Community and the United States based on official exchange rates (1) and actual purchasing power parity (2) in prices of 1954 dollars.*

	Community		Index 1950 = 100	U.S.A.		Index 1950 = 100	Proportion Community: USA Index USA = 100
YEAR	(1)	(2)		(1)	(2)		
1950	604	862	100	2126	2126	100	41
1951	648	919	107	2253	2253	106	41
1952	661	940	109	2283	2283	107	41
1953	693	905	114	2329	2329	110	42
1954	729	1035	120	2259	2259	106	46
1955	780	1109	129	2353	2353	111	47

* Source: OEEC, *General Statistics*, January 1957; and OEEC, *Comparative National Products and Price Levels*, by M. Gilbert and Associates, Paris, 1957.

countries of the ECSC amounted to less than half of the corresponding American figures in the period from 1950 to 1955. On the other hand, the indices reveal that after World War II economic growth was more rapid in Western Europe than in the United States.

Some of the most important reasons for the American lead are worth mentioning. The United States is better equipped with sources of energy and raw materials than Europe. Until recently the marginal productivity of labor rose, with increas-

it, will be substantially impeded by the narrowness of European markets. The technological revolution initiated by atomic energy would shatter our obsolete economic structure in a couple of years." Report of the Leaders of the Delegations to the Government Committee Appointed for the Conference of Messina, Brussels, 1956, pp. 9ff.

ing production, in most of the raw materials-producing industries; this applies to coal, petroleum, natural gas, iron ore, and
pig iron. Measured in labor productivity, the comparative advantage of the United States in these basic industries is almost
twice that in most of the processing industries. This advantage
is reflected in the relative costs of steel and other metals,
electricity, and other types of energy; and causes to some extent a reduction in the costs of capital goods. On the other
hand, insofar as relative prices influence the structure of production, the European price structure favors consumption
rather than investment.[7]

Consequently, the American entrepreneurs faced a situation
in which labor became scarcer, in relation to other productive
factors, than was the case in Europe; hence, they used more
capital and in particular more energy per labor hour than did
European entrepreneurs. As a result, American productivity
in the basic industries is not only greater than in Europe but
also greater than in the manufacturing industries of the United
States itself. However, the availability of raw materials and
certain sources of energy is gradually becoming smaller and
requires increasing investment if the increase in productivity
is to be kept up. But even when the rate of growth in the raw
materials-producing industries diminishes, this still does not
mean a decline in the comparative advantage of the American
versus the European economy in this sector. Coal mining has
fallen behind manufacturing industry in Europe, though coal
is the most important European source of energy. Moreover,
the United States is in a better position than most of the European countries to solve its energy problems by technical improvements and, thanks to its high reserves of foreign exchange,
by imports.

In general, it is assumed that competition is less keen in

[7] Cf. A. Maddison, "Industrial Productivity Growth in Europe and in
the U.S.A.," *Economica* (1954), pp. 308ff. M. Gilbert and I. B. Kravis,
*An International Comparison of National Products and the Purchasing
Power of Currencies*, OEEC, 1954, page 33.

West Europe than in the United States; but this assumption has never been proved and can only be based upon differences in the institutional framework. First, the past economic expansion in the United States proceeded chiefly with geographic expansion, or at least with the relocation of population and urban centers. The growth in demand therefore came largely from the increased demand in new regions and could easily be satisfied by the firm that settled first in the new localities. The saving of transport costs and other advantages of market proximity sufficed to undo consumers' preferences for long-established producers in other regions. Consequently, there is some similarity between the expansion of the United States and the economic growth of underdeveloped countries: the erection of mass production plants was not hindered by competition with old established firms. Unlike the situation in the underdeveloped countries, however, bottlenecks in the supply of raw materials and semi-manufactures were of less importance in the United States because of its great natural wealth.

On the other hand, few West European countries were and are large enough to enjoy the advantages of a regional development within their national borders. True, the European countries experienced an industrial revolution and, thereafter, temporary periods of accelerated growth. But this expansion cannot be compared with the regional development of the United States; in Europe, industrialization was retarded by insufficient international mobility of capital, labor, know-how, and often of raw materials, too.

Another factor which also contributes to the advantage of the American over the European competitor is the highly developed distribution system of the United States. This network permits even small firms to service numerous retail dealers over a large market; at the same time, the system makes competition more impersonal. A great number of more or less anonymous rivals face the individual producer and it is not difficult for him to penetrate the market of his competitors, since the losses thereby incurred by his rivals are shared by a great number of producers and consequently do not weigh too heavily on any one. On the other hand, the European producer is in general linked up with a less rational and rather regionally organized system of distribution. His sales media are less numerous and his retail dealers are concentrated in a small geographic area. Relationships among competitors are therefore quite different in Europe than in the United States. The distance between European competitors is smaller and there is a lack of anonymity and consequently of willingness to penetrate a new market. The structure of European competition is at the same time more oligopolistic than in the United States. Under these circumstances, expansion of the market of an individual producer is difficult. Inside the geographic borders of his inherited market it is thwarted by the oligopolistic relationship with his competitors, and outside these borders it requires the troublesome and expensive establishment of relations with unknown retail dealers. Moreover, every expansion of the market injures a small number of competitors.

There is also a difference between the United States and West Europe in the character of the firm. In a stationary economy, an enterprise which changes over to mass production cannot capture a new market but must acquire a larger share in markets traditionally served by its competitors. Such a process develops rather smoothly in an economy in which marginal producers are willing to give up or to rearrange their production. The high rate of turnover among existing firms and the frequency of mergers suggest that this willingness is present in the United States. A quite different picture emerges from comparable West European data. The rate of business failure is probably less in England, France, and Germany than in the United States, and, so far as mergers are concerned, they are numerous only in West Germany.

On the whole, the family enterprises in West Europe have in general a power of inertia by far exceeding their natural lifetime. There are several reasons for this. First, the preference for an independent position is stronger in Europe, where social status still has a special meaning, than in the United States. Second, European experience of prolonged unemployment has led the small entrepreneur to place a high value on independence and the security of employment that goes with it. Third, some West European countries have experienced pronounced inflation, which has led from time to time to an expansion of income from profit and a contraction of income from securities bearing a fixed interest. That, too, has favored the independent earner over the employee. Fourth, closing down an enterprise causes a capital loss; there is a strong temptation to postpone this as long as possible and to wait for a rise in prices. On the other hand, in the United States it is easier to obtain information on technical improvements and the business outlook. Consequently, the owners of small and outdated enterprises see their actual situation more clearly and are therefore more willing to take a capital loss. Furthermore, the European way of doing business is influenced to a greater extent by traditional motives than the American way, so that it is fully conceivable that a family enterprise is carried on solely in deference to the past. Moreover, labor is in some European countries still not as well organized as in the United States. Consequently, there is a chance that the entrepreneur can compensate low productivity by low labor costs. Finally, numerous European governments adhere to a social policy directed at the preservation of small enterprises.

Since the turn of the century, the United States has had a larger domestic market than any European country.[8] The size of the economy influences the degree of standardization of individual products and the specialization of enterprises, plants, workers, entrepreneurs, and whole branches of industry. The advantages of such specialization increase with an expanding economy. It is occasionally emphasized that the advantages of producing standardized commodities in large quantities can also be obtained in small countries,[9] so that a small country

[8] Cf. A. Maddison, op.cit., page 315.
[9] J. Viner, The Customs Union Issue, New York, 1950, page 46; also

could, for instance, maintain an optimal auto-assembly plant. However, a product often requires constituents or capital goods —for instance, machine tools, large presses, etc.—the acquisition of which exceeds by far the capacity of a small country. Of course, such countries can import those products; but the producer who supplies the finished product will hardly benefit from the advantages of mass production if his own (finished) product is not homogeneous with commodities produced elsewhere. Also, when a small country is large enough to set up plants of maximum size for all the products that it manufactures, it will often not be able to afford several big enterprises with a highly developed system of competition. Consequently its market will be dominated by a monopolist who is protected by tariff walls and will have little incentive to increase his productivity. A large country or a larger integrated market will always be favored when there are savings from the standardization of products. For, under those circumstances, large enterprises generally dominate only a part of the market and consequently—because of competition—show a strong interest in technical improvements and increased productivity. In any case, it is not accidental that, so far as productivity in the manufacturing industry is concerned, the United States has the greatest advantage over Europe in standardized mass-products such as radios, cars, rubber tires, electric bulbs, food cans, glass containers, etc.

Moreover, the American entrepreneurs faced a market which expanded much faster as a result of population growth than that of any country in West Europe. Their expectations for the future were therefore more optimistic than those of European entrepreneurs, though the 1930's smothered this optimism. They could thus maintain a higher rate of investment and a higher rate of depreciation.

H. G. Johnson, "The Criteria of Economic Advantage," *Bulletin of the Oxford University Institute of Statistics* (1957), page 34; F. Gehrels and B. Johnston, "The Economic Gains of European Integration," *The Journal of Political Economy* (1955), pp. 275ff.

The rate of investment has been very high in most of the European countries since the end of World War II and that is undoubtedly one of the principal reasons for the rapid growth in productivity during this period. However, it will probably be politically difficult for the governments to maintain a high rate of investment when they are at the same time forced to adopt large military expenses. In countries like France, this has been achieved by continuous inflation. Under inflationary pressure, moreover, investments are not always made in the most productive direction (this applies also to repressed inflation).

American investments in the development of technology have for a long time been larger than European ones. Institutions of higher learning educate a larger part of the population in the United States than in Europe. The number of college graduates per capita is about three times as high in the United States as in Great Britain, and the expenditures of American universities on scientific research amount to seven times those of Britain. The share of the American population in higher education has risen extremely fast in the last fifty years and it is likely to continue to rise in the future. In 1950 the per capita number of teachers in Great Britain at institutions of higher learning (with students aged 18 and over) was 32 per cent of the corresponding American figure; in France it was 7 per cent and in Germany 18 per cent.[10] The level of American higher education is on the average lower than that of most European countries, but it is probably higher in the fields of technology and business administration. The enlistment of a large number of college graduates by American industry has obviously raised productivity to an extent that has helped to develop a willingness to adopt new ideas and to propagate the employment of the best methods of production. But the support of a large number of students would be a much heavier burden on the relatively poor economies of Europe than it is on the American economy, if higher education in

[10] M. Gilbert and I. B. Kravis, *op.cit.*, page 180.

Europe were organized in conformity with that of the United States.

Finally, the United States has benefited from its smaller dependence on foreign trade. In many European countries structural distortions have often been caused by changes in trade relationships. Many industries also suffered sudden setbacks in their foreign markets, so that a large share of their capacity remained unused. The governments tried to protect industries in such situations or carried out adjustment plans to facilitate the continuation of non-profitable enterprises. In the United States only a few industries run into trouble as a consequence of losing foreign markets.

All these factors have contributed to the small rate of investment and the low productivity of capital equipment in Europe.

The higher real income per capita in the United States, however, cannot be attributed only to the presence of a common market; this has also been pointed out by the Economic Commission for Europe.[11] It is quite possible that the capital wealth of the country or the other factors mentioned above are important reasons for higher productivity. But all these factors, some of which are attributable to a common market, do not suffice to explain why the European standard of living lags behind the American. The American economy therefore points the way for Europe, by clearly demonstrating the superiority of a single Continental market over comparted individual national economic systems. This superiority is based, among other things, on the undisturbed free trade among the individual states of the American federation. This free trade increases productivity by promoting specialization in the form of a more intensive division of labor, by permitting the advantages of mass production to be exploited, and by increasing competition among entrepreneurs and, with it, the disposition to innovate technologically.

[11] Cf. ECE, *Economic Survey of Europe in 1956*, Geneva, 1957, ch. IV, page 17.

CHAPTER I

UNIVERSAL FREE TRADE

1. THE PREREQUISITES TO FREE TRADE

THE FUNDAMENTAL THESIS of the theory of international trade is that free trade leads, under certain assumptions, to the highest possible standard of living. But the assumptions are as important as the thesis itself; they are:

(1) There must be full employment and no excess capacity. (2) Prices must be equal to marginal costs. (3) Temporary difficulties in adjusting the structure of production must be disregarded. (4) For reasons of computation, welfare, or the standard of living, is considered equal to the value of production at free trade prices.

If these four conditions are satisfied, every utilization of productive factors that is not in conformity with the law of comparative costs will be less advantageous than the allocation of resources under free trade.[1]

Condition 1 was not mentioned in the classical theory of international trade, since it was implicitly assumed that it was always satisfied. However, it follows from Keynesian theory, as Modigliani and Leontief have shown, that the possibility of unemployment exists under the assumption of a labor supply function which has infinite elasticity in relation to money wages.[2] Since, according to our assumptions, standard of living and value of production are considered to be synonymous and an increase in the rate of employment results in a rise in pro-

---

[1] Cf. J. Tinbergen, *International Economic Integration*, Amsterdam, 1954, pp. 54ff.

[2] In technical language, the labor supply function is homogeneous of zero degree in relation to money wages. In the terminology of Irving Fisher, workers, as suppliers, are subject to a money illusion. Cf. F. Modigliani, "Liquidity Preference and the Theory of Interest and Money," *Readings in Monetary Theory*, London, 1952, page 186; and W. Leontief, "Keynes' General Theory and the Classicists," *The New Economics*, ed. by S. E. Harris, New York, 1948, pp. 232ff.

duction, it is impossible to have maximum welfare with unemployment and excess capacity.

Condition 2 implies that there is perfect competition, in the sense that neither buyers nor sellers of factor products or commodities are able to influence the market price of the products. On the one hand, the marginal disutility of labor must be equal to the real wage in this situation, and the marginal disutility of liquidity or—depending on the theory of interest employed— the marginal rate of time preference must be equal to the rate of interest;[3] these equalities determine the supply of productive factors. Furthermore, factor prices must be equal to the value of the marginal product of the factors concerned; these equalities determine the demand for productive factors. On the other hand, the marginal production costs of a commodity must be equal to its price; this equality determines the supply of commodities. Finally, the marginal utility of consuming a commodity must be equal to its price; this equality determines the demand for it.

It follows from these equalities that the marginal disutility of labor or of forgoing liquidity must be equal to the marginal utility of the marginal product of the productive factor. But this equality is in reality never fulfilled, mainly for three reasons: (1) There is in reality never perfect competition. (2) There are in reality "external" and "internal economies" and "diseconomies," i.e., there is a divergence between the social and the private products of a productive factor.[4] If, for instance, a landowner drains his land to increase his wheat production, his wheat production will indeed increase; but as a consequence of the drainage the land of his neighbor can also become more fertile without using additional factors. The social product then equals the increase in the wheat production of the two landowners together. (3) Government intervention for

[3] Land and capital are treated as individual, homogeneous factors of production.

[4] We mean by the social product of a factor the yield of a factor for the benefit of the community as a whole, while the private product of a factor accrues to the purchaser of the factor product.

reasons of economic policy may upset the aforementioned equalities.[5]

Condition 3 requires that the losses suffered as a result of a change toward free trade by the enterprises that were hitherto favored by a protectionist trade policy be smaller than the increase in welfare enjoyed by all the free trade countries together. This can be achieved by an appropriate choice, during the transition period, of adaptive subsidies, etc.

Condition 4 implies that the relationship between the distribution of income and the level of the standard of living is ignored. Hence, it is assumed that the marginal utility of individual incomes is independent of their size and is the same for all persons. The volume of production can then be used as a yardstick of welfare. For the sake of clarity, it should be mentioned that the paradoxical possibility exists that the national income of a country will rise as a consequence of a change toward free trade and at the same time the income from labor will decrease. On the basis of the assumptions already mentioned, we must also in this case speak of an increase in welfare.[6] Measuring welfare by *production* at free trade prices has the further advantage that it can be applied to countries which are in a position to influence their terms of trade. This would be impossible if welfare were measured by total *expenditures* at free trade prices.[7]

Hence, free trade leads to an increase in the standard of living by increasing efficiency. This is achieved in two ways: by optimization of trade, and by maximization of production.[8]

[5] Cf. J. E. Meade, *Trade and Welfare*, London, 1955, pp. 12ff.

[6] Cf. J. E. Meade, "Probleme der Wirtschaftsunion souveräner Staaten," *Probleme nationaler und internationaler Wirtschaftsordnung*, Zürich-Tübingen, 1955, page 133.

[7] Viz., there is no "optimum tariff." This would maximize the volume of production *and* of free trade, which is, however, only possible at the expense of other countries. The measurement of prosperity by production at free trade prices is, on the other hand, compatible with the maximization not of national but of world production.

[8] The way that this mechanism works has been investigated, in the case of the sector integration of the Coal and Steel Community, by K. K. F. Zawadzki, "The Economics of the Schuman Plan," *Oxford Economic*

Optimization of trade has been attained when, for each consumer, differences in commodity prices correspond to differences in the marginal utilities of these commodities, and when the commodities can be freely exchanged between countries at the same price relationships. In this case, total utility is increased without a regrouping of the productive factors. Trade is not optimized so long as it is possible to improve the position of one consumer without worsening that of another. This situation would include the possibility that there are commodities which differ as to the ratio between their marginal utility and the marginal disutility of labor and of the other necessary factor contributions. The total utility of a given pattern of production could then be increased by a variation in the volume of trade. Only when it is impossible to benefit from increased exchange is trade optimized. This result would be automatically obtained in an international commodity market with perfect competition, for it is sufficient for the fulfillment of the condition that the prices at which these commodities can be purchased bear the same relationship to each other for all consumers.

The following example will give meaning to these rather abstract statements. The ratio in country A between the price of a suit and that of a barrel of butter is ¼ of the ratio in country B so long as no trade exists. Hence a buyer in country A can purchase at these ratios of exchange one barrel of butter or two suits; in country B, two barrels of butter or one suit. Since it is possible in this case to reap trade profits, an opening-up of trade will increase welfare. We will assume that the consumers in A value two additional suits as highly as one additional barrel of butter, and those in country B one additional suit as highly as two additional barrels of butter. Now, if one suit were exported from A to B and two barrels of butter from B to A, the welfare of the citizens of B would remain unchanged, while that of the citizens of A would increase. A con-

Papers, 1953, pp. 157ff.; also H. Jürgensen, *Die westeuropäische Montanindustrie und ihr Gemeinsamer Markt*, Göttingen, 1955; idem, "Die Montanunion in den Funktionsgrenzen der Teilintegration," *Wirtschaftsdienst* (1955), pp. 623ff.

sumer in B would have to consume one suit more and two barrels of butter less, and, by hypothesis, one additional suit just offsets for him the loss of two barrels of butter. A consumer in A has to give one suit for two barrels of butter, but since, by hypothesis, he is willing to give two suits for one barrel of butter, his welfare will clearly increase. The exchange ratio will, at a certain point, have fallen so far in A and have risen so far in B that it will be the same for both countries. The volume of trade will not increase further; trade is optimized. (Transport costs have been disregarded here.)

The starting-point of a process of *maximization of production* is a situation in which the ratios of marginal production costs of two or more commodities are different in two or more countries. The productive factors should be employed in such a way that it is impossible to produce more of one commodity or less of another. Production is maximized once this condition is fulfilled. The question arises as to what ratio exists between maximization of production and international mobility of productive factors. Factor mobility generally is a condition for maximization of world production. However, Samuelson has shown that mobility of commodities is, under certain assumptions, a perfect substitute for factor mobility. This is therefore a sufficient but not a necessary condition for maximization of production. In the following example, we will assume that productive factors are internationally immovable.

As before, the world consists of two countries, both of which produce suits as well as butter. Let the price ratio between suits and butter in country A be ¼ of the ratio in country B before the beginning of trade. As a consequence of perfect competition, there are no divergences between the marginal utilities of the commodities and the marginal disutilities of the factors employed in the production of the commodities. Consequently the ratio between the marginal production costs of a suit and of a barrel of butter in B is four times as high as in A. Now, if B expanded its butter production (the costs of which are low) and contracted its suit production (the costs of which are high), and A changed its production structure in the opposite way, it would be possible for both countries together to produce more of both commodities than before. The adjustment goes on until complete specialization occurs in one country or in both countries together, or until the ratio between the marginal costs of both industries is the same in both countries. (Again, transport costs are neglected.)

Both of the free trade mechanisms for the optimization of trade and the maximization of production that have just been described lead to maximum efficiency in the world economy and therewith to as high a welfare as possible so long as the marginal utility of income is considered to be independent of its level. If this restrictive assumption were dropped, welfare at the highest possible degree of productivity could be further increased by a *redistribution of income.* Only when the distribution of income is such that the transfer of income from one person to another cannot increase the latter's satisfaction more than it decreases the former's will optimum distribution prevail. While the productivity of the world economy can be measured in terms of prices and marginal costs—essentially measurable quantities—the measurement of increasing welfare would require indices of marginal utility.

Thus far, we have made an implicit assumption that the *supply of factors of production* was constant. Actually, the size of a population changes and, along with it, the supply of workers; the quantity of capital goods will also increase when the population saves. Hence, economic welfare is also influenced by government actions to regulate the rate of population growth and the rate of capital accumulation. Under certain circumstances, a developing economy justifies deviations, if not from free trade, then from unrestricted international factor mobility.

2. LIMITATIONS OF THE PRINCIPLE
OF FREE TRADE

Under ideal conditions, free trade theoretically maximizes world income. However, in the first place, these conditions are

hardly ever fully realized. Second, maximization of world income does not necessarily also mean maximization of the income of each individual country. Third, trade policies can
serve other than economic objectives.

Most of the *non-economic motives* to restrict international
trade are of a *political nature*. For instance, the authorities of
one country could impede trade in certain—e.g., strategic—
materials with another country to decrease the military potential of the latter. The embargo placed by the NATO countries
on trade with the Soviet bloc is an example. On the other hand,
countries with close political relationships could favor each
other in international trade at the expense of third countries.
The German Customs Union or the Ottawa preferences of the
British Commonwealth are examples. A country may also be
obliged to deviate from the principles of free trade to improve
its bargaining position. The revision of the Swiss tariffs as a
condition for Switzerland's joining the General Agreement on
Tariffs and Trade (GATT) is an example of this.

Since maximization of world income does not necessarily also
imply *maximization of national incomes*, it might possibly be
advantageous for an individual country to forgo the principle
of free trade. It can be shown that even under ideal conditions
—i.e., with free competition and in the absence of external
economies—a country can gain by restricting its exports and
imports. It must, however, be assumed that the elasticity of
the demand of foreign countries for the exports of the country
in question is less than infinite, and that its trade partners do
not retaliate. A large country could reduce the demand for
certain import commodities by levying a tariff and consequently get them cheaper than a nation without such a tariff.
Moreover, it could use the instrument of tariffs to maximize the
volume of commodities that can be obtained from production
and trade. The tariff that maximizes this volume is called the
"optimum tariff."[9] The height of the optimum tariff depends
on the elasticity of the foreign demand and the shape of the

[9] Cf. J. Tinbergen, *op.cit.*, pp. 55ff.

domestic transformation curve. The so-called "terms-of-trade agreement," which was formulated by John Stuart Mill and is accepted by modern economists, should not, however, be misused for all possible protectionist purposes. The gain from an optimum tariff is in any case at the expense of other nations.

Another argument in favor of protection can likewise be advanced under the assumed ideal conditions. It is based on the assertion that a deviation from free trade would change the distribution of income in a desirable way. If, for instance, it can be shown with the help of the Stolper-Samuelson theorem that free trade tends to decrease the real income of labor in one country (insofar as labor is in short supply relative to other factors of production and in comparison with other countries),[10] this fact could be considered a sufficient justification for protection, although the total real income of the nation in question would suffer thereby. This argument supports to a certain extent the traditional attitude of American labor unions toward the foreign trade policy of the United States (wage-dumping).

The terms-of-trade agreement and the Stolper-Samuelson theorem illustrate that a protectionist attitude could be considered sensible, at least from a theoretical point of view, on grounds of income distribution. In the first case, it relates to international and, in the second case, to intranational distribution of income.

Moreover, each *deviation from the ideal conditions* results in justifications for intervening in one way or another in free trade. Particularly important deviations are rigidity of prices and wages and involuntary unemployment. In a depression, national policy to counteract unemployment can degenerate into a "beggar-my-neighbor" policy, as does every artificial stimulation of exports and/or contraction of imports. Internal stabilization would then be obtained at the expense of the rate of employment abroad.

[10] Cf. W. F. Stolper and P. A. Samuelson, "Protection and Real Wages," *Readings in the Theory of International Trade*, Philadelphia-Toronto, 1949, pp. 333ff.

Even when there is internal equilibrium, the balance of payments need not be in balance, for the deflation necessary to adjust the balance of payments cannot take place if prices and wages are rigid. If sliding wage scales are operating, it becomes impossible to reduce the real income from wages and alteration of the rate of exchange is ineffective. In both cases, the balance of payments cannot be brought into equilibrium by methods of price adjustment that are compatible with the principle of free trade. Direct controls in one form or another must therefore replace them. Moreover, the sum of the import elasticities of the trade partners must be larger than one in order to adjust the balance of payments by way of the price mechanism. If this sum is smaller than one, direct controls are needed to restore the equilibrium of the balance of payments.

Finally, deviation from the principle of free trade is theoretically plausible on the basis of structural considerations. Individual branches of an industry or even an entire industry can often be stimulated to a greater degree by a policy of protection and subsidization than by a free play of market forces. This should be done in such a way that the assisted industries have a comparative advantage at the end of the period of protection and are then strong enough to meet foreign competition without protective tariffs. This condition is usually considered to be a necessary, but not always sufficient, criterion of the success of a protectionist policy. It is not necessarily sufficient because the advantage gained by the temporary support of the industry has to be weighed against the temporary loss in national income.

The best-known argument for deviations from free trade on the basis of structural considerations is Friedrich List's proposal of an infant-industry tariff, an argument which is closely related to the possibility of external economies and of decreasing marginal costs for the society concerned.[11] Basing the principle of free trade on the theory of comparative costs has al-

[11] Cf. G. Haberler, *A Survey of International Trade Theory*, Princeton, 1956, page 53.

ways been criticized because of its static nature and its neglect of problems of development. On the other hand, the infant-industry argument, like all structural reasons for protection, takes account of long-term changes in basic conditions. However, it is not true that an infant industry as such automatically justifies government protection. That would be the case only if the new industry created external economies, in the sense that other industries could benefit from the experience of the new, protected industry. For, as Meade says, "The temporary subsidization of the first firm may be socially desirable; but this would be so not because infants have to learn but because infants teach each other."[12]

Another argument that is often adduced in support of governmental assistance to new industries is related to the increase of the number of industries in a country. Here, in contrast to the infant-industry tariff, the necessity for permanent protection can be advanced. A country may want to set up new industries in order to decrease its dependency on imports, even though it could import the products concerned more cheaply from abroad. It might thereby escape future uncertainties of supply as a consequence of foreign shifts in demand; an external economy has then been created by protection.

Another form of external economies is relevant. The production costs of a single firm may be considerably smaller when it is located in the middle of an industrialized region than when it is isolated. The cost of transportation between firms whose products are in some way related to each other becomes cheaper; the supply of highly skilled labor is increased; technical training, experience, and innovations are advanced by a closer contact among firms and among employees.

Such external economies are not incompatible with perfect competition. The reduction in costs that results from them represents, for reasons independent of the single enterprise, a downward shift in the marginal cost curve when the industry grows as an entity. This is not to say that under these circum-

[12] Cf. J. E. Meade, *Trade and Welfare*, page 257.

stances free competition will always result in an optimum production structure and the best possible division of labor; and protective measures may become necessary if these economies are to be realized.

Internal economies, on the other hand, are incompatible with free competition. Nevertheless, internal savings could furnish a motive to bring about structural adjustments with government help. However, the following point must be considered: Take the case of a commodity in the production of which decreasing average costs have manifested themselves and which so far has been produced in *one* country only. If another country begins to manufacture it, the advantages of mass production so far reaped by the first country will diminish, since it will be forced, as a consequence of the decrease in demand, to produce on a smaller scale and at higher output costs than before. The loss neutralizes part of the savings of the second country. The justification for protecting a new industry depends not just on the advantages of mass production, but also on the question of whether these advantages are secured at a medium scale of production or whether they require large-scale production.

However, theoretical considerations of location must also be taken into account in these cases. Even at decreasing costs, production is profitable only when it develops in a favorable natural, social, and political environment. It makes no sense, for *instance, to produce bananas at the North Pole, even though* the average cost of producing ten bananas would be lower than that of producing five.

Hence, the advantages of mass production do not exempt a country from taking account of the law of comparative costs in protecting an industry. Production should not only take place in an appropriate environment but also concentrate on those commodities which the country could produce at relatively least cost on the basis of its factor supplies. If the manufacture of butter requires little labor but much land and the production of clothing little land but much labor, the production of butter will be cheap in a less densely populated country and the manufacture of clothing cheap in a more densely populated country. In the first country, which is relatively rich in land and poor in labor, rent will be low and wages high. It follows that in this country the cost of the production of butter will be low in comparison with the manufacture of clothing, which requires much labor and little land. In the second country, it will be the other way around, so that the first country should promote the production of butter and the second that of clothing.

Finally, transport costs should not be neglected. If they are so large that they counterbalance the advantages of mass production, suitable environment, and factor supply, there are good reasons for starting production in the country in which the final product will have its market. It would not be justifiable to manufacture refrigeration equipment in Greenland even if the costs of transporting it were high. But the final product is not the only commodity that has to be transported. Raw materials and semi-manufactured goods enter into international trade, too. While the cost of transporting manufactured goods tends to draw production to the marketing countries, the cost of transporting raw materials tends to concentrate production near the raw-material sources; which of the two tendencies will be stronger will depend on the nature of the product. Some products contain virtually all the raw materials that are needed for their manufacture. Since there is no loss of cotton in the manufacture of a skirt, for instance, no savings in the cost of transporting the raw material can be obtained if one sets up textile factories in the region in which cotton is grown. The cost of transporting cotton would indeed fall, but an approximately equal cost would be incurred in transporting the skirts to the ultimate consumers. Other products, however, do not contain all the raw material needed for their manufacture—i.e., their production is characterized by a weight loss. Pig iron, for instance, does not contain the coal that is used to smelt iron ore. Therefore, transportation charges are saved if blast furnaces are built in the neighborhood of the coal mines. Of course, transport costs depend not only on the weight of the commodities but also on their form, volume, perishability, and other properties. The resultant of all transport costs theoretically determines the place where an industry which manufactures several products from several raw materials can be established at minimum transport costs.

All these factors have to be considered before one decides whether the advantages of mass production justify government protection. Only temporary measures should be taken to protect an industry which promises to yield the advantages of mass production, even if the structure of transport costs, factor endowment, and the general environment are favorable. The duration of the protective measures will be highly dependent on development costs necessitated by the introduction of new production methods, the retraining of workers, etc. The higher these costs, the longer government support will have to last. However, one should never forget that development costs alone do not sanction government intervention.

3. THE TECHNIQUES OF TRADE AND PAYMENTS CONTROLS

So far the arguments for deviating from the principle of free trade have been discussed. Nothing has yet been said about methods of protection, and various means of government intervention will now be examined. However, we will limit ourselves in the following to those means of intervention which have a direct effect on foreign trade.

Government trade policies are always aimed at influencing the volume or the value of imports and/or exports, so that the volume and direction of international trade will be diverted from a free trade pattern.

First, one can divide the means which a government has at its command to shape trade policy into financial and commercial controls. The *financial controls*, which will be dealt with first, are subdivided into monetary and fiscal controls. Systems of foreign exchange control and multiple exchange rates are monetary controls, while the fiscal controls comprise taxes, tariffs, and subsidies on special items in the balance of payments. Quantitative restrictions and government trade monopolies are *commercial controls.*[13]

If the volume and quantity of imports are to be restricted for economic, political, or institutional reasons, this can be achieved first by a system of *rationing foreign currency.* Each purchase or sale of foreign exchange by residents of the country concerned which is not settled through the medium of the control authority is declared illegal. The currency of the country that enforces such rationing is not convertible by its residents, but on the other hand it is convertible by foreigners.

Under such a system of foreign exchange control, every resident who has to make a payment in foreign currency must purchase the corresponding foreign exchange from the controlling body or from an authorized agent. Moreover, every resident who has obtained foreign currency in the form of export proceeds must sell the corresponding foreign exchange to the control authority or its agent at the official exchange rate. Hence, the foreign exchange market is monopolized by the control authority. This body decides for which imports the foreign exchange can be used that has accrued from exports. The system requires an all-embracing bureaucratic apparatus.

Curbing imports through monetary controls can be more highly differentiated and at the same time be made more effective by the use of a system of *multiple exchange rates.* In purchasing or selling foreign exchange, the controlling body can differentiate the exchange rate according to countries or commodities. For instance, the imports of essentials could be permitted at an exchange rate of 4:1, while imports of luxuries could be financed at a rate of 3:1. This method implies a value duty of 33⅓ per cent on imports of luxuries. The same result

[13] The following exposition is based on J. E. Meade, *The Balance of Payments*, London, 1951.

could be obtained if foreign trade transactions were settled at an exchange rate of 4:1 and at the same time a duty were levied on the import of luxuries. This system could replace a license system for imports if the controlling body sold the currency of country A, which it had obtained from the exporters at a rate of 4:1, to importers of essential goods at the same rate but to importers of, say, automobiles at a rate of 3:1. Conceivably, if foreign exchange were auctioned off, the exchange rate to be established for the import of luxuries would of its own accord reach a level which would make quantitative import restrictions redundant. Moreover, the control authority could use the profit from selling the currency of country A at a higher rate to the importers of luxuries to offer the exporters a more favorable exchange rate for the foreign exchange they received. This method would be in keeping with a subsidy ad valorem, for, under a system of multiple exchange rates, there is no reason to subsidize each type of export to the same extent. It is much more desirable to stimulate the export of those commodities for which foreign demand has a very high elasticity. Even a small subsidy would considerably increase the proceeds of foreign exchange from these exports. On the other hand, it would be possible to thwart exports by a negative subsidy—i.e., an export duty in the form of an unfavorable exchange rate—if the demand for the commodities concerned were inelastic. Foreign exchange proceeds would also be increased thereby. If the system of exchange rates were set in such a way that the value of imports would be sufficiently reduced and the proceeds from exports sufficiently increased, quantitative restrictions would become redundant. And if the profits and losses that resulted from the application of a system of flexible exchange rates balanced, the budget would not be burdened. Instead of placing a monopoly of the foreign exchange trade in public hands, it is also possible to permit exporters to sell part of the proceeds of foreign exchange in the foreign market. The importers of essential goods could then purchase the foreign exchange at official rates from the control authority, while importers of luxuries would have to meet their exchange requirements in the free market. Consequently, the system entails a combination of subsidies in favor of those exporters who are allowed to sell foreign exchange in the free market, and of duties detrimental to those importers who have to obtain their foreign exchange in the free market. Hence, each system of multiple exchange rates corresponds to a system of tariffs and subsidies in combination with a single exchange rate.

Besides these various means of restricting imports and promoting exports by monetary controls, there are *fiscal procedures* that may serve this purpose. The most obvious examples are import duties aimed at the reduction of demand for foreign commodities, and export subsidies to promote the exports. As already stated, these procedures correspond in many ways to a system of multiple exchange rates. What criterion determines the choice of the most suitable method? The rationing of foreign exchange and in particular the application of multiple exchange rates are impossible without an all-embracing control of current payments and a monopoly of the foreign exchange market. Without these steps there will be arbitrage transactions benefiting from local differences in exchange rates. On the other hand, tariffs can be levied and subsidies be paid without setting up a new bureaucratic apparatus. However, it is very difficult to tax or subsidize some items in the balance of payments. This is particularly true of tourist expenditures abroad. The authorities of country B must know how much each tourist spends in country A in order to levy a 10 per cent ad valorem tariff on all expenditures of tourists from B in A. This can be achieved only by an all-inclusive administration of foreign exchange. Hence, a tariff on expenditures of tourists abroad corresponds in every respect to a special exchange rate; the foreign exchange is issued in this case to tourists at a price increased by 10 per cent. For these reasons, visible imports and exports are the most suitable objects for tariffs and subsidies. Contrary to services, commodities can be taxed or subsidized at the very moment that they pass the border.

On the other hand, invisible imports and exports require administration of foreign exchange transactions.[14]

Besides financial controls, *commercial controls* are often employed. Value and/or quantity of imports and exports can be directly limited by *quantitative restrictions.* These measures are most applicable to trade in visible commodities. The starting point of our analysis is that the imports of country B are to be restricted. Restriction can be aimed either at the volume of import of a certain commodity or at its value. It can take the form of an "open," or "global," quota, which means that the border will be closed for further imports once the quota has been exhausted. Quantitative restrictions can, however, also be administered by issuing import licenses to individual importers. For instance, W, X, Y, and Z are each allowed to import an automobile, but the licenses of W, X, and Y are related to imports from the United States and that of Z to imports from France. The purpose of this restriction is to limit the value of imports. This result will definitely be obtained when a limit is set to the import value itself, but if a limit is set to the quantity, the result is uncertain.

First, let us consider the problems posed by the quantitative restriction of imports, and start from the assumption that import licenses are issued to the importers of cars in country B which limit the *number* of cars imported from A to, for instance, four. If the price of a car in country A is 100 A-currency units ($), the producers of A could sell five cars in B. However, *since the volume of the transactions has been limited to four cars,* the consumers in B are willing to pay a scarcity price of $133⅓. Hence, for an import quantity of four, the import value would be $533⅓. But since the producers in A supply the cars at $100, the total value of imports is only $400. There is a total difference of $133⅓, or $33⅓ per car, between the price which the consumers are willing to pay and the price

---

[14] This applies to an even greater extent to capital movements. But since the entire analysis has been made on the assumption of international immobility of productive factors, we abstract from this case.

asked by the producers. Restriction of imports always brings about an increase in the demand price over the supply price. If the imports were curbed by import duties or by the application of multiple exchange rates, the resulting difference would automatically accrue to the treasury as tariff revenue, or to the control authority as profit from the trade in foreign exchange. However, in the case of quantitative restrictions, it is no longer certain who ultimately benefits from the margin between the supply and the demand price. There are five possibilities:

(1) If import licenses are issued to dealers, part of the $33⅓ which is the value of a license can be used to bribe the officials who decide which dealer will be granted $100, or a license for a car with the value of $100.

(2) If the administration is honest and no import licenses are issued, the margin of $33⅓ per car between the supply and the demand price of the curbed import will bring an extra profit to the dealers.

(3) The extra profit of the dealers can be eliminated by price control. However, since the difference between supply and demand remains, all the symptoms of repressed inflation would result. Because the demand of the consumers cannot be satisfied at the fixed price, the consequences will be rationing, standing in queues, black market prices, and the like.

(4) Under certain conditions, the exporters in A may be able to secure the extra profit.

(5) The treasury can take possession of the extra profit by levying an import duty to the amount of the margin.

If the treasury does not secure the extra profit, whether the value of the import will be reduced as desired will depend on whether the profit accrues to the importers or the exporters. Suppose the number of imported cars is reduced from five to four by quantitative restriction and the consumers are willing to pay $533⅓ for these cars, although they have previously obtained five cars for only $500. The value of the imports of B is then reduced from $500 to $400 if the importers are able

36

to secure the extra profit. However, if the profit benefits the exporters in A, then the value of imports by B will increase from $500 to $533⅓, although the import quantity has been restricted successfully.

The result of the analysis is the same when the value of imports is restricted. In one case, the profit from the difference between demand and supply prices accrues to the importers in B. However, if the exporters in A can secure the extra profit, the imports of country B will decline, but B's terms of trade will deteriorate.

If the quantitative restriction is administered in the form of an open or global quota, then for importers and exporters it is a case of first come, first served. As soon as the quota is exhausted, trade comes to an end. In this case it is impossible to establish a general rule as to who makes the profit from the quantitative restriction. The rush to the borders could in the end prove to benefit the importers as well as the exporters.

4. UNIVERSAL OR REGIONAL FREE TRADE?

The described controls have become increasingly important in the course of time, so that the present situation differs fundamentally from that of universal free trade. It is an illusion to believe that the system of general free trade such as existed in 1914—and which is still advocated by Wilhelm Röpke[15]—can be easily restored by a turn of the hand. The present world is divided into two parts: one pursues an international trade policy that is primarily based not on economic, but rather on political and ideological, motives; and the other, divided in itself, lacks a uniform policy in international trade. A prominent American economist tersely summarized the difference between the period prior to the First World War and the present in the following words: "The world has changed greatly,

[15] Cf. W. Röpke, "Integration und Desintegration der internationalen Wirtschaft," *Wirtschaftsfragen der Freien Welt*, Frankfurt a.M., 1957, pp. 493ff.

and is now a world of planned economies, of state trading, of substantially arbitrary and inflexible national price structures, and of managed instability in exchange rates. The classical theory is not directly relevant for such a world, and it may be that for such a world there is and can be no relevant *general* theory."[16]

In view of the present political situation, it would be irresponsible to direct all efforts exclusively to the re-establishment of universal free trade. It would be better to concentrate our efforts on a more intensive exchange of commodities between nations—a goal that lies much closer to reality. In particular, those countries which are united by geographical situation, cultural relationships, and common interests could and should intelligently coordinate their economic policies. The abstract and quite vulnerable principle of free trade by itself will not convince the European nations of the necessity for close cooperation, nor will it meet the surprising and drastic changes in economic structures. Success depends on an economic, social, and political objective that appeals directly to politicians and peoples. It is impossible in the present world to construct a liberal international economic order through free trade among sovereign nations; a more positive approach is required, one which is directed toward an international economic institution—if not toward a supranational economic authority. In the modern world, the purely negative device of suspending protectionist measures or limiting their use requires international supervision, if not supranational powers which have until now been reserved to national governments. Moreover, if it is true that a liberal economic order can be constructed successfully in the modern world only to the extent that national governments refrain from certain kinds of policies at home, it is evident that some degree of continuous intergovernmental discussion about related domestic policies or their control by a supranational government is necessary.

[16] Cf. J. Viner, *International Economics*, Glencoe, Ill., 1951, page 16.

But further action is needed. There are at present certain functions which require positive international or supranational measures. To be sure, it is difficult to draw a line between the negative act of merely refraining from particular domestic policies and the positive one of adopting domestic measures which are in agreement with economic integration. Some examples may demonstrate the problem.

Synchronized actions are, for instance, necessary to influence the distribution of income among countries. Structural changes and economic development involve common interests of both developed and underdeveloped countries; and this is a domain that, by its very nature, requires government planning and therefore needs international treatment.[17] Furthermore, many countries feel obliged at this time to plan their defense programs together. This includes sharing the burden of defense expenditures, establishing certain industries on the basis of economic and strategic considerations, and choosing the sources of supply for current defense programs. For these reasons, the reinstatement of a liberal economic order cannot, in the present world, be expected to result solely from the negative act of *laisser faire*; it requires to a considerable extent the development of an international, if not supranational, economic organization. It makes more sense therefore to apply the principle of free trade in a framework which assures a better coordination of economic policies than would be possible in a coalition that included the whole non-Communist world.

These considerations provide one of the arguments in favor of regional—in our case, Continental—free trade. In itself, it is a sufficient counterargument to the absolute and uncompromising demand for world-wide integration. The thesis of the superiority of universal free trade under the present circumstances is advocated by numerous authors with liberal

[17] E. Salin recommends the same for the supply of energy; cf. "Über die Notwendigkeit langfristiger Energiepolitik," *Wirtschaftsfragen der Freien Welt*, pp. 333ff.

tendencies like Röpke,[18] Haberler,[19] and Kindleberger.[20] The project of an Atlantic Union, proposed by economists like Meade[21] and Robbins,[22] is also too far-fetched. Still, the idea of an Atlantic Community of Nations is more realistic than a scheme involving solidarity between Europe and Japan. That Britain, faced with the alternatives of a European economic union or maintenance of the *status quo*, would vote without any hesitation for the economic order that exists at the present is understandable. It is indeed difficult to imagine that Britain would be willing to exchange the indisputable advantages of its central position inside the Commonwealth for the hypothetical advantage of a political union with Europe. For, as Robbins writes, most of the help that Britain received during the Second World War did not come from Europe; the United States and the members of the Commonwealth were the countries from which Britain in the last resort asked for and obtained help. She forged with these powers the closest alliance that history has even seen. It is therefore difficult to believe

[18] Cf. W. Röpke, *op.cit.*

[19] Cf. G. von Haberler, "Die Wirtschaftliche Integration Europas," *Wirtschaftsfragen der Freien Welt*, pp. 521ff. It seems that Haberler still adheres to the opinion he expressed at the beginning of the 1930's: "Not that a European customs union would not be preferable to the present state of affairs; however, the objective—as an ideal—has not been set high enough and is at the same time even more difficult to attain than the ultimate goal to which it is subordinated. Hence it means a detour which is, moreover, more difficult to follow than the direct way. It is hard to see why the abolition of tariff barriers should stop at the borders of Europe. In general it is dilettantish . . . to think in terms of geographic continents. . . ." (Haberler, *Den internationale Handel*, Berlin, 1933, page 288.)

[20] Ch. Kindleberger, "European Economic Integration," *Money, Trade and Economic Growth*, in honor of J. H. Williams, New York, 1951, pp. 58ff. Kindleberger poses the equilibrium of the balance of payments between Europe and the United States as an objective of international economic policy of the highest priority.

[21] J. E. Meade, *Problems of Economic Union*, London, 1953; cf. also idem, "Economic Problems of the Atlantic Union: A British View," *Readings in Economics*, ed. by P. H. Samuelson, R. L. Bishop, J. R. Coleman, New York, 1952, pp. 325ff.

[22] L. Robbins, "Auf dem Wege zur atlantischen Staatengemeinschaft," *Aussenwirtschaft*, St. Gallen, 1950, Vol. 4.

that any British government would of its own accord cut or loosen its ties with Ottawa and Washington in order to form new ties with a European Department of State or Defense. The interest that Britain lately showed in a European Free Trade Area was to no small degree attributable to the fear that a European Common Market might prove to be such a strong organization as to deprive the British economy of its European market. Even in the envisaged Free Trade Area, Britain reserves the right to preserve the Commonwealth preferences. But the Free Trade Area is above all based on free trade among the participating countries—a freedom of trade which can hardly last for long without extensive integration—and hence implies a rather loose form of cooperation, dependent on the loyalty of its members to the treaty. The only grouping of powers in which Britain could unconditionally cooperate without threatening its existing ties is a union as extensive as an Atlantic Pact. Since she will not accept a closer link with the Continent than the Free Trade Area and since the United States cannot be expected, in the framework of an Atlantic Economic Union, to cede sovereign rights to a supranational authority, only the formation of a common domestic market among the Continental states has a genuine chance of realization. It is therefore significant that the most far-reaching attempt at an economic union up to now has come from six Continental European states. It is also revealing that GATT, despite its multilateral character, did not dispense with bilateral trade treaties and has shown, by its unwieldy organization, that agreements which are complicated and difficult to master from an organizational viewpoint can successfully be achieved only within a narrower framework. For instance, the negotiations on an eventually free currency were not held at the International Monetary Fund, with world-wide membership, in Washington, but at the Organization for European Economic Cooperation in Paris.

Regional economic arrangements, like customs unions, free trade areas, and economic unions, are often objected to on the ground that the discrimination against outsiders ("third countries") which accompanies them leads to a distortion of world trade relationships and thus tends to decrease world economic welfare and eventually also the welfare of the partners. According to this view, a partial union on a broader basis would be preferable to closer cooperation among a smaller number of countries.[23] As will be shown later, however, this argument is not generally correct even when only economic effects are in question.

Moreover, political considerations are more important than economic ones. Since the existence of Europe is at stake, integration is more of a political than an economic desideratum. Political integration can be facilitated by economic cooperation, but mere economic union is unthinkable.[24] If the preservation of the European way of life is at stake, a solution which from an economic viewpoint is only second best is preferable to a political decline while waiting hopelessly for the establishment of universal free trade. Stated more generally, one should not place the achievement of an economic prescription above the claims of vital human needs. As the greatest economist of our generation wrote: "But, chiefly, do not let us overestimate the importance of the economic problem, or sacrifice to its supposed necessities other matters of greater and more permanent significance."[25]

This more broadly formulated concept of a European union lies at the base of the arguments which will be presented below, from a purely economic point of view, on behalf of regional integration. It must be stressed that, despite all arguments against the principle of free trade, this principle represents the most important economic justification for regional integration. The mechanisms for optimization of world trade and

[23] J. E. Meade, *Problems of Economic Union*, page 9.
[24] Cf. R. Aron, "A propos de l'unité de l'Europe: La dialectique du politique et de l'économique," *Mitteilungen der List Gesellschaft* (1957), pp. 266ff.
[25] J. M. Keynes, "Economic Possibilities for Our Grandchildren," *Essays in Persuasion*, London, 1931, page 373.

maximization of world production will also increase the prosperity of a limited number of countries. *Integration* may be said to be the *creation of the most desirable international economic structure by removing artificial barriers to the optimum operation of free trade and by introducing all desirable forms of cooperation and unification.*[26] Hence, the problem of integration is only part of a more general problem—namely, the formulation of the best possible economic policy. At the same time, in formulating recommendations regarding economic policy, one leaves the domain of objective science, or must at least admit that exogenous factors play a role.

Now what is the objective of the best possible economic policy? A well-known formulation of that objective is the maximization of the welfare of society, or an increase in the general well-being. This means, first, a high level of production; in other words, all available capacities should be used in the most economical way. However, as we have shown, an increase in productivity is not enough to meet this requirement. The problem of distribution of income cannot be neglected in this connection. The difficulties which arise in determining optimum distribution and in weighing freedom against security have already been mentioned. Taking these points into consideration, we can state the objectives of the best possible economic policy as follows:

(1) All productive forces should be fully utilized. Instability of production should be avoided as much as possible. (2) Productive factors should be employed where their yield is highest. (3) Income should be redistributed more evenly among individuals and countries so long as a strong inequality exists. (4) Government intervention should occur only if there are obvious disequilibria and dislocations to be prevented or removed. Though the definition of some of the concepts that lie behind these four objectives depends on public opinion and political decisions, nevertheless these objectives are useful as criteria.

[26] J. Tinbergen, *op.cit.*, page 95.

In order for these objectives to be effectively attained on an international level, the interested states must be willing to delegate part of their sovereign rights to a supranational body. This is, within the framework of the integration, the special aspect of the "best possible economic policy" and it was this necessity of which those who initiated the European Common Market were aware from the beginning. According to Tinbergen, international or supranational authorities must be created to fulfill the following functions, among others: control and removal of trade restrictions; regulation of the markets for raw materials; control of currency convertibility; control of monetary equilibrium and employment policy; and supervision of capital investments in order to stimulate development and regulate migration.

CHAPTER II

REGIONAL FREE TRADE

1. TRADE-CREATING
AND TRADE-DIVERTING EFFECTS
OF A CUSTOMS UNION

WHILE A CERTAIN UNIFORMITY exists in the convictions of scholars regarding free trade as a principle for organizing the world economy, there is a divergence of opinion regarding free trade within smaller areas. Some serious objections have always been raised to the global principle of free trade in favor of temporary deviations from it; we investigated earlier to what extent these objections were sound. The usefulness of applying the free trade principle regionally is, however, contested on several grounds by authors who believe strongly in the global application of this principle. The main argument along these lines has been advanced by Jacob Viner.[1]

Viner has investigated whether or not a customs union will bring us somewhat closer to the results of world-wide free trade. In this instance, we mean by a customs union an association of a limited number of countries, who have removed mutual trade barriers but discriminate against third countries. The most-favored-nation clause is therefore applied only inside the union. Whether the third-country restrictions have been made by each member country separately or by the union as a whole according to mutual arrangement will be passed over for the moment, so that the following investigation applies to a free trade area as well as to a customs union proper. While it is clear that in the end all countries will have to take the same steps as the members of a customs union to obtain universal free trade, it can be doubted whether a limited customs union would improve the division of labor. In some cases this will occur. If shoes are produced more cheaply in A and

[1] J. Viner, *The Customs Union Issue.*

45

glass in B, it is possible that the removal of trade barriers be-tween these two countries may lead to a more rational struc-ture of production. But as a consequence of mutual preferen-tial treatment, a tariff against third countries may also lead to an increase in the butter production in A, though country C was potentially the cheaper supplier. The first would be, ac-cording to Viner, a *trade-creating* effect of a customs union, the second a *trade-diverting* effect. Which of the two effects is more important depends on the actual circumstances.

In the following analysis, we will assume complete employ-ment of all productive factors in all countries linked together by trade relationships and ask ourselves whether the removal of tariff barriers between A and B would lead to a more or a less profitable use of the factors of production in the trading countries.[2]

Let us assume that before the formation of the union A levies an ad valorem tariff of 100 per cent on the import of steel from every country of origin. Further, let us assume that the costs of producing one ton of steel amount to $100 in C, to $150 in B, and to $250 in A. Taking into account the tariff before the formation of the union, the price in A of steel from C is $200 and that of steel from B is $300, compared with do-mestic steel at $250. Hence, C-steel will be the cheapest, price-wise as well as costwise, and the consumers in A will buy C-steel. But if the steel from B is now freed from the tariff, its price in A will drop from $300 to $150. The consumers in A will therefore shift their demand from C-steel to B-steel and the consequence will be an uneconomic diversion of produc-tion from the cheaper steel of C to the more expensive steel of B. Viner calls this occurrence "trade diversion." It is uneco-nomical and wasteful and causes world production to decrease,

[2] For the following, cf. J. E. Meade, *The Theory of Customs Unions*, Amsterdam, 1955. Our argument is based on this publication. See also H. Makower and C. Morton, "A Contribution Towards a Theory of Customs Unions," *The Economic Journal* (1953); R. G. Lipsey, "The Theory of Customs Unions: Trade Diversion and Welfare," *Economica* (1957), pp. 79ff.

since the factors of production are no longer optimally employed and somewhere the general standard of living must fall.

However, this is not the only possible result. It is necessary to change only one figure in the previous example to arrive at totally different results. If, *ceteris paribus*, country A originally levies an ad valorem tariff of 200 per cent on all imports of steel, then the price of steel from C will amount to $300 and that from B to $450, while domestic steel—as before—works out at $250. Before the formation of the union, A will therefore import neither C-steel nor B-steel, but use its own cheaper steel. Now, if the tariff on the steel of B is removed, its price in A will drop to its actual cost of $150. Hence, the residents of A will use cheap steel from B instead of the expensive domestic steel. Clearly, the removal of the tariff with which A taxed the steel from B has created a new import. In this case, the customs union leads to a creation of international trade, since one of the trade partners can undersell an already existing industry in the other country. This development represents a reallocation of productive factors into a more efficient structure. Whether in the end trade has been increased or diverted depends on the original height of the import duty of A. This seems to be one of the few generalizations about a customs union which can be supported: namely, that with the formation of a customs union, the higher the original duties which the partner countries remove, the more the economic welfare increases.

The seemingly simple distinction between trade creation and trade diversion possesses various shortcomings which result from restrictive and partly implicit assumptions. First, it says nothing about how the economic gains from certain consequences of the "trade creation" should be weighed against the economic losses from certain other consequences of the "trade diversion." Let us assume that country A, as a consequence of the customs union, buys expensive steel from B instead of cheap steel from C. In this case there is an economic loss as a result of diverting trade from a cheap to an expensive source of supply. But let us also assume that, because of the customs union, country B now imports cheese from country A which it itself produced before. The abolition of the tariff of B on imports from A has removed an obstacle which hitherto kept the cheap cheese of A away from the market in B. This trade creation results in an economic gain. What are the criteria for deciding whether the losses from the uneconomic trade diversion in the steel sector are greater or smaller than the gains from the newly created international trade in cheese?

On the basis of Viner's distinction, one might be tempted to believe that there is on balance a trade diversion of $70 million if a trade volume in steel of $100 million is shifted from the cheap source of supply in C to the expensive one in B, and new trade is created in steel between the cheap country A and the expensive country B to the amount of $30 million.

This conclusion would be false, and it would hardly be in agreement with the ideas which are at the base of Viner's argument. In order to determine whether a customs union increases or decreases the total cost of producing a given quantity of commodities, we must not only consider the total volumes of trade in the two groups of commodities whose production costs have risen or fallen as a result of the shift in trade. We must also take into account the extent to which the costs of each unit of the diverted trade have risen and the extent to which the costs of each unit of the newly created trade have fallen.

In the previous example, in which there was a diversion of the steel trade to the amount of $100 million and a creation of new cheese trade to the amount of $30 million, it was assumed that the production costs of steel from B were 50 per cent higher than those of steel from C. But if at the same time the production costs of cheese in B exceed those in A by 200 per cent, then a loss of only $50 million as a result of additional costs in steel production (50 per cent of 100 million) would be matched by a saving of $100 million as a result of a reduction in the costs of cheese production (200 per cent of

$30 million). On balance there would therefore be a cost saving, despite the fact that the value of the newly created trade would be considerably smaller than the value of the diverted trade. Weighing the newly created and the diverted trade by the *average* costs of production before and after setting up a customs union is a big improvement over a rough comparison of the volume of diverted and newly created trade.

Moreover, Viner's analysis rests on the assumption that all *demand elasticities* are zero and all *supply elasticities* are infinite. This assumption is identical with the hypothesis of fixed quantities of demand and fixed marginal production costs in each country. Calculation of the advantages of a customs union becomes much more complicated if one or both of these conditions are not satisfied. In our first example of trade diversion, the steel price in country A amounted to $200 per ton before the formation of the customs union (i.e., it was equal to the costs in C of $100 plus the ad valorem tariff of 100 per cent); after the formation of the customs union it dropped to $150 (i.e., to the duty-free price of B-steel). Let us assume that the demand for steel in A has a very high elasticity and that, as a result of the fall in price, the demand of the consumers in A rises from one million to three million tons. The result is that while before integration country A imported one million tons of C-steel, the production costs of which were $100 per ton, after integration it imports three million tons of B-steel at $150 per ton. This does not necessarily mean a deterioration of the situation. One can say that there is a loss of $50 per ton, or a total of $50 million, on the one million tons of steel that has been diverted from the cheap country C to the expensive country B. But we cannot neglect the fact that B produces and sells to A an additional two million tons. A simpler cost comparison cannot be set up for these additional two million tons, for A had not previously ordered this quantity of steel; the quantity in question is additionally consumed by A and has to be added to the earlier world production of steel. In order to find out whether the shift represents a gain, we must therefore compare the value of this additional steel to the consumers in A with the production costs of the steel mills in B. It is unfortunate, however, that we cannot restrict ourselves to the relatively objective problem of comparing the costs of production of a given commodity output in production facilities with different geographic locations. We have to take into account the utility, the ophelimity, or the well-being that the residents of A derive from the extra consumption of steel instead of something else. If we wish to determine whether a customs union would be good or bad, we must inevitably introduce aspects of welfare theory. The additional two million tons of steel clearly add $300 million to the costs of country B. But what is their value in A? Before the union, the steel price in A was $200 at an ad valorem tariff of 100 per cent on imports from C. The value of an additional ton of steel would at that time in all probability be $200 for the consumers in A. The steel price in A drops as a result of the integration, the consumers increase their purchases, and the more they buy the more the value of an additional ton of steel drops. At the end they will buy three million tons of steel at $150 per ton, which could mean that an additional ton of steel has for them at this point a value of $150. The value of the additional two million tons therefore probably lies between $400 million (two million tons at the original and highest marginal value of $200 per ton) and $300 million (two million tons at the ultimate and lowest marginal value of $150 per ton). Let us assume that the additional two million tons of steel have for the consumers of A a value of exactly $350 million. The producers in B, however, have sacrificed $300 million to produce this quantity. The increase in the consumption of steel in A, as a consequence of the abolition of the import duty on B-steel, therefore leads to the conclusion that the value to the consumers exceeds the cost of production by $50 million. The gain from expanding the trade therefore balances the loss of $50 million resulting from the diversion of trade from C to B. This is an element in the calculation of the profits and losses of integration that favors a customs union and that seems to be over-looked by Viner.

This example is based on the assumption that the customs union has a trade-diverting effect. The analysis of a customs union which has a trade-creating effect would, under the same assumptions, lead to the conclusion that the gain from the newly created trade is greater than the value of the newly created trade alone. The customs union would be judged even more favorably in this case.

Another point has to be taken into consideration. The formation of a customs union implies the drying-up of the *source of income* which the tariffs represented for the governments of the participating states. Let us assume that these governments continue expenditures as before and do not change the balance between total receipts and total expenditures. The revenue obtained from the tariffs must then come from another form of taxation. If the tariff revenue is replaced by imposing a tax on the consumption of another commodity, this will cause a greater divergence between the marginal utility and the marginal costs in that other branch of economic activity. The loss resulting from the contraction of trade in these products has to be weighed in part against the gain from the expansion of the trade in those products which have been freed from the tariff. If the loss of the tariff revenue is compensated by a progressive income tax, this will result in a greater divergence between the marginal revenues and the marginal disutility of employing capital, labor, land, and entrepreneurship. A certain decline in the supply of productive factors as a consequence of higher direct taxes must then be weighed against the expansion of the trade in commodities which are freed from the tariff. It is very unlikely that the new source of taxes will do as much harm as the tariff did before. By hypothesis, the tariff has been levied for reasons of commercial policy. Chances are very slim that the duty will represent the tax which achieves the financing of expenditures in the least harmful way. Replacing the tariff by a tax that minimizes divergences between marginal utility and marginal costs, on the one hand, and marginal revenue and marginal disutility, on the other, means that the effects of the trade expansion resulting from the removal of the tariff will probably be more pronounced than the contraction of the best alternative method of raising revenue.

Viner's assumption of supply curves with an infinite elasticity also needs to be critically examined. Let us assume that A can manufacture only a single product—viz., cheese; B is able only to produce lace, and C can only produce toys. We will assume throughout the argument that there is full employment everywhere—which means, in other words, that the elasticity of supply of these products is equal to zero. Every country uses all its productive factors, available in a constant quantity, for the manufacture of a constant output of a single product. Viner's question as to whether a customs union would lead to a more or a less economical structure of world production is in this case irrelevant, since the structure of production is fixed. However, we can examine whether the formation of a customs union between A and B would lead to a more or a less economical structure of world consumption. We start with a situation in which each country levies a non-discriminating ad valorem tariff on imports from both the other countries. The tariff rate of A amounts to 10 per cent, that of B to 20 per cent, and that of C to 30 per cent. In the framework of the integration, A removes its tariff of 10 per cent on lace imports from B, but not the tariff on toys from C, and B eliminates its tariff of 20 per cent on cheese imports from A, but not on the import of toys from C. These actions will stimulate the trade in cheese and lace between countries A and B. At the outset, the market price and therewith the marginal utility of lace will be higher, in relation to the marginal utility of cheese, in A than in B—first, because the tariff of A on lace from B has kept it scarce in A, and, second, because the tariff of B on cheese from A has made it scarce in B. Expansion of the trade between A and B can therefore increase the standard of living in both countries. This result would certainly occur when the increase is not offset by a decrease in the trade between A and C or B and C. If the residents of B simply buy cheese from A instead of lace from B, and the residents of A simply buy lace from B instead of cheese from A, new trade would be created only between A and B. But that is hardly the end of the process. If the price of lace from B in A drops as a consequence of the removal of the tariff by A, then the residents of A, under certain circumstances, need buy additional lace from B only partly at the cost of cheese from A; they could at the same time shift their demand for toys from C, the price of which has not dropped, to lace from B. The increased purchases of lace from B by the residents of A would at the same time reduce the supply of lace from B in the world market and the exporters in B would probably sell more in A, at the expense not only of their sales in the home market but also at the expense of their sales in C, on which there is still a tariff. In the same way, the residents of B would buy more cheese from A at the expense of their consumption of toys from C and only partly at the expense of their consumption of lace. The cheese exporters in A would at the same time be induced to shift their exports from the tariff-burdened markets in C to the tariff-free markets in B. So it is possible that after the formation of the customs union, there will be a smaller export of cheese from A and of lace from B to country C and a smaller export of toys from C to countries A and B. This contraction of trade means an actual economic loss. The decline of the trade between A and C, on the one hand, and between B and C, on the other, could result in a fall in the standard of living in the states that take part in this trade.

Whether the losses exceed the gains or the other way around depends on two circumstances: first, on the *structure of the tariff systems* with which we started; and second, on the *structure of demand* in the countries concerned.

The difference in the ratio between the price of cheese from A and the price of lace from B in country A and country B determines how much can be gained by expanding this trade by one unit. This price difference itself is determined by the sum of the original tariff of A on lace and the original tariff of B on cheese. If the import duty in A amounts to 10 per cent, then the price of lace in A will be 10 per cent higher than in B, while the cheese price in B will be 20 per cent higher than in A if the import duty in B amounts to 20 per cent. This means that the ratio between the price of lace and that of cheese in A is about 30 per cent higher than in B. This provides us with a yardstick for the possible improvement in the standard of living in both countries which can be attained by expansion of the trade between A and B by one dollar. However, it must not be overlooked that this yardstick for the increase in welfare is actually related to only the first units of the expansion of the trade between the two countries.

A customs union between A and B can come about through a sequence of partial reductions in tariffs. For instance, A could lower its 10 per cent duty on lace in ten consecutive steps of 1 per cent each and B could lower its 20 per cent tariff on cheese in ten steps of 2 per cent each. As shown before, the utility of each additional unit in the amount of mutual trade at the beginning of the successive tariff reductions can be evaluated at 30 per cent. After accomplishing the first step, the tariff in A still amounts to 9 per cent and in B to 18 per cent, so that the utility of an additional unit in the mutual trade still amounts to 27 per cent before the second step is taken, etc. After the tenth tariff reduction has taken place, no additional utility gains will be obtained. Similar calculations can be made of the lowering of the standard of living which results from a contraction of the trade between C and A by one dollar, on the one hand, and between C and B, on the other. However, the tariff rate of A on toys from C and the tariff rate of C on cheese from A, and similarly the tariff rate of B on toys from C and the rate of C on lace from B, remain the same in this case during the development of the customs union between A and B. Consequently, the weight in measuring the decrease in welfare resulting from a contraction of the trade between C and A by one unit remains fixed at about 40 per cent for all steps; similarly, the weight in measuring the decrease in welfare resulting from a contraction in trade between C and B by one unit remains fixed at about 50 per cent. Two conclusions can be drawn from this: First, as a consequence of a customs union, the lower the tariff rate of C is in comparison with those of A and B, the sooner will the standard of living increase. A customs union between two countries which levy abnormally high tariffs will be more advantageous than one between two countries which have, compared with other countries, low tariffs. Second, one may assume that, in forming a customs union, the first steps in the preferential reduction of tariffs on mutual trade will yield more utility than the later steps. From the viewpoint of welfare, the expansion of trade caused by the first preferential reduction of tariffs will yield a greater benefit than that resulting from the ultimate elimination of duties. Hence, if there are no special reasons to assume that the trade with third countries will contract more after the first steps of the formation of the union than after the later ones, it follows that the first steps will probably yield more utility (or cause less damage) than later ones.

However, in order to evaluate the effect of a union on economic welfare, we cannot limit ourselves to taking into account only the weights to be attached to each unit of the trade that is expanded or contracted. The extent to which the customs union causes the trade to expand or contract must also be considered. Let us assume that cheese and lace are good substitutes for each other, while toys are bad substitutes for cheese as well as for lace. If, in this case, A and B lower their tariffs at the same time, a major part of the trade will be expanded and only a minor part contracted. The residents of A will buy more lace from B mainly at the expense of their own cheese consumption; their demand for toys from C will be reduced very little because the price of lace has fallen. Similarly, the residents of B will increase their consumption of cheese from A at the expense of their consumption of the lace which has now become available for export to A. They too will reduce their demand for toys from C by only a little. Hence, a large increase in the trade between A and B in lace and cheese and a small decrease in the exchange of toys for cheese from A and lace from B by country C will be registered. The situation would be quite different if cheese and lace were poor substitutes and toys, on the other hand, good substitutes for cheese as well as for lace. Then the increase of the cheese export of A will be small, but the cheese could be sent to B instead of C in order to obtain the lace, which is now cheaper, instead of toys, the price of which has remained the same. Also, the export of lace by B need not increase much, but the lace could be sent to A to finance the purchase of cheese, which has now become cheaper, instead of to C, the price of whose toys has remained the same.

We can therefore conclude from our simple model, in which the trade advantages consist only of an increased satisfaction of demand at constant supplies, that a customs union will raise the standard of living the more, (1) the higher the original tariffs of the uniting countries; (2) the lower the tariffs in the outside world; (3) the greater the substitutability of the products of the countries in the union; and (4) the less the products of the countries in the union can substitute for the products of the outside world.

Since our restrictive assumptions (inelastic supply, each country producing one commodity only) do not exist in the actual world, the model will be brought closer to reality in the following. Let us assume that each country produces more than one commodity, that on the demand side there are different degrees of substitutability and complementarity, and that on the supply side the marginal costs are an increasing function of production. Countries A, B, and C all produce cheese, lace, toys, etc. Each country exports some commodities and imports others and each levies a non-discriminating tariff. What will happen if A and B remove their tariffs reciprocally but main-

56

tain them with respect to C, while C adheres to non-discriminating tariffs on imports from A and B?

In view of the complications which are involved in this problem, we shall limit ourselves to the question of whether a *small preferential tariff reduction* is good or bad. Will the standard of living rise or fall if A slightly reduces its import duty on a product of B—for instance, beer—without also reducing the duty on other products from B or on all commodities from C? For the sake of simplicity, we will assume that the marginal utility of the incomes of all income-earners in all countries is the same. Furthermore, we will assume a situation of perfect competition in which there are no external economies or diseconomies of production. The result will be an increase in the import of beer by A from B. The price of beer in A will fall as a consequence, and the marginal costs and therewith the price of beer in B will rise as a result of an increase in export production. The price in A will fall and the price in B will rise, until the smaller excess of the price in A over the price in B is equal to the lower duty on the sale of beer from B in country A. Since the tariff which A levies on beer from C does not change, the lower beer price in A means that C has to export to A at a lower price in order to withstand competition. The beer production in C will contract until its marginal costs have fallen so much that it is able to compete with beer from B in country A. These changes in the supply and the price of beer in the three markets may have all sorts of reactions on the supply and demand conditions of other products in those markets and on the trade among them. The question is whether the net result of these changes tends to raise or lower economic welfare.

If there are no indirect taxes levied inside the countries— i.e., the prices paid by the buyer are equal to the prices paid by the seller—we can neglect all changes occurring in the domestic trade of the corresponding countries as a consequence of the tariff reduction. Of course, all sorts of changes can take place in domestic trade; but since the marginal utility of the employed factors of production equals the marginal utility of the commodities in domestic trade, marginal changes will have no effect on the internal welfare of the country. For, by hypothesis, domestic trade remains optimized as before, despite the tariff reduction—that is to say, the algebraic sum of the marginal disutilities of the employed factors of production and the marginal utilities of the consumption of the product remains zero. However, in view of the existence of monopolies, taxation, external economies, and diseconomies in the domestic trade, it seems extremely unrealistic to assume that in the domestic trade there will actually be no divergences between marginal disutilities and marginal utilities. One must judge the value of a customs union according to the extent to which it expands or contracts in each country the domestic production and consumption in those sectors in which such divergences are substantial. But divergences which stem from taxation on international trade are often grafted onto domestic divergences. For instance, the marginal costs of production of a commodity can be lower than the marginal utility to domestic consumers as a consequence of an excise tax or a monopoly. If, in addition, an import duty is levied on this product in other countries, the marginal utility of this commodity will be still higher for the consumers of the importing country. The divergence between the marginal disutilities and the marginal utilities in export production will then exceed the divergence in production for domestic consumption. For these reasons, the divergences between marginal disutilities and marginal utilities tend to be larger in international trade than in domestic trade. Our simple assumption that these divergences exist in international but not in domestic trade therefore draws attention to some important relationships in the real world.

We must now take into account all changes in international trade which stem directly or indirectly from the tariff reduction of A on behalf of the beer from B, evaluate each change according to its supply price in the exporting country, weigh them according to the ad valorem tariff rate of the importing country, and add the resulting amounts for all increases as well as decreases in trade. If the sum of the trade increases exceeds that of the decreases, welfare has risen, and vice versa. We will limit ourselves to a description of some obvious effects, since a computing machine would be able to cope with all arithmetic problems.

Meade distinguishes these reactions as *primary, secondary, and tertiary effects of a tariff change* on the trade.

The primary effect of a tariff reduction by country A on beer from B is an increase in the imports of A when all incomes and all prices are constant, with one exception: the price of beer from B decreases in A and increases in B. The higher the elasticity of the demand in A and the supply in B, the more the imports of country A will expand. The primary change will therefore always be advantageous. The greater the primary expansion of trade and the higher the original tariff rate of A on beer from B, the greater the primary gain in economic welfare.

The secondary effects deal with changes in the international trade of products which are good substitutes for or good complements of beer from B in A or in B, so that the trade in them is directly affected by the changes in the price of beer from B as a result of A's reduction of the tariff. Meade lists eight of these secondary reactions: (1) If beer from B is a good substitute in A for beer from C, then the decrease in the price of beer from B as a result of A's reduction of the tariff will divert the demand in A for beer from C. This is, in Viner's terminology, the familiar case of trade diversion: a secondary contraction of the import trade of A. (2) If beer from B is a good substitute in A for domestic alcoholic beverages, which are themselves an important export of A, the shift in A's demand from such beverages to beer from B will result in a decrease in A of the price of alcoholic beverages, of which a larger quantity can now be sold in C. If C levies a duty on alcoholic beverages from A, this secondary expansion in the export trade of A will cause a shift in the market for alcoholic beverages from a low price to a high price, and the consequence will be an increase in economic welfare. (3) The reduction of the tariff levied by A on beer from B can raise the total demand for beer from B and thereby its price in B. Now, if the beer from B sold in A is a good substitute in B for the beer that is sold in another export market, the increase in price which the breweries of country B may cause in A can lead to a reduction of the quantity sold to C. Moreover, if the beer export of country B to C is subject to duty, this secondary contraction of the export trade of B will result in a loss in economic welfare. (4) Domestic beer may be a good substitute in B for wine from C. The increased exports of beer from B to A would cause a decrease in domestic demand in favor of wine from C as a consequence of scarcity and price increases in B. If B levies a tariff on wine from C, this secondary expansion in the import trade of B will represent an increase in economic welfare, since a larger quantity of wine from C will move from a market with a low price in C to a market with a high price in B.

These four cases of secondary reactions deal with substitution among different commodities. Another four cases can be set up for relations of complementarity. If, for technical reasons, beer from B has to be exported in barrels and bottled in A, then beer bottles in A are complementary to beer imported from B, while in B beer barrels are complementary to exported beer. The following additional reactions may occur: (5) If A imports beer bottles from C, the additional import of beer from B in A will bring about an increased demand for beer bottles from C, and thus a secondary expansion of the import trade of A. (6) If A normally exports beer bottles to C, the additional import of beer from B will bring about an increased demand for beer bottles in A for domestic use. Fewer bottles will be available for export to C; the result will therefore be a secondary contraction of the export trade of A. (7) If B exports beer barrels to C, the additional export of beer from B to A will require more beer barrels from B, so that there will be fewer barrels available for export to C—a secondary contraction of the export trade of B. (8) If B imports beer barrels from C, the increased export of beer from B to A will raise the demand for beer barrels from C—a secondary expansion in the import trade of B.

Of course, not all of these eight cases possess the same degree of probability. Let us call the commodity on which the duty has been reduced the "primary commodity." The cases which will probably occur most frequently are those in which the primary commodity is a substitute for other imports in the importing country (case 1) and for other exports in the exporting country (case 3). Let us examine these two cases more closely.

Since A can obtain its beer not only from B but also from other countries, its imports from B compete to a considerable extent with its imports from other countries. The possibility of replacing beer imports from B by those from C results not only from the similarity of the needs which can be satisfied by the competing imports. Substitution can play a role on the production as well as on the consumption side. For instance, a country can be endowed with much land, in relation to capital and skilled labor. Such a country will probably produce an export surplus of agricultural products and an import surplus of industrial products. That country, for instance, will export wheat and potatoes and import nylon stockings and machinery. Nylon stockings and machines hardly satisfy the same needs, but the imports of both products can be good substitutes. Let us consider the case of a country with an import surplus of these two products. This country may have a small protected industry whose products compete with import products. This industry can partially meet the country's need for nylon stockings and machines and absorb the total supply of capital and skilled labor. If the duty on machinery which is imported, for instance, from Germany is reduced, the increased imports would outsell the domestic supply of machines. Capital and skilled labor would become idle in the importing country and these productive factors could then shift to another suitable industry—for instance, the production of nylon stockings. An increased import of machinery from Germany could in this way induce a decrease in the demand for nylon stockings imported, for instance, from the United States. This result is to the detriment of the customs union. It has a still wider significance if, for similar reasons, the primary commodity can be a good substitute for other export products in the exporting country.

All this shows that the imports of each country from various sources can to a great extent be substituted one for another; there will also be a high degree of substitution among the products which a country exports to various destinations. On the other hand, the probability is small that the imports as such will be good substitutes for the exports as such. But in some cases normal competition exists between the imports and exports of a country. In international trade a raw material must be regarded as a more or less good substitute for the finished product that contains this raw material. For instance, a country may import the finished product as well as the raw material if it has a small textile industry which is unable to meet the total need for clothing. It may import cotton from Egypt for its domestic industry and clothes from England for the rest of its domestic needs. Now, if this country reduces its duties on merchandise from England, this will result in a larger import of clothing from England. This will cause a contraction of its own textile industry and therefore lead to a reduction in its demand for Egyptian cotton. The substitution relationships between imports and exports in the trade in finished products are still more important for countries like Switzerland, Germany, Japan, Great Britain, Belgium, and Holland. The imports of raw materials and the exports of finished products compete keenly with each other in these countries. England imports raw wool from Australia and sells woolen textiles to the United States. If England abolishes its duty on Australian wool, it will import more wool and thereby stimulate exports to the United States. Instead of a contraction of England's import

trade, there will be a secondary expansion of her exports. Or
the other way around: if the United States abolishes its duties
on English products, it will import more English woolen textiles, which will lead to an increase in English imports of
Australian wool. Instead of a diversion of England's export
trade, an expansion of her imports will occur. This type of relationship is undoubtedly important, but it is virtually irrelevant in connection with a customs union, since tariffs on raw
materials are normally very low or do not exist at all.

Therefore, let us return to our earlier problem of the substitution of export commodities for each other, and of import
commodities for each other. Reduction of the import duties
on merchandise from B by country A will result, as we have
shown, in a decrease of imports by A from third countries and
a decrease of exports by B to third countries. If third countries
place an import duty on products from B, these products will
have a higher value in third countries than in B. Hence, as a
consequence of the normal diversion of the exports of country
B to A, there will be a loss in welfare (at constant costs, there
is no negative effect of the export diversion). As soon as we
allow for the possibility that trade will be diverted on the demand side in the importing country and on the supply side
in the exporting country, it is clear that abolition of duties on
imports can do considerable damage: Country A abolishes its
duties on imports from B. The residents of A can now buy from
B commodities which they have previously bought somewhere
else, and the residents of B can export to A commodities which
they previously sold somewhere else. If the import commodities of each country evince a pronounced substitutive character, A will import from B instead of from the outside world,
and country B will export to A rather than to third countries.
Under certain circumstances, the losses from the combined
diversion of imports of A and exports of B could outweigh the
gains from an expansion of the trade between A and B. The
validity of this general thesis is strongly restricted, as will be
shown if it is applied to our earlier examples. Country A re-

moves its import duty on beer from B but not on beer from C. The distortion of the import trade implies that A obtains more beer from B and less from C. The distortion of the export trade implies that B now sells its beer in A instead of in C. Stated otherwise: in order to have a distortion in import as well as in export trade, country C must, in the original situation, export beer (or good substitutes for it) to A and at the same time import beer (or good substitutes for it) from B. The fundamental objection to a customs union, formulated before, is based on the general assumption that the imports of a country can be substituted for each other, and so can the exports of a country, but the imports can hardly substitute for the exports. Now, if we examine the trade relationships between these countries, this assumption seems to lead to a contradiction. If the imports of A from B compete with the imports of A from C and the same exports of B to A compete with the exports of country B to C, the imports of C from B will probably be in the same class as the exports of C to A and they will compete with each other. The rule that the imports of a country cannot compete with its exports is inconsistent when applied to three countries at the same time.

On the other hand, the objections to a customs union gain weight if one takes into account that the world outside the customs union does not consist of only one country, but of a number of them—for instance, the countries C and D. While C will hardly export beer to A and at the same time import it from B, it is quite possible that A imports beer from B and C and country B exports to A and D. The removal of the tariff on beer from B by country A can then decrease the demand for beer from C in A (in which case the loss in welfare depends on the tariff which A levies on beer from C); it will also reduce the sale of beer by B to D (in which case the loss in welfare depends on the tariff which D levies on beer from B). The introduction of a second outsider, D, has further consequences. Even if the trade inside each country is completely free, it can hardly be assumed that free trade exists between C and D. If this is the case, we have to include in our gain and loss account the changes in the trade between C and D which stem indirectly from the removal of tariffs on products from B by A.

Another possible effect which argues against a customs union should be mentioned. If the residents of C can sell less beer to A and the residents of D can obtain less beer from B, country C will look for other beer consumers and country D for other beer suppliers. The export of beer from C to D will increase. If D levies a duty on the import of beer from C, a gain will result to the amount of the increase in the export of beer from C to D multiplied by the ad valorem tariff rate in D. If D replaces the reduction in its purchases of beer from B completely by an increase in its purchases of beer from C and applies the same tariff on beer from C as on beer from B, the decrease in welfare as a result of the drop in the exports of B to D will exactly equal the increase in welfare as a result of the rise in the exports of C to D. But the reaction on the trade between C and D need not take this form at all. Beer from B and beer from C need not be consumption substitutes, and differences in transport costs could mean that these two sources of supply are not equivalent for the importers in D. The residents of D cannot simply shift their demand for B-beer to C-beer. As soon as one assumes that in C or in D, or in both, some imports compete with some exports, cases arise in which the net effect is not an increase in the trade between C and D, but a decrease. Let country D export wine to C. Let domestic beer and wine from D be good substitutes in C, while in D domestic wine and beer from B compete with each other. Now, if the residents of D obtain less beer from B, they will consume more domestic wine and consequently export less of it to C; if the residents of C can sell less beer to A, they will drink more domestic beer and import less wine from D. The exports of D's wine to C will fall and welfare will decrease insofar as C levies an import duty from D. The damage of a customs union between A and B will therefore be enormous: it will be detrimental to the beer sales of C in A, the beer sales of B in D, and the wine sales of D in C. If heavy duties weigh on all these trade relations, the residents of A must increase their beer consumption fantastically or restrict their beer production radically so that the trade-increasing effects of a tariff reduction will offset all these unfavorable reactions.

This rather gloomy result shows that, in judging a customs union, everything depends on the circumstances. If our casual assumptions were replaced by other ones, a customs union might appear in a more favorable light.

So far we have tacitly assumed that trade barriers consist of import duties, while in reality quantitative restrictions are widely prevalent at present. The results of our analysis undergo a change as soon as we replace duties by quantitative restrictions. Let country A import steel from B and C, and assume that there are quantitative restrictions on the imports from both countries. What happens if these restrictions are removed on the imports of steel from B but not on those from C? We will assume that at the start the restrictions are effective for both countries, in the sense that prices and marginal utilities of the steel in B and C are lower than in A, and that an increase in the imports from both countries is prevented only by the quantitative restrictions on the imports. Let the removal of the restrictions in A take the form of a sequence of gradual enlargements of the quota for steel from B in A until the allowed import in A is larger than the unimpeded demand, so that all quantitative restrictions become completely unnecessary. If the quota of country A for steel from B is enlarged, more steel can be obtained in A; the steel price will tend to drop and this will tend to decrease the demand for steel from C. However, there will not be a direct reduction of the quantities of steel imported from C; the immediate effect will only be that the price of steel from C in A will approach the lower price for steel in C. But so long as the price and marginal utility of steel in A are higher than in C, the whole quota of permitted imports of steel from C will be exhausted and the quantity of steel moving from C to A will remain unchanged. Hence, there is no secondary contraction of imports of C-steel in A, though the steel from C competes keenly with that from B. It is possible to enlarge the quota of A for steel from B to such an extent that the price and marginal utility of steel in A will fall to the level of C. In this case, each further increase of the quota for steel from B will tend to decrease the price of C-steel in A below the level in C and the steel exports of C to A will diminish. Hence, there will be a secondary contraction of the imports of C-steel in A. But, since the price of steel from C in A is no longer higher than in C, the marginal utility of steel in A will no longer exceed that in C. Hence, welfare will not decrease as a result of this contraction of trade. The following conclusion can be drawn from this example: If the imports of steel from C in country A are fixed by quota, there will be no decrease in the steel exports of C to A so long as A's quota effectively restricts the demand for steel from C. If this demand diminishes, this means that the quota has become ineffective and could be removed, so that a possible reduction in the trade leaves economic welfare undisturbed. Hence, if all trade barriers take the form of fixed quotas, a customs union will raise economic welfare. The primary expansion of the trade between the partners would incontestably increase welfare and there would be no repercussions except in markets in which there are no or ineffective quotas. In any case, these reactions do not affect economic welfare.

So far, we have interpreted the customs union as a system that discriminates among countries. This is not the only discrimination possibility. The European Coal and Steel Community is an example of the combination of a preference system of several countries with discrimination among products. Let us assume that all the countries of the world decide to reduce their trade barriers against coal and steel and form, so to speak, a World Community for Coal and Steel: the problem of import and export diversion then becomes irrelevant, since no nation is outside the union. But a diversion can now set in against other products, since the trade barriers have not been removed for all goods. As an example, A removes the tariff on steel from C without removing the tariff on machinery. The fall of the steel price in A reduces the production costs in its machine industry; consequently, its output rises, so that the import of machines from C can be reduced. If the tariff rate of A on machinery is much higher than the original tariff rate on steel, these developments are possibly uneconomical. True, the increase in the steel exports of C to A means the shift of a product from the market in C, in which it was cheaper, to a market in A, in which it is expensive. But this gain can be overcompensated by the fact that fewer machines are exported from C, where they are produced at low costs, to A, where costs are high. This is one of the cases in international trade in which a raw material (steel) and a finished product (machines) have to be considered as good substitutes. Of course, discrimination among products can have repercussions which are analogous to those that result from discrimination among countries.

2. JUSTIFICATION OF REGIONAL INTEGRATION

The starting point of our study of the effects of a customs union on economic welfare was the difference between trade diversion and trade creation. In the course of the analysis it has been shown that this simple distinction is an inadequate criterion for judging the effects of a customs union. Actually, the problem is very complex. However, some general conclusions can be drawn.

First, each customs union requires a reduction of trade barriers. This circumstance will always lead to a primary expansion of trade, almost always accompanied by a considerable increase in welfare.

Second, the formation of a customs union will lead more rapidly to an improvement in the standard of living if at the beginning the economic structures of the partners are very similar to each other (substitutable), but can potentially supplement each other well—that is to say, the two economies are potentially very complementary. In this case, a sharp expansion of their mutual trade is possible without diverting their imports or exports from other markets.

Third, the higher the original tariff rates on imports from the partner countries, the more the customs union will raise economic welfare.

Fourth, a customs union will raise economic welfare if each country is the other's principal supplier of the products which it exports, and if each country is the other's principal market for the products which it imports. If A is the principal market for certain products from B, then there is less opportunity to divert the exports of B from other markets to the market of A. Or, if B is the principal supplier of certain products to A, then A has less opportunity to import the products of countries other than B. Of course, the extent to which these conditions are satisfied depends on the structure of trade between the two countries at the moment in question.

Fifth, the greater the share that a customs union has in the production, consumption, and trade of the world, the sooner it will lead to a rise in economic welfare. Ultimately—that is, when all countries of the world are joined together in one union—diversion of import and export trade will no longer be possible. The larger the area comprising the union, the more trade in this area will expand and the less trade will be diverted from the outside world.[3]

Sixth, the lower the tariff rates in the outside world and the larger the number of independent customs areas into which the outside world is divided, the sooner the formation of a customs union will raise economic welfare. A reduction of the tariff on beer from B by country A can cause a diversion of the exports of B's beer from the market in D, but the lower the beer tariff of country A, the smaller the loss resulting from this distortion.

[3] Cf. also J. Tinbergen, "Customs Unions: Influence of Their Size on Their Effect," *Zeitschrift für die gesamte Staatswissenschaft* (1957), pp. 404ff.

The tariff reduction of A can at the same time cause a diversion of its beer imports from the market in C; as a consequence, C will export more beer to D.

Seventh, the more frequently trade barriers take the form of fixed quantitative restrictions rather than tariffs, the fewer will be the unfavorable secondary effects of a customs union on the economic welfare of the world.

Eighth, the greater the possibility of obtaining the advantages of mass production in those industries that are now able to expand by underselling similar industries in the other member countries of the union, the sooner the formation of a customs union will raise economic welfare.

Ninth, a partial but non-selective reduction of the tariffs on imports from partner countries will be more favorable than the final, complete removal of these tariffs. In this sense, a general system of partial preferences would be preferable to an all-embracing customs union. A mutual reduction of the import tariffs by the partners will raise their mutual trade, but it can also divert imports and exports. Trade expansion will always mean an increase in welfare, but the lower the tariffs on this trade, the smaller the gain will be. However, since the tariffs of the other countries on the exports of the union states and the tariffs of the union states on imports from the outside world could remain the same, the loss of welfare resulting from each unit of trade diversion need not change during the process of forming the customs union. This argument does not mean that a partial tariff reduction within a group of countries would be preferable under all circumstances to a complete tariff reduction. What can be concluded from it is only that the first stages in the process of forming a customs union influence welfare more strongly than the later stages.

From the standpoint of pure logic, the conclusion from the previous analysis is that the best principle in removing trade barriers would be an agreement—including all countries and all products—to lower all tariffs on a non-discriminatory basis below a given maximum. In the framework of such an agreement, the highest tariffs would be reduced (whereby the high-

70

est possible gain would be reaped from each unit of primary trade expansion) and the reduction would be non-discriminatory (whereby a minimum of trade distortion would be entailed). However, Meade, to whom we owe this thorough investigation of the theoretical aspects of a customs union, himself departs at this point from the domain of pure theory by indicating the political and the geographical limits set to the theoretically highest possible welfare: "While this is a logical conclusion from our analysis, it is not, of course, a condemnation of smaller economic unions, since the political conditions may not exist for obtaining any far-reaching action on the more universal scale. . . . I know very well that I should be an ardent proponent and supporter of the building of Benelux even if a careful and unbiassed application of the criteria which I have just enumerated suggested that its formation was more likely to reduce than to raise economic welfare in the rather narrow sense in which I have been using that term. Why would I adopt this attitude? It is becoming a truism that with modern developments of transport, communications, and technology larger social and political units are likely to be more viable and self-reliant politically and strategically. I am quite certain that there is a need for a greater integration of the countries of the free world. Politically it would give greater coherence and strength. Economically any move towards economic union covering a large number of countries would undoubtedly serve to raise standards of living."[4]

The second-best solution of a union within relatively narrow geographical limits, whose realization several institutions are prepared to strive for, is definitely preferable to an illusive and passive waiting for a free trade regime embracing all the countries of the world.

3. REGIONAL UNIFICATION AND DISCRIMINATION

In the last section we examined the problem of universal free trade versus free trade on a regional basis. In the process,

[4] J. E. Meade, *The Theory of Customs Unions*, pp. 114f.

various forms of regional free trade were neglected. The only characteristic of regional unification that we touched upon was one of trade policy; we assumed that intraregional trade received preferential treatment—that the countries which form the union apply lower import and export tariffs, and higher quotas or lower export subsidies, in their mutual trade in some or all products than they levy on trade in the same products with the outside world. The regional system of preferences therefore signifies discrimination among countries or among products so far as the outside world is concerned.

Discrimination is incompatible with the fundamental clause of the General Agreement on Tariffs and Trade (GATT)—namely, the most-favored-nation clause. This clause requires that all special advantages granted by one state to another in international trade must also be granted automatically and unconditionally to those states with which trade agreements have been concluded on the basis of the most-favored-nation principle. The purpose of this clause is to put all participating states on an equal basis—i.e., to prevent discrimination. Since GATT is a world-wide organization, the ban on discrimination can also be applied in principle to Continental (regional) trade agreements. Contrary to the intentions of the founders of GATT, the most-favored-nation principle has proved in the last few years to be more of a deterrent than a stimulus to effective tariff reductions. For this reason, the West European countries have availed themselves of the exception clauses of the GATT agreement in which the customs union and the free trade area are excluded from the ban on discrimination. In both cases, the participating countries can mutually lower their tariffs without being obliged to lower them simultaneously for third countries. In the previous section, we have therefore considered these two cases together as a "customs union."

A customs union as well as a free trade area will normally have a discriminating effect on trade with the outside world. The discriminatory practice is, however, not limited entirely to regional systems of preference. The special aspects of discrimination as they appear in the case of general free trade among a restricted number of countries have been examined in the previous chapter. Discrimination in regional preference systems has not appeared to be as harmful as the objections against such unions depict it, but the problem is always present in examining directly controlled trade among more than two countries. It is indeed impossible to establish an unambiguous criterion of non-discrimination.

The way in which discrimination works can best be demonstrated by some examples:

(1) Let us assume that a system of import duties or quantitative import restrictions has a varying influence on the import of certain commodities. Country A restricts the import of cars, while wheat imports are not controlled. On the face of it, there seems to be no discrimination against certain countries. The producers of every country could export cars and wheat to A under the same conditions, but it is possible that B produces only cars and no wheat, while C perhaps produces only wheat and no cars. The authorities of A do not intend to treat the suppliers in B differently from those in C; it is conceivable that imports of cars are restricted for reasons which have nothing to do with the country of origin.[5] Nevertheless, the producers in B become fully aware of the effect of the restrictions, while the producers in C are not directly affected at all. Moreover, it is impossible to determine the motives that make the government of A restrict imports in the indicated way; in reality, the reason may very well lie in an intention to discriminate against a source of supply. The possibilities of this situation are very numerous as a result of the difficulty of defining any particular commodity exactly. The definition can of course be made so exact and meticulous that it applies exclusively to one source of supply. An example of this can be found in Haberler's book, *Der internationale Handel.* Haberler cites a clause in the German tariff of 1902 which refers unambiguously to Switzerland and Austria. In it, a certain tariff is levied on brown or spotted

---

[5] Cf. J. E. Meade, *The Balance of Payments,* page 380.

cattle that have been bred at an altitude of at least 300 meters above sea level and have grazed for at least one month during the summer at an altitude of at least 800 meters above sea level.[6]

(2) Another example of potential discrimination occurs when a duty is levied on a specific instead of a value basis. The difficulty here is to measure the degree of import restriction for various commodities. But, apart from that, the problem of discrimination occurs even in the case of a single commodity. For instance, a duty need not specify a tax of, say, 10 per cent on the import value of a certain cloth. It is also possible to levy a duty of one dollar per imported yard of this cloth. An expensive cloth of good quality that, for instance, costs $10 per yard will then be subjected to a tax that corresponds to an ad valorem duty of 10 per cent. On the other hand, a cheap cloth that, for instance, costs only $2 per yard will then be subjected to a tax that corresponds to an ad valorem duty of 50 per cent. It is possible that B specializes in the production of high-quality cloth and C in the production of cheap cloth. As a consequence of the specific way of levying duties, there is then discrimination against the producers of cloth in country C.

(3) A similar case occurs when import licenses are fixed not by value but by quantity. Here, too, the producers of high-quality commodities are favored. A license which permits an importer to import 100 yards of cloth enables him to import goods to the total value of $1,000 at $10 per yard, or of $200 at $2 per yard. If the same profit rate applies to both qualities, the importer will use the license to import the more expensive cloth since it allows him to realize a higher turnover. The producers of the superior quality, who are possibly residents of B, then benefit at the expense of the producers of the inferior quality, who are possibly residents of C.

(4) If import restrictions are administered as open quotas, a maximum is fixed for the import value or the import quantity. All exporters, irrespective of their domicile, can then export to

[6] Cf. G. Haberler, *Der internationale Handel*, page 251.

A, but the borders are closed to a commodity as soon as its quota is exhausted. The method seems to be non-discriminatory, since no preferential treatment is given to certain exporters or importers. In reality, however, those suppliers benefit who are closest to the consuming market.

(5) To eliminate these difficulties, import licenses could be issued to certain dealers in A, enabling them to decide freely which source of supply they will use. Frequently, it is possible to obtain by this method a good approximation of the principle of non-discrimination, since it may be assumed that the dealers will consider the cheapest producers. However, this need not be the case. The dealers can specialize in the import of products from certain countries or from certain markets or of certain qualities. The distribution of licenses among the importers therefore does not solve the problem of non-discrimination.

(6) The authority in charge of import restrictions can itself determine the source of supply and try to prevent discrimination by permitting all exporters in the various countries to export a certain percentage of the deliveries during a certain base period. Nevertheless, non-discrimination is not guaranteed, for three reasons: First, there is the problem of the representative base period. If a period is chosen in which the exports of B to A were high, the producers of B are favored, etc. One cannot tell which period is the right one. Second, the supply and demand conditions change even when the base period is really representative for the past. A quota fixed on this basis discriminates against a producer whose production costs have fallen or against commodities which have become increasingly fashionable. But, if the quota has to be adjusted to such changes, then there is the problem of which adjustment accords with the principle of non-discrimination. Third, it cannot be said that a uniform percentage reduction of the imports from all countries of origin does not cause discrimination even when the base period is representative for the past and supply and demand conditions have not changed. It is possible that the producers of B may be able to reorganize their production

more quickly or to serve another market than the producers of C.

It follows from these examples that discrimination also is the rule and non-discrimination the exception in the trade policy of a single country. The reservations relating to regional preference systems therefore represent an aspect which is not an exclusive characteristic of a customs union or a free trade area.

4. FREE TRADE AREA AND CUSTOMS UNION

For these two types of unification, GATT has an exception clause permitting the participating countries to reduce their tariffs among themselves without being obliged to lower them for third countries as well. The distinction made between a customs union and a free trade area is the following: the customs union applies a common tariff rate to third countries (according to Art. XXIV, Sect. 2b, of GATT, the outer tariffs and other international trade regulations of a customs union should, in total, not be higher or more restrictive than before the formation of the union), while the countries which form a free trade area can maintain their national tariff rates for their trade with third countries.[7]

These two systems no longer belong wholly in the realm of abstract deliberation. On the one hand, the six countries of the European Coal and Steel Community have already participated for some years in one common market, which has the features of a customs union to the extent that trade barriers between participating countries will be removed step by step, and at the same time a common tariff for trade with third countries will be created. The union of "Little Europe" has been carried over into a more global integration by the European Organization for Economic Cooperation (OEEC). On the other hand, these attempts have caused the member countries of the OEEC

[7] For the following, cf. G. Keiser, "Das System der Freihandelszone als ein Weg au grösseren Märkten," *Wirtschaftsfragen der Freien Welt*, pp. 602ff.

to consider, within the framework of the organization, the establishment of a Free Trade Area for the territory of West Europe which would include the Common Market of the six countries of "Little Europe." If these efforts are crowned with success, tariffs among the West European countries will eventually disappear completely. Exceptions are being considered for the agricultural sector and the underdeveloped countries ("countries which are in the stage of economic development"), according to the report of the research committee of the OEEC.[8]

The representative of Great Britain in that research committee observed that the definition of a free trade area—as can be found in, for instance, GATT—demands the removal not only of import duties but also of other trade restrictions. He pointed out that the obstacles to intra-European trade in agricultural products were not caused so much by duties and quantitative restrictions (as is the case with industrial products) as by protectionist measures inside a country. The removal of duties and quantitative restrictions would therefore miss its mark, and consequently agricultural products should be excluded from the proposals for a free trade area. On the other hand, the representatives of the predominantly agricultural countries pointed out that the exclusion of agriculture would be incompatible with the regulations of GATT. These regulations demand a removal of duties on more than 90 per cent of the products that are produced in the member countries.

Moreover, the research committee expressed its opinion on the question of whether all member countries should participate at the same time and in the same way in the Free Trade Area. The representatives of the relatively underdeveloped countries pointed out that they were forced to maintain in toto, or at least partially, their present protective measures against imports. The reason why Great Britain has proposed not a customs union but a free trade area for this all-European pref-

[8] Cf. OEEC, *Report on the Possibility of Creating a Free Trade Area in Europe*, Paris, 1957.

erence system is, as we have said, that only in this way can it maintain its preference system with the Commonwealth.

Many specific problems of the Free Trade Area are primarily of a technical nature. The continuance of different national tariff rates against third countries has the danger that cheap commodities from the outside world will be imported by way of the member countries with low tariffs against third countries (low-tariff countries) into the member countries with high tariff rates. To prevent this, the customs borders between the member countries have to be maintained and, in addition, a workable system of certificates of origin has to be put into practice. The problem of certificates of origin occurs in any regional agreement that is characterized by discrimination against outsiders. In brief, it consists of distinguishing the product of one country from that of another. But what percentage of the value of the finished product has to be produced in country X in order to be marked "Made in X"? Some kind of arbitrary criterion must be employed. The certificate of origin is a simple matter so long as the finished products of third countries are at issue. Japanese textiles and American machines, for instance, could be recognized with the help of the principle of certificates of origin and be taxed with the current national tariff even when they are imported by way of a country with low tariffs against the outside world. The problem becomes more complicated when one deals with a product that has actually been manufactured in a country of the area, but in the manufacture of which raw materials or semi-manufactures have been used which originated in third countries. If, as is the case in West Europe, the countries individually levy different tariffs on these raw materials and semi-manufactures, then the countries with the lowest tariff rates for basic materials from outside the area have a competitive advantage, if the finished product is traded duty-free inside the area. This situation can give rise to specific processing industries in the countries with low outer tariffs and can lead to a curtailment of similar industries in the countries with high tariffs.

The system of certificates of origin must therefore give those countries in the Free Trade Area that have a high tariff on the import of a certain product the chance to discriminate against member countries with a lower tariff on the same product. For instance, Switzerland, unlike Italy, has no automobile industry of its own; however, American cars are assembled in Switzerland. Since Italy levies a protective tariff on American cars, the American cars assembled in Switzerland will be cheaper in Switzerland than the American cars exported to Italy will be in Italy. Hence, in a prospective Free Trade Area, Italy will discriminate against American cars with respect to Switzerland. Moreover, if Italy imports American cars which are assembled in Switzerland, there is the problem of the certificate of origin and the way in which the cars will be taxed. Are the cars assembled in Switzerland to be evaluated as American or as Swiss products? In the latter case, they could be imported duty-free in Italy and the protective rate on American auto imports would be ineffective. The Swiss assembly plants would expand and a potential Italian assembly industry as well as the Italian automobile industry in general would incur the risk of contraction. Different tariffs in Italy and Switzerland on the import of cars from the United States would therefore make no sense.

In the domain of agriculture, the problem is still more serious. From the viewpoint of farm policy, there are at the moment in Europe two distinctly different groups of countries. One group protects production which is basically agricultural by tariffs on cereals and other feedstuffs, and levies correspondingly high duties on finally processed agricultural products. The other group of countries does not restrict the import of feedstuffs and consequently can produce the refined agricultural products more cheaply. If the Free Trade Area were fully realized, there would no longer be tariffs on refined products within the area. The countries without duties on feedstuffs could then flood the other countries with cheap refined products, while in the latter fodder prices would remain high because feedstuffs are mainly imported from third countries against which the former customs duties remain in force.

The research committee of the OEEC proposed a series of solutions to the problem of the distortions which can result from the various nations maintaining different outer tariffs. The system that is practiced at the moment in the Commonwealth could constitute a solution. The duties on the commodities traded among the contracting countries of the Commonwealth are either removed or reduced, while the individual member countries autonomously levy duties on trade with third countries. Thus American commodities on which Canada imposes no or low duties could theoretically be exported duty free via Canada to England. The Commonwealth has protected itself against this by stipulating that, in the case of each commodity that claims the advantage of the preference system, it must be proved that a certain percentage of the value of the commodity, ranging from 25 per cent to 75 per cent, has been produced in the Commonwealth. The shortcoming of this system is that, for a certain percentage of the value of the commodity, no account is taken of the effects of different tariff rates if basic materials imported from third countries are used.

Hence another system has been evolved, according to which each country of the Free Trade Area would require from the exporter proof as to whether basic materials have been used that were imported from third countries and were liable to a tariff. In that case, the duties applicable to the basic materials according to the national tariff rates would be levied pro rata. Of course, the tariffs to be paid by the exporter at the time of the import of the raw materials would have to be refunded to him in his home country. This complicated system, if properly maintained, would guarantee that shifts in production would not occur as a result of differences in the national tariffs against third countries. The system could also be put into effect in agriculture by levying a tariff, for instance, on the quantities of feedstuff necessary for the production of a certain number of eggs if the eggs were imported by a country with protective tariffs on feedstuffs. Naturally, input-output relationships would have to be ascertained for the feedstuff requirements per refined product.

Finally, a third solution might consist of making tariffs uniform in all cases in which varying tariffs on raw materials and semi-manufactures could lead to shifts of production to the countries with the lowest tariffs. In any case, the investigation of the OEEC has shown that, from the viewpoint of tariff technique, there is always the possibility of preventing or moderating disturbances and dislocations caused by the maintenance of different tariffs against third countries.

Apart from these technical problems, a free trade area also differs in an economic aspect from a customs union. Customs duties influence the terms of trade, the price level, and therewith real wages and eventually also money wages. If a group of countries mutually removes trade barriers, but each country maintains its own tariff rates against the outside world, it is possible that a price divergence will be carried over into the area. The countries with the lowest level of tariffs against third countries have an advantage in competition with the countries levying protective tariffs. If these cases are not adjusted from the very beginning by a change in the exchange rate or the price level and the nominal wages, long-term shifts of production from the high-tariff to the low-tariff countries will result which have nothing to do with differences in factor endowment, but are simply and solely based on differences in national tariffs against the outside world. The smaller the domain of the free trade area—i.e., the more significant the trade with third countries—the stronger these tendencies will be. However, the purchase of commodities from third countries that are subject to duties are of secondary importance in the industrial sector for the West European Free Trade Area, as it is currently envisaged.[9] True, a large part of the raw ma-

[9] Cf. G. Keiser, *op.cit.*, page 605.

terials that are used by West European industry (cotton, wool, rubber, non-ferrous metals, etc.) originates in third countries, but the import duties on raw materials are generally low—a mercantilist relic.[10] Maintaining national outer tariffs for semi-manufactures and manufactured goods should therefore have hardly any effect on the price levels of the member countries in the planned West European Free Trade Area.

The situation is different in the agricultural sector. A considerable share of the demand for a whole series of products is met by imports from third countries. Differing outer tariffs in the agricultural sector would therefore lead to a continuation of the national differences in price levels; for this reason, the leveling effect of a removal of the inner tariffs within the Free Trade Area should remain rather limited for this sector. However, since import duties are only one of the numerous instruments for fixing agricultural price levels according to political desiderata, Great Britain as well as Switzerland should be permitted to exclude the agricultural sector from the Free Trade Area.

It can be accepted that, in a Free Trade Area, strong forces will work in the direction of a gradual removal of the differ-

[10] This appears from the following tabulation:

Import Duties at the Beginning of the Common Market of the European Coal and Steel Community
(in per cent)

	France	Benelux	Germany	Italy
Coal	0	0	0	0
Coke	0	0	0	5–10
Iron ore	0	0	0	0
Pig iron	(5)	0–1	(12)	11–20
Basic and semi-manuf. steel	(7–10)	1–2	(15–18)	11–15
Hot-rolled steel products	(10–18)	1–6	(15–25)	15–20
Finished steel products	(16–22)	6–8	(15–28)	15–23

The figures in parentheses stand for duties which were suspended in the trade with all countries before the establishment of the Common Market. It is therefore certain that the establishment of the Common Market of the Coal and Steel Community has had only a very small direct influence on the trade barriers of the Community. Derived from Horst Mendershausen, "First Tests of the Schuman Plan," *The Review of Economics and Statistics* (1953), page 273.

ences in the price and cost levels which might result from maintaining separate national tariffs against third countries. The Free Trade Area will therefore tend to transform itself gradually into something that is virtually the same as a customs union.

CHAPTER III

METHODS OF INTEGRATION

1. FUNCTIONAL AND INSTITUTIONAL INTEGRATION

To BRING THE ECONOMIC INTEGRATION of several countries closer to realization and to safeguard this integration, two principal types of methods can be distinguished. According to the first, integration is established through administrative measures, and can only be maintained by continuous administrative action. The second involves the liberalization and ultimately the complete elimination of these administrative measures, through mutual agreement, in order to free the exchange of goods across the borders of the member states and so form a larger market in which the laws of supply and demand can be effective without regional administrative intervention.[1]

The first type can be defined as the institutional method of integration, the second as the functional method. The functional method meets only the first criterion of our definition of integration by limiting itself to the mere removal of artificial trade barriers; the institutional method, however, introduces in addition the desirable elements of coordination and unification. Hence, if the problem of integration is seen as part of the more general problem of formulating the best possible economic policy, the functional method is unsatisfactory.

The advocates of the *functional method*—for instance, Röpke —lean toward a purely historic conception of integration: "Hence, if anything deserves the name of international economic integration, surely it is the world economy as it developed up to 1914."[2] Röpke starts from an integrated de-

---

[1] Cf. K. Albrecht, *Probleme und Methoden der wirtschaftlichen Integration*, Kiel, 1951; idem, "Integration auf vielen Wegen," *Wirtschaftsdienst* (1955), pp. 449ff. F. Perroux, *L'Europe sans rivages*, Paris, 1954, page 432; R. Aron, "Problems of European Integration," *Lloyds Bank Review* (April 1953).

[2] Cf. W. Röpke, "Integration und Desintegration der internationalen Wirtschaft," *Wirtschaftsfragen der Freien Welt*, page 494; on the other

veloped economy and denotes as its characteristic feature "a market and price community which rests on a payments community and, unhampered on this ground, a localization of production in keeping with the idea of a rational division of labor." According to this view, the ideal case of complete economic integration occurs when free competition prevails in all markets—in particular, in the market of productive factors—and a common currency system is in effect. The cases of integration which one finds in the real world therefore represent more or less significant deviations from this hypothetical ideal. Hence, despite frequent limitations on competition, integration is in effect in developed economies. Correspondingly, it can be said that international economic relationships before 1914 were "integrated" in the sense that as a "world economy" they fulfilled the requirements of such a "national economy" on a global level. "An international currency system, the gold standard, which made national currencies freely convertible into each other and into a common standard metal—moreover, at stable exchange rates—secured a perfect 'virtual multilaterality' which, in its turn, produced the international market and price community that distinguishes the world economy quantitatively but not qualitatively from a national economy." This analogy applies, according to Röpke, to the international mobility of productive factors in the period before 1914. Of decisive importance for the "integration" of that time was a structural feature of the world economy "on which the existence or non-existence of international economic integration is dependent": the free convertibility of currencies. Indeed, the disintegration of an international economy can then be denoted as the decomposition or destruction of the "market, price, and payments community" through new methods of trade policy aiming at new economic and currency objectives.

Such a definition of international integration obviously colors proposals for restoring trade among the Western nations in a

---

hand, cf. E. Salin, "Wandlungen der Weltwirtschaft," *Wirtschaft und Staat*, Berlin, 1932, pp. 15ff.

particular way. We are ignoring for the moment the fact that the advocates of the functional method in general prefer world-wide to regional solutions. These authors—above all, Röpke—see the source of international disintegration in the coming to the fore of those national forces which they denote by the vague term of "collectivism." National collectivism "necessarily destroys the international integration of economies, but, on the other hand, to repair the damage by means of international collectivism also necessarily fails, since it requires a maximum of international social integration. And that at a moment when the degree of international social integration achieved by nineteenth-century liberalism has declined, and has done so partly as a result of collectivist trends. From this twofold paradox of collectivism . . . follows compellingly the incompatibility of collectivism and international economic integration except in the case of a collective world despotism."[3]

At the moment, according to this view, the task therefore consists of overcoming the continued disintegration of the world economy by a national and international return to a market economy, on the one hand, and by repairing the outer economic framework, on the other. Röpke believes that under the present circumstances this task can be achieved only in the way attempted by the OEEC; for the OEEC is an organization which tries, by binding resolutions, to bring the individual countries to relinquish national economic intervention. European integration should therefore be attained by reducing the number and the impact of government interventions in the area of international trade. The endeavor to establish a "market and price community" merely through eliminating trade barriers and renouncing government interventions typifies the functional method of integration. In contrast to the OEEC, Röpke denounces the organization of the Coal and Steel Community, regardless of the fact that it limits the possibilities of national intervention, since it opens the door wide to intervention by a supranational authority. How to overcome nation-

[3] Cf. W. Röpke, *op.cit.*, page 498.

alism in economic matters, not by transferring national sovereignty rights to a supranational body, but by renouncing the use of these sovereign rights in foreign trade policy is therefore the leading question for the advocates of the functional method as well as for those of classical liberalism. The gist of their argument is that the transfer of national sovereignty rights leads to the formation of a bloc which it is impossible for other countries to join, if not in theory, at least in practice. This is due to the fact that the number of countries eligible for entry is limited from the beginning by the area over which the principle of supranational sovereignty can be extended. Another reason is that, as in the case of the Coal and Steel Community, a "compact industrial body" is forged which makes an extension, with its new adjustments, seem like an annoying disturbance. On the other hand, the renunciation of national sovereignty rights in foreign trade policy, as agreed upon in the framework of the OEEC, leaves open the possibility of moving from a system of preferences to a non-discriminating system including all the countries of the world. Since the advocates of the functional method are also supporters of global integration, the institutional solution is, according to them, to be repudiated the more.

The exponents of the *institutional method*, unlike those of functional integration, take account of the fact that integration requires, under present circumstances, coordination and unification of economic and social policies. They are more realistic, in the sense that they regard historic developments as irreversible and, furthermore, do not consider the world economy of the period before 1914 as an ideal situation and therefore as an objective to be pursued by the integration movement. In comparison with the situation in 1913, the present disintegration is more apparent than real, according to Myrdal. Prior to 1914, only part of the world was to some extent integrated; the most important of the colored peoples, the colonies, and the backward areas were excluded. Capital movements, movements of people, and international trade among the small group of advanced countries, on one hand, and among them and small enclaves of the rest of the world, on the other, functioned relatively undisturbed. The "world" of 1913, like Athens in the days of Pericles, in many respects appears to have been an exemplary civilization if one forgets the fact that it excluded from its blessings the major part of humanity. According to Myrdal, "Any new international system ensuring stability, broadly shared progress, and a commonly felt confidence in the future must be attained on different terms, since the peoples who were then excluded are unwilling to resume their earlier passive role."[4] Myrdal therefore defines integration quite differently from the advocates of the functional method: "Economic integration is the realization of the old Western ideal of equality of opportunity."[5] A national or a world economy is therefore not integrated so long as all opportunities are not open to everyone and so long as all equal productive factors do not receive equal remuneration. For Myrdal, the most important objective of the integration movement will be achieved when the distribution of income has become as equal as possible. However, objectives like an equal distribution of income, full employment, etc., cannot be achieved by the functional integration method. Free mobility of productive factors among countries must be added to freedom of international trade and convertibility of currencies, for commodity trade is only to a very limited extent a substitute for mobility of productive factors. At any rate, no liberalization of international trade can eliminate the present disintegration and the present differences in national welfare. "Migration, capital movements, international aid, and trade are not the primary means of achieving this closer integration. In a real sense they are the products of integration, not the cause. They can help, but they cannot be relied upon to do the job. The major task is first to force economic development in the underdeveloped countries. . . ."[6]

[4] G. Myrdal, *An International Economy*, London, 1956, page 1.
[5] *Ibid.*, page 11.   [6] *Ibid.*, pp. 3-4.

As experience shows, mobility of productive factors would not suffice to bring about an equalization in the welfare of the West European countries. At any rate, to solve the problem of Southern Italy not only international but also intranational mobility of capital has been insufficient. Before the unification of the Italian states (1859-1870), the southern regions of Italy were, it is true, already agriculturally oriented and backward in comparison with the other regions of Italy and the rest of Europe. Still, they possessed an industry which was protected by high duties. It was at that time considered certain that the creation of a common national market, accompanied by political unification, would accelerate the economic development of these regions, which had previously been politically autonomous. For instance, it was assumed that capital investments would be made within the new national framework and that the relative poverty of the South would present not a deterrent to industrialization but, on the contrary, an advantage, since the relatively low wages would stimulate investments. This conception did not leave room for any form of government policy for the development of Italy. In actual fact, the elimination of the tariff walls between the southern and northern regions led to the ruin of the industry of South Italy, while the industry of the North, which was originally only slightly protected, benefited from the newly created national market. The industrial regions of the North received a new impetus from the introduction of an extremely protectionist tariff system between 1883 and 1888. However, since no special steps were taken to promote the development of South Italy, stagnation continued in that part of the country, and at the same time the standard of living went down as a result of a deterioration in the terms of trade (the ratio between the agricultural and industrial product prices) caused by the introduction of protective duties on industrial commodities. During both world wars industries were established in the North, and in the course of the postwar inflations considerable amounts of capital went from the South to the more promising North.[7]

In the underdeveloped countries, restrictions must therefore be imposed on the export of capital. The possibility exists that the advantages of mass production may not be fully utilized and that the productivity of capital as well as of labor will remain low so long as certain basic requirements in the transport and energy sectors (so-called infrastructural investments) are not fulfilled. Yet the savings of the underdeveloped countries may turn out to be insufficient to meet these requirements. At this stage of development, the yield of private capital abroad is probably higher than in the underdeveloped regions themselves. The wealthy people in the underdeveloped countries will therefore export their capital despite an advantageous endowment of productive factors. Restrictions imposed on the mobility of capital should serve the purpose of raising domestic investments in the underdeveloped countries to the level of domestic savings. However, these measures must be supplemented by precautionary ones to prevent the use of capital for unproductive investments or for financing consumption. It is also improbable that private capital from other countries will move in to finance the necessary investments in these underdeveloped regions, for the same reasons which lead to undesirable exports of capital. The capital which can be mobilized for these purposes in the developed countries should probably be transferred through international transactions agreed upon by the interested governments.[8]

Hence, if the objective is to equalize welfare in the West European countries, a European investment bank in one form or another must inevitably be established. If it is left to each

[7] Cf. International Labor Office, *Social Aspects of European Economic Co-operation*, Report by a Group of Experts (and Bertil Ohlin), Geneva, 1956, pp. 14ff.; also "Memorandum über die gesamtwirtschaftliche Integration," Wirtschaftsabteilung der Hohen Behörde, EGKS, Luxembourg, 1955, page 26.

[8] For the problem of capital exports, see W. Guth, *Der Kapitalexport in unterentwickelten Ländern*, Tübingen, 1957.

country to determine the direction and the volume of its capital exports, there is no guarantee that the investments will be made in the countries in which the proceeds will be highest from the point of view of the region as a whole. Moreover, the underdeveloped countries will not be able to make plans for their development which are based on confidence in the future. South Italy provides an example of the case in which the functional method of integration falls short, and in which only the institutional method offers a possible solution.[9]

It is highly significant that what is termed "international disintegration" by the exponents of the functional method is called "national integration" by Myrdal. The Western countries which come closest to his ideal of national integration are the United States, the West European nations, Australia, and New Zealand. The relatively complete national integration in all these countries is a new phenomenon; none of them has been socially and economically integrated for as long as a century, and this process has greatly accelerated in the last fifty years. The Industrial Revolution reached these countries several generations ago. The large labor reserves in the formerly agricultural regions of West Europe permitted the establishment of industries with a high rate of expansion and the accumulation of large amounts of capital. The real income of the majority of the people increased relatively slowly at first. The policy of redistribution, which has been a central element of national integration during the last two generations, was not initiated before the area's productivity had reached a level much higher than it was before the Industrial Revolution. After World War II, full employment was by and large general in these integrated economies, a fact of decisive importance for rapid economic growth. In the past, the periods of mass unemployment, with their destructive social and economic effects, were considered the Achilles' heel of industrial countries. Effective full employment since World War II and the

---

[9] Cf. F. Hartog, "European Economic Integration: A Realistic Conception," *Weltwirtschaftliches Archiv* (1953), pp. 165ff.

determination of governments to make mass unemployment impossible in the future can therefore be considered the highest achievement of the national integration process.[10]

Sweden is typical of these nationally integrated countries. Contrary to most other countries of the group, there was no contraction of the Swedish economy during the 1930's and its terms of trade developed favorably. Social and political problems are practically solved in this country; every citizen is to some extent ensured against the chief economic hazards and opportunities are open to all. Consequently, Sweden as a typical "welfare state" comes very close to the ideal of national integration. At the same time, a national disintegration process can be observed in France. The economic behavior of the French population has been influenced by a continuous process of stagnation and lacks flexibility even within the state. The connection between national integration and economic growth can also be seen in the example of the United States. Stagnation occurred in the southern part of the country from the Civil War until the middle of the 1930's. The population of the southern states has always been in a position to move to the industrial centers of the North. Their American citizenship and knowledge of the English language gave Southerners an enormous advantage over the European immigrants who flocked to the labor markets of the North. Nevertheless, a heavy emigration from the South did not occur and the stagnation of the southern states was overcome only under the impetus of World War II. It can also be seen from this historic example that a connection exists between economic stagnation and insufficient flexibility.

The process of national integration in the developed economies has been expedited by numerous actions of the public authorities. The present situation could not have been attained

[10] In 1914 J. Schumpeter wrote: "I am not of the opinion that unemployment as well as poverty belongs to those evils which the development of capitalism can abolish *on the basis of its own strength.*" J. Schumpeter, *Kapitalismus, Sozialismus und Demokratie,* Bern, 1950, page 117 (italics added).

simply by a policy of non-intervention. One of the most important means of equalizing economic opportunities was the elimination of differences in income and wealth. The steps that were taken to this end included progressive taxation and the establishment of a system of social security.

As one prerequisite to national integration, the citizens of a country must be convinced that it is worth while to bear part of the common burden of financing an integrated economy. This feeling of solidarity results from a long period of common experience and continuous participation by the individual in the formulation of national policy. The frail social basis of national integration in countries like France, Italy, and Greece is reflected in the inability of those countries to eliminate large-scale evasion of taxes and to carry through progressive taxation. On the other hand, the setting-up of a system of direct progressive taxation in the United States is a continuation of the strong tendencies toward national integration in this country.

Before World War I there was not much difference between the national and international integration of economies. The rapid economic development in the countries under discussion was the cause and at the same time the effect of their striving for national integration. This economic growth was only possible owing to, among other things, the relative mobility of labor and capital and the unrestricted exchange of commodities among the industrial countries. But from 1914 on, a contrast between the two processes of integration became noticeable. International mobility of productive factors and freedom of international trade became more and more restricted, in particular after the outbreak of the Great Depression. It is tempting to picture this trend of international disintegration simply as the result of false steps in economic policy, but that would be too optimistic. For in the course of the numerous political and economic crises of the last century there was usually no other course open to the governments concerned than the steps which they actually took. Moreover, government intervention has since become a fixed part of the programs of political parties, since it usually serves the purpose of realizing the objectives of economic equality and security.

The main reason for the disintegration of the world economy owing to the policies of the welfare states is that the policy of redistribution was not limited to a direct transfer of income by a system of taxes and social security, but penetrated the whole area of national economic policy and changed the fundamental conditions of the price mechanism. Labor in the United States considers protective tariffs on the whole industrial sector as legitimate weapons for the protection of the standard of living (or at least did so until recently). The fact that this argument is not fully tenable shows that nationalism and solidarity are in certain cases stronger than logic. But if redistributive policy has a definite effect on other economic policies, this cannot be attributed to an intellectual aberration, as it usually is, but to totally rational motives. In almost all developed countries, the farmers need government support to keep their standard of living more or less on the level of that of other groups, and the non-agricultural majority of the population everywhere has, for the sake of national solidarity, accepted the far-reaching modifications of the price mechanism resulting from it. This type of agricultural policy has become a cornerstone of the economic policy of most of the welfare states, but so far few have demanded that this solidarity be extended beyond national borders. The same combination of a national feeling of solidarity and an almost complete indifference to the interests of the outside world can be observed in most areas of economic policy. A willingness manifests itself everywhere to improve the economic basis of national production, largely motivated by the ideal of social equality. This applies to coal policy in Great Britain, regulation of the fisheries in Norway, and viniculture in France. This world-wide conflict between national and international integration obviously cannot be settled in favor of the latter merely by preaching internationalism and condemning nationalism. Not a single country is prepared to give up the fruits of national integration or even to undertake this risk. Most of the industrial nations may have a true desire to give up the controls on trade and payments which are necessitated by balance-of-payments difficulties. However, lack of equilibrium in the balance of payments is often the result not only of disturbances such as war, but of the trend toward national integration and of the government measures inherent in this trend, instituted to ensure stability and equality. Governments are unable to give up these measures, which usually realize very important national objectives, even when their effects are disastrous to international integration. In America, the Randall Committee Report has this to say on the matter: "The fact is that we have moved far from a world in which complete international specialization of labor is possible. Some of the rigidities . . . are here to stay . . . this means that completely free trade is not feasible."[11] Therefore it is fruitless to regard international integration as anything else than an extension of national integration beyond the borders of individual countries. But at the same time, we must draw the further conclusion that international integration must consist of something more than merely pulling down national barriers. An attempt must be made to coordinate the economic measures of the individual countries.[12] At present, national markets almost everywhere have been organized by the state and by groups of interested persons. Therefore, what is necessary is the internationalization of these national measures in such a way that all the benefits obtained by them for the nation are guaranteed.

If the national governments could agree upon this more ambitious form of cooperation, some of the present national measures would clearly become redundant. In many other cases, it would turn out that national protective measures sup-

[11] United States Commission on Foreign Economic Policy, *Report to the President and the Congress,* January 1954.

[12] Cf. also "Memorandum über die gesamtwirtschaftliche Integration," *op.cit.,* page 9.

port interests which, it is true, are not unimportant to the individual country, but are of less importance than the results which could be obtained by a mutual agreement to renounce the means of intervention in question. On the other hand, other forms of intervention—for instance, the protection of agriculture or of infant industries—are imperative from a national viewpoint. On the basis of international solidarity, it would be possible to stipulate that no attempt would be made to shift the burdens resulting from these measures from one country to another.

A primary objective should be the creation of stable international markets and the stabilization of production in general. A large number of national interventions would also become redundant to the extent that the efforts to achieve these ends were successful. Like the process of national integration, international integration could be carried on with success only in a period of economic growth. A mutual readiness to cooperate, without which the integration process would soon fail, can be mobilized only in an expanding international economy.[13] Myrdal therefore comes to the conclusion: "The whole movement towards international integration along these lines will have to be argued in positive terms of the wider community of interests and aspirations, not the negative ones of wanting to break up the defenses of national integration."[14] The task is

[13] The Coal and Steel Community had this experience. It owes its establishment at least in part to the fact that prosperity has lightened the functioning and the development of sectoral integration. The High Authority said on this point: "The Common Market could be established without disturbing competition or closing down factories to a greater extent than usual. The actual stoppages resulting from it involved only a very small number of workers; putting the treaty into effect has alleviated its enforcement and has mitigated its consequences. An important lesson can be learned from this for the establishment of the General Common Market: If the rate of expansion can be kept sufficiently high, large reductions in production can be avoided and unequal efficiency of enterprises will be expressed more in their unequal share in the over-all development than in a reduction of the activity of individual enterprises or in comprehensive adjustment processes." *Fünfter Gesamtbericht über die Tätigkeit der Gemeinschaft*, Luxembourg, 1957, page 17.

[14] G. Myrdal, *op.cit.*, page 51.

much heavier than any which the old internationalists who saw the problem only as one of removing national barriers ever tried to perform.

Hence, institutional integration tends to the creation of an economic union in which the functions of coordinating economic policies have been delegated to an authority superior to the national organs.[15] Domestic and foreign economic policy are unified by restricting national autonomy in the framework of an economic union. The logical consequence of this postulate in the area of foreign exchange would be a currency union with a common currency; nevertheless, other solutions are possible, as will be shown later. The sacrifice of autonomy in the area of foreign economic policy, on the other hand, requires a customs union; this implies that foreign economic policy as a whole and foreign trade policy in particular will be drafted in one place. The trade barriers inside the economic union have to be removed; moreover, the objective of maximizing production requires, in general, mobility of the factors of production among the member countries. As the example of Switzerland shows, an economic union need not necessarily include centralization of the financial system; however, if financial policy is to be federalist in nature, large-scale coordination on financial matters among the national governments is required (see Chapter V). From the foregoing, it can be concluded that an economic union requires a central organ of economic policy, comparable in authority and executive power to the corresponding ministries of the federal government of the United States or Switzerland.[16] But the eco-

[15] Cf. also J. E. Meade, "The Building of Benelux," *The Banker* (1956), page 760.

[16] Cf. Hans Bachmann, *Westeuropäische Wirtschaftsunion oder wirtschaftliche Zusammenarbeit?*, Zürich and St. Gallen, 1950, page 2.

In federalist but integrated national economies, decisions on economic policy are also made by majority rule. However, majority decisions are a feature of institutional integration. From this it follows that even federalist states are institutionally integrated. In contrast, the principle of unanimity in making decisions adopted by the OEEC *is* in conformity with functional integration. In this connection it is worth mentioning, as

nomic union could be brought fully into line with the principle of decentralization on which the federalist form of government is based. This principle requires that everything that can be delegated without too much damage to the smaller units—the member states, the province or the canton, the city or the municipalities—should be handled by those units. The requirements of a modern economic organization, resulting from the advantages of mass production, could in this way be linked to the principle of national, regional, or local self-government.

2. THE COAL AND STEEL COMMUNITY
AS AN EXAMPLE
OF PARTIAL INTEGRATION

Institutional integration has been realized in a broader sense, first, by way of sectors within the framework of the European Community for Coal and Steel.[17] The plans that emerged after World War II for a customs union including a large number of countries in West Europe soon proved to be utopian, and the European study group which investigated the project of a customs union did not come up with a workable proposal. In the case of smaller customs unions, the results were disappointing, too. As soon as the step was taken from general pronouncements to actual operations, the obstacles proved insurmountable. The only exception to this rule has been the customs union of the Benelux countries. A definite trade expansion could be observed in the three member countries after the founding of the union—though it is still too early to give an opinion upon the shifts which have taken place in market positions and in industrial specialization. The greatest obstacles to further liberalization of the trade among

---

an historic parallel, that in the Swiss confederacy domestic tariffs were dropped at the time that the Confederation of States, organized according to the principle of unanimity, gave way to the Federal States, which are governed on the basis of majority decisions.

[17] Cf. *Vertrag über die Gründung der Europäischen Gemeinschaft für Kohle und Stahl.*

the three member countries sprang from differing production conditions in the agriculture of Belgium and the Netherlands, as well as from the differing monetary and fiscal policies of the member countries, which made an adjustment of prices and wages more difficult. Though it was decided in 1948 to coordinate investment policies, no decisive steps have been taken toward carrying out this decision. Consequently, integration of the three Benelux countries is still in its first stages. The liberalization program of the OEEC was of much more importance for the expansion of inter-European trade, and in 1949 and 1950 was therefore considered to be the most promising way toward integration. That experiment soon ran afoul of limitations. In the first place, it proved to be extremely difficult to make real progress in the removal of quantitative restrictions on agricultural products. In this field, the connection between trade policy and purely national economic policy is so close that few countries were inclined to accept the risks of an international market. In the second place, the problems of heavy industry—in particular, the coal and steel industries—could not be solved by a simple liberalization. There is in this sector a close connection between trade policy and the efforts of the producing countries to preserve production and special cost advantages. For these reasons, the necessity arose of taking other and more positive steps than the mere removal of restrictions. But even in the domain of manufactured goods, great obstacles stood in the way of liberalization as soon as industrial interests of even a secondary order were threatened.

The obvious limitations of trade liberalization steered integration policy into new channels. "Integration by sectors" became the new slogan and it was not accidental that the areas that first received attention were those of the coal and steel industries—sectors in which simple liberalization had failed. Apart from the political factors behind the formation of the European Coal and Steel Community, the coal and steel industries were for purely economic reasons a natural object for the experiment in integration by sectors, particularly be-

99

cause the necessity for coordination was seen very clearly in both sectors and was at the same time administratively capable of solution. The necessity followed from economic and geographical facts.[18] For centuries the coal and steel industries of the member countries have been concentrated in a relatively small region and in a relatively small number of concerns; moreover, these industries, despite their indisputable significance, employ only from 2 per cent to 3 per cent of the national labor force. There was therefore the prospect that the markets of both industries could be unified without first solving the larger problem of a coordination of the entire economic policies of the member countries.[19]

In the following, we will survey the particular powers which have been transferred to a supranational body, the High Authority of the Coal and Steel Community, in the framework of this first effort to apply the institutional method. At the same time, it will be shown how in the European Coal and Steel Community the institutional method has been linked to the partial (sectoral) method of integration.[20]

The carefully balanced powers of the High Authority in the domain of investment policy represent an interesting attempt at international planning under the assumption of competition. Decisions to invest can be influenced by the High Authority

[18] Cf. N. J. G. Pounds and W. N. Parker, *Coal and Steel in Western Europe*, London, 1957.

[19] Sources: *Fünfter Gesamtbericht über die Tätigkeit der Gemeinschaft*, page 333. For the quantitative significance of the steel industry in the framework of the entire economy, cf. W. Isard and R. E. Kuenne, "The Impact of Steel upon the Greater New York-Philadelphia Industrial Region," *The Review of Economics and Statistics* (1953), pp. 289ff.; W. D. Evans and M. Hoffenberg, "The Interindustry Relations Study for 1947," *ibid.* (1952), pp. 97ff., especially the tables on page 24; H. W. Broude, "Bottleneck Phenomena and Cyclical Change: The Role of the Iron and Steel Industry," *The Quarterly Journal of Economics* (1954), pp. 437ff., as well as the literature quoted there. Cf. also J. B. Parrish, "Iron and Steel in the Balance of World Power," *op.cit.*, and the literature quoted there.

[20] The following exposition is based on United Nations Economic Commission for Europe, *Economic Survey of Europe Since the War*, Geneva, 1953, pp. 230ff.

in three ways: by advice, by prohibition of undesirable investments, and by granting loans or guarantees in the case of
promising investment projects.[21]

First, the treaty compels all firms in the coal and steel industry to submit their investment plans to the High Authority.
The role of obligatory advisor assigned to the High Authority
has made this body a center of information on the coal and
steel markets. Besides its advisory function, the High Authority has also been given by the treaty the power to prohibit
investments when there is reason to assume that the projects in
question require discriminatory measures or that they are uneconomical and can only be sustained with the help of subsidies or protective tariffs. But this power is limited to investments which have to be financed by borrowed money. In
many cases, this prohibition will indeed suffice to prevent the
establishment of uneconomic new enterprises. But in at least
a portion of the member countries the self-financing of expansion and modernization has become rather significant, and the
limitation imposed on the High Authority's veto power on
investments therefore cuts down its opportunities to intervene
in the investment policies of its members.

On the other hand, the High Authority cannot prevent those
investments which, though remunerative for an individual
firm, would lead to social losses. From the point of view of
perfect control on investments, it may seem incomprehensible
that the High Authority cannot prevent overinvestment—i.e.,
excessive modernization. Still, there are good reasons for this.
In the first place, it is more desirable for control of investments to be too loose rather than too restrictive. If the High
Authority were in a position to prevent modernization, there

---

[21] This attempt has been successful: "The investments reported so far
to the High Authority prove . . . that the advice of the High Authority
is effective. A reorientation of investments has become apparent which
warrants a better equilibrium for the future." Cf. *Fünfter Gesamtbericht
über die Täkigkeit der Gemeinschaft*, page 263; also Europäische Gemeinschaft für Kohle und Stahl, *Die Investitionen in den Kohle- und
Stahlindustrien der Gemeinschaft*, Luxembourg, 1956.

would be the danger that one group of producers could force a restrictive investment policy on other producers. In the second place, since it merely has "sectoral" powers, the High Authority is unable to weigh the desirability of investments in the coal and steel industries against those in other sectors.[22]

Finally, the High Authority has at its disposal both its own and borrowed money which it can use to finance investments or to provide guarantees for investments which it considers particularly desirable. This is the more necessary since it is possible that the national governments may decide on a new investment program as the result of the creation of a common market. From fear of the consequences of international competition, the national governments might possibly favor investments which would assure the preservation of sub-optimum enterprises rather than increase the productivity of firms which can face international competition anyway. The financial functions transferred to the High Authority could therefore have a compensating effect. Moreover, the fact that the High Authority itself is in a position to finance investments should increase the willingness of firms to heed its advice.

As a result of the acute cyclical fluctuations in the basic industries, some sort of market-regulating body is inevitable in the coal and steel sectors. To this end, the High Authority has been granted far-reaching powers which replace the national governments' previous power to intervene and also the functions which were usually exercised by cartels. During the scarcity periods after World War I, the national governments regularly attempted to secure raw materials for domestic industry by way of rationing and price controls. On the other hand, in times of overproduction there was a tendency to reserve the domestic market to the national industry. The official actions of both sectors therefore displayed autarchic traits. At the same time, the national and international cartel agree-

[22] W. Röpke makes this point when he tries to prove the infeasibility of a supranational investment policy. Cf. W. Röpke, "Europäische Investitionsplanung: Das Beispiel der Montanunion," *Ordo*, Volume 7 (1955), pp. 71ff.

ments on these markets which were concluded in the years between the wars were aimed at limiting production. The national cartels which had existed since the end of the nineteenth century organized equalization funds, paid subsidies to marginal producers, and had often a deterrent effect on plans for expanding enterprises. The first international cartel agreement (1926) even contained a clause according to which supply would be limited by output quotas in periods of increasing demand. The collapse of this agreement in the Great Depression caused the industries to sell at dumping prices on the export markets, while the prices on the domestic markets were stabilized by national cartels. (During the recession of 1949 an attempt was made to revive the international cartel system of the prewar years. The boom coming in the wake of the Korean War led to an abandonment of these efforts.)

By setting up the High Authority, international powers have been created instead of national ones, and public law has taken the place of private cartels. The powers of the High Authority in regulating the market have two aspects: first, the reestablishment of private cartels or other monopolistic agreements is to be prevented and, second, action is to be taken in periods of scarcity or overproduction.

The exclusion of monopolistic practices is, of course, of fundamental importance for the entire organization of the European Coal and Steel Community. The opportunities for intervention given to the High Authority in this area are considerable indeed, but the obstacles opposing almost every such action are equally important. It should not prove difficult to punish firms which conclude an agreement of merely local significance. On the other hand, there will be great difficulties in ferreting out secret and informal agreements between major enterprises.

In the event of a market crisis or a shortage, the High Authority can act in the same way as a cartel usually does. Minimum prices, production quotas, or restrictions on imports from third countries could be fixed, and in the case of scarcity a distribution system and production priorities as well as maximum prices could be enforced. But it is a great advantage that all these powers are exercised by a supranational authority and that its actions must be aimed at the economic welfare of the Community rather than at the well-being of only the coal and steel producers.[23]

If partial integration is compared with a global integration that includes all sectors, it becomes clear that the partial method leads to an economic disequilibrium.[24] The general wage level will be higher in the countries with protective tariffs than where there are no protective tariffs, and production is less attractive in the integrated sectors of such a country. In the integrated sectors of a country with a protective tariff, the volume of production therefore tends to a more severe contraction than would be required by the international division of labor in the event of all-round integration. Equilibrium will be restored only after the abolition of tariffs on the products of the remaining sectors. If the integration of the remaining sectors is postponed too long, the tensions could become excessive: an attempt would eventually be made to lower wages

[23] Europäische Gemeinschaft für Kohle und Stahl, *Bericht im Namen des Ausschusses für Fragen des Gemeinsamen Marktes über die Zusammenschlüsse von Unternehmungen in der Gemeinschaft*, Gemeinsame Versammlung, May 1957; EGKS, Verhandlungen der Gemeinsamen Versammlung, Ausführliche Sitzungsberichte, May 16, 1957.

[24] The High Authority of the European Coal and Steel Community is alive to this danger. For this, see *Fünfter Gesamtbericht über die Tätigkeit der Gemeinschaft*, pp. 34ff. "The meaning of the treaty is not to try to integrate Europe piecemeal by individual sectors, but to lay the material foundations for a general integration and to gain experience in a restricted domain. This partial integration has already succeeded in influencing the general expansion favorably by overcoming the reluctance of enterprises which feared that a further expansion of their production and their plant would be risky in view of too small markets. . . . But this particular method cannot be applied on a larger scale. For it contains the contradiction that industries which remain linked to completely different economic systems, which in particular exclude the outside world to a varying degree and have as a result different wage and price levels, will face competition without the protection that they formerly had. This daring experiment has to be followed up by a more comprehensive action. Expanding the common market into an over-all integration responds to the inner meaning of the treaty and will make its application easier."

in the integrated sector. From a social standpoint, this would be only after prices, and therewith the cost of living, had sunk to a level that corresponded to a situation with over-all reduced tariff rates. For this reason (and also because of the danger of trade diversion previously discussed), partial integration must be followed as soon as possible by an integration of the other sectors, or at least by a general reduction of tariffs. The positive aspect of partial integration is therefore its inner dynamics which tend unambiguously to an over-all integration. Only complete integration will remove the disequilibrium between the integrated and the remaining sectors. The founders of the European Coal and Steel Community, perhaps less for economic than for political reasons, originally counted on the effectiveness of these immanent forces: "There is inherent in the Schuman Plan a dynamism, a force toward expansion, produced by necessities of varying degree but of equally compelling strength: in unifying the management of coal and steel production one will be obliged, at the risk of failure, to proceed with other schemes of unification, which will gradually extend themselves."[25]

3. TRANSITION DIFFICULTIES OF A REGIONAL PREFERENCE SYSTEM

It is the essence of institutional integration that it is capable of mitigating the inequities resulting from the transition to a Common Market as well as of taking steps to achieve that end without losing sight of the objective of an optimum division of labor. Probably the most important obstacle in the way of freeing international trade is the fear that liberalization will influence unfavorably the income and rate of employment of the industries which are thus exposed to keener international competition. The extent of these negative consequences is often exaggerated, since the compensating effects emanating from economic growth are neglected. The numerous adjustments to

[25] Paul Reuter, *La communauté européenne du charbon et de l'acier*, page 32.

an optimum structure of production will, in the case of an expanding economy, be restricted to a more rapid expansion of industries capable of meeting competition. The sub-optimum firms or industries will merely experience a reduction of their share in total production, which need not result in an absolute contraction of their rate of employment and production. Moreover, there is a possibility in some industries of shifting over to the manufacture of new products without a radical reorganization, merely ceasing production of those commodities in which it has become more difficult to compete as a result of the liberalization. As the change-over from wartime to peacetime production showed, such reorganizations do not necessarily require the building of new factories, and it is even possible that there need be no change in the type of work to be done. Despite these reservations, some firms will, however, have to face a contraction of their markets as a result of the transition to freer trade, and this is a real problem.

The principal economic objective of free trade consists of a more rational use of productive factors. This cannot be achieved without changes in the production pattern. This means, however, that certain regions will experience a contraction of their traditional industries as soon as a Common Market has been created, since the commodities they have hitherto produced may be manufactured more cheaply in other regions. The entrepreneurs as well as labor will fight against sudden dislocations which result from international specialization and against the reduction in income which goes with them, even when they admit that these changes are in the interest of the Community in the long run. The opposition coming from this quarter is often very strong, since the groups concerned are in many cases trade unions, employers' organizations, and political parties which can bring pressure to bear on those officials who conduct the foreign economic policy of their country. The large group of consumers who benefit from the lower costs and prices and obtain a higher real income through the liberalization of trade is, on the other hand, far less well-organized. The disadvantages to local interest groups caused by freer trade therefore carry more political weight, in comparison with the advantages of a better international division of labor, than they would if profits and losses were compared more objectively. But this is not to imply that the difficulties of the transition period will not cause real damage if no steps are taken to prevent it. The abolition of trade barriers must therefore be supplemented by measures which will mitigate these inequities.

In the first place, this is desirable for reasons of justice. Protected industries are not necessarily unproductive or badly managed. Protective tariffs are often instituted in order to enable governments to promote the development of particular branches of industry for reasons of defense or employment policy. When these motivations have lost their force and the abolition of tariffs seems to be desirable, elementary social justice demands temporary assistance for workers who have become unemployed for reasons beyond their control. Moreover, society benefits from an integration policy which minimizes losses in capital and technical experience. Still, the losses of firms or industries of a size which cannot withstand the cold wind of international competition will be more than compensated in the long run by the over-all increase of real income. But the transfer of factors of production from one industry to another takes time. Apart from the serious social disadvantages of unemployment, it is also preferable for purely economic reasons that productive factors be employed until new opportunities for employment have been found.

The next method of overcoming the transition difficulties consists of a step-by-step removal of trade barriers.[26] All industrial countries have for quite some time gone through a continuous process of structural change and thereby have overcome transition difficulties which were much greater than

[26] Cf. ILO, *Social Aspects of European Economic Co-operation*, page 52; also "Memorandum über die gesamtwirtschaftliche Integration," *op.cit.*, page 22.

those which would occur as a result of lowering trade barriers. Practical experience has shown that reorganizing the structure of production can be accomplished without major disturbances if a gradual transition to new methods of production is possible. A similar process will be initiated by the lowering of trade barriers—i.e., it should be possible to avoid mass unemployment. During the transition process, capital and labor will slowly shift from the contracting to the expanding industries. Stated more precisely, what will happen in an expanding economy is not actual movements of productive factors between firms or industries, but shifts in the output composition within firms or industries. In this process, newly formed capital and new workers entering the labor market will be directed first of all to the expanding sectors. The GATT allows for a step-by-step process to the extent that not only the present customs union is exempted from the non-discriminating clause, but also a customs union-to-be during the transition period (Art. XXIV, 5 [C]).

If, in difficult cases, an appeal can be made to exemption clauses in order to guarantee special treatment to individual countries or industries (for instance, a later start or a longer duration of the liberalization process), step-by-step realization of the Common Market would ward off the danger of endless bargaining for numerous "special cases." The entire program would be endangered by this. In those cases where a gradual lowering of trade barriers would lead to serious disturbances, some sort of special support would be preferable, but this support should be in the form of a subsidy rather than of exclusion of certain sectors from the liberalization program.

Losses during the transition period can be completely avoided if the new workers entering the labor market are employed in the new industries, and if the invested capital is not written off prematurely, but rather the normal annual amounts for capital replacement are invested somewhere else. Losses from a sub-optimum division of labor among the member nations during this transition period must, however, be taken into account. Hence, a middle course has to be found between the Scylla of transformation losses and the Charybdis of the losses resulting from a sub-optimum division of labor. Since, as a rule, it takes about twenty years for invested capital to be entirely written off and for old workers to be fully replaced by new ones, a transition period of ten years has frequently been recommended.[27] (The treaty for the European Economic Community prefers a period of from ten to fifteen years.) In shaping the transition period, benefit can be derived from the experience gained from setting up the European Coal and Steel Community. In the clauses of the agreement dealing with the transition period, there are some provisions for sudden and painful adjustment difficulties: Italian industry will be further protected by tariffs during a period of five (under certain circumstances, even seven) years. In the same way, provision is made for a rapid contraction of the Belgian and French production of coal, as well as for the protection of Italian coke ovens and coal mines. An additional protective action has been taken by postponing the harmonization of transport costs. Special adjustment provisions for the reemployment of workers who might become unemployed during the transition period have been made in the Schuman Plan treaty.[28]

All these provisions for bridging transition difficulties will suffice to induce submarginal enterprises to cease production or encourage a willingness to invest in developing industries.

There must, therefore—and this distinguishes institutional integration fundamentally from functional integration—be some guarantee that the reorganization and the new pattern of specialization will have a permanent character.[29] While, in the

---

[27] Cf. ILO, *Social Aspects of European Economic Co-operation*, page 55; J. Tinbergen, *International Economic Integration*, page 120.

[28] Vertrag über die Gründung der Europäischen Gemeinschaft für Kohle und Stahl, Abkommen über die Übergangsbestimmungen.

[29] Cf. T. Balogh, "Liberalization or Constructive Organization?," *Bulletin of the Oxford University Institute of Statistics* (1957), page 47: "An entry into the Free Trade Area, if it is to have any favourable impact on productivity, must be non-reversible, otherwise no-one will invest

OEEC, for instance, every member has the liberty to go back on the liberalization measures, the European Coal and Steel Community has protected itself against this danger by the extraordinarily long period of fifty years covered by the treaty. It is in the spirit of the contract that the transfer of power from the national governments to the supranational authority is irrevocable.[30]

---

in rationalising production." Cf. also "Memorandum über die gesamtwirtschaftliche Integration," *op.cit.*, page 7.

[30] Cf. the Preface by Robert Schuman to Paul Reuter, *op.cit.*

CHAPTER IV

CURRENCY SYSTEMS AND
STABILIZATION POLICY

1. INTERNAL AND EXTERNAL
EQUILIBRIUM

THE RELATIONSHIP between internal and external equilibrium must first be examined before we can deal with the problem of the foreign exchange policy of an economic union.

Keynes has shown that the market economy in itself has no automatic tendency toward a macro-economic equilibrium. If the economic authorities do not take stabilizing actions, situations of under- or overemployment can occur. If targets which require the full use of economic capacity are set in the framework of a closed economy, this can lead to situations of external disequilibrium in a world in which the national economies are linked to each other by international trade. Since the deficit in the balance of payments involved in disequilibrium cannot be tolerated indefinitely, economic policy must aim at achieving an optimum approximation of complete internal *and* external equilibrium. But even if no policy of internal stabilization is pursued, external equilibrium will not be automatic.

External equilibrium means equilibrium in the balance of payments. The latter is composed of the current account and the capital account. The current account usually includes receipts and payments of a country for international transactions in commodities and services. The capital account consists of unilateral payments (gifts, reparations, official gold transactions, etc.) and capital transactions (loans, repayments on debts, sale of securities to the residents of another country). The balance of payments is in equilibrium if no payments are needed for settlement. These balancing payments are distinguished from the other items of the balance of payments by

111

the fact that the only reason for their existence lies not in the purchase of a commodity, the rendering of a service, or the intention to invest outside the country, but in a deficit in the balance of payments. The ordinary items of the balance of payments therefore have an autonomous character, while the payments for settlement are induced by deficits in the balance of payments. The essential feature of a disequilibrium in the balance of payments therefore consists of the fact that the autonomous receipts on current and capital accounts are smaller or larger than the autonomous payments during the period of settlement.

Only in one case does external stability establish itself automatically after a disturbance occurs. In the following we will assume that the capital account of a country is in equilibrium, so that if the balance of payments eventually becomes unbalanced, this will be attributable to the current account alone. Let us denote the national income of a given country by Y, its exports by X, and its imports by M. Let the marginal propensity to consume domestic commodities and services be c, the marginal propensity to save be s, and the marginal propensity to import be m. The algebraic sum of the three marginal propensities is equal to one. If the foreign demand for commodities of the analyzed country increases by dX, then the national income of the analyzed economy increases by

$$dY = \frac{1}{1-c} dX.$$

The change in income induces an increase of imports by

$$dM = m.dY = \frac{m}{1-c} dX.$$

Clearly dM, the increase in imports, is equal to the increase in exports, dX, and the balance of payments remains in equilibrium only if

$$m + c = 1; \text{ for only then does } \frac{m}{1-c} = 1.$$

Since $c + s + m = 1$, this condition implies $s = 0$. In this static model, therefore, the balance of payments automatically remains in equilibrium only when the marginal propensity to save is equal to zero—that is, in a stationary economy. But it is typical of the modern economy that it is in a state of development. Realization of equilibrium in the balance of payments therefore requires additional mechanisms or measures.

First, a balance of payments which becomes upset because of spontaneous disturbances (for instance, because of an autonomous *change* in domestic or foreign *expenditures*) can be brought into balance again by income and price adjustments. With the help of a model of a "neutral" economy, in which no other disturbances appear, we will now investigate under what circumstances these adjustments will suffice. To show the pure *income adjustments*, we first eliminate price adjustments. The following assumptions must then be made: (1) The tax rates and the tax system as well as the size of government expenditures remain unchanged. (2) The interest rate is constant (in the case of several interest rates, the structure and the heights of the interest rates do not change). (3) Money wages remain unchanged, independent of the rate of employment and the price level. (4) Exchange rates remain constant. (5) Trade policy also remains unchanged. Furthermore, it is assumed that no foreign exchange controls and quantitative import restrictions exist. We start with a "world economy" which consists of two countries. The two economies each produce only one commodity or, if they produce several, the relative prices remain constant.[1]

We will now assume that the investment expenditures in country A increase for one reason or another. We have shown before that income adjustments do not suffice in this case to secure external equilibrium after a new internal equilibrium has been reached. The new equilibrium position of countries A and B looks something like this: In A the national income has risen. Part of this increase in income has induced income to rise in B, and, since in both countries the marginal pro-

[1] For the following, cf. J. E. Meade, *The Balance of Payments*, pp. 43ff.

113

pensity to save is greater than zero, B's rise in income has led to an increase in its imports from A which is only a fraction of that rise in income. The current account has developed favorably for B—i.e., the imports of A have increased more than those of B. The reason for this is that, as a result of a positive propensity to save in B, not all of the increase of its imports is composed of imports from A.

Besides these effects on the current account, the capital account must be examined, too. On the assumption that the proportional increase in the income of A is greater than in B, two factors are relevant: on the one hand, the profitability of industry in A will probably increase more than in B. On the other hand, savings in A have probably risen more than in B, proportionately speaking. If the savers in A as well as in B have a constant marginal propensity to export capital, the capital exports from A to B would, under these assumptions, increase more than the capital exports from B to A. Hence, opposite tendencies come into effect and it cannot be assumed in general that the deterioration in the current account of A will be neutralized by an improvement in its capital account.

So far we have neglected *price adjustment* to an autonomous increase in expenditures. Our conclusions must therefore be modified in view of the fact that the income changes in A and B will change the price ratio between A-goods and B-goods— i.e., the terms of trade are altered. The remaining assumptions hold.

At a given level of money wages, commodity prices in both countries could also rise as a result of an increasing rate of employment, since the marginal productivity of labor will decrease in the short run and, as a consequence, the marginal costs of production will rise. The result of increased expenditures in A will at first be an increase in demand for the commodities of A, and, when the marginal propensity to import is greater than zero, of B as well. If the real elasticity of supply in both countries is smaller than infinity (i.e., if the marginal productivity of labor decreases with an increasing rate of employment), the prices of commodities in both countries will rise with the increasing demand, despite a constant level of money wages.

If, as we have assumed, the demand in A rises autonomously, and if, in addition to this, it can be assumed that the production functions in both countries have a similar shape, it is probable that the prices of the commodities in A will rise more than in B. The reason is that a spontaneous increase in expenditures in A will, for the major part, be spent on domestic commodities. Let us assume that the value of the production of country A is $20,000 and that of B $80,000. The buyers in A will then probably spend less than 80 per cent of their income on commodities of B, though B's share amounts to 80 per cent of world production. On the other hand, the consumers in B will spend less than 20 per cent of their income on commodities of A. National preferences and transport costs explain this state of affairs. Moreover, numerous products like houses and services cannot be transported and therefore do not enter international trade. The relationship mentioned here between average propensities to consume domestic commodities and to import probably also holds good for marginal propensities.[2]

Now, if the marginal propensity to import in A is smaller than the ratio between the value of the production of B and that of the world, then—as a result of a small increase in the domestic expenditures of A—the demand for A's commodities will increase more than the demand for B's commodities. If the production functions of both countries do not differ too greatly, commodity prices in A must, as a result, increase more than commodity prices in B. This change in the terms of trade between A and B will evoke a shift in demand from the goods of A to those of B. This price effect on the balance of pay-

[2] Contrary to Meade, we define the marginal propensity to import as the first derivative of the imports as a function of national income. Hence, if M stands for imports and Y for income, $M=f(Y)$, and the marginal propensity to import is $M'=dM/dY$.

115

ments depends on the extent of the shift that results from the change in the relative prices of A's and B's commodities. It can be shown that, regardless of the income effects, the change in the terms of trade will favorably affect the balance of payments of that country whose commodities have become more expensive, if the sum of the price elasticities of the demand for imports is smaller than one. The balance of payments is not affected if this sum is equal to one. If the sum of both price elasticities is greater than one, the balance of payments of the country whose commodities have become more expensive will be unfavorably affected by the increase in autonomous expenditures.[3]

It is possible, though not probable, that the price effect of the increase in demand in A will counteract the income effect. This will happen if three conditions are fulfilled: (1) The marginal propensity to import must be small in A. (2) The marginal productivity of labor in A must decrease sharply with an increasing rate of employment, so that the increase in demand in A leads to a proportionately higher increase in prices than in production. (3) The sum of the price elasticities of the demand for imports in both countries must be considerably smaller than one, so that as a result of a change in the terms of trade there will be no substitution of commodities of country B for commodities of country A. However, if the sum of the elasticities mentioned is greater than one, the price effects will work in the same direction as the stabilizing income effects. If the income effects do not suffice to restore equilibrium in the balance of payments, then the price effects can do the rest. Following Meade, we are assuming in general that the last situation is the normal one.

Consequently, if the function of restoring equilibrium in the balance of payments is left to the price mechanism, the

[3] This so-called "Marshall-Lerner condition" holds in the indicated form only if one starts from an equilibrium in the current account. Moreover, this condition is a sufficient but not necessary one. Cf. G. Haberler, "The Market for Foreign Exchange and the Stability of the Balance of Payments," *Kyklos* (1949), page 207.

magnitude of the import elasticities is the decisive factor. This can be influenced in various ways. In the first place, the greater the rate of substitution of one commodity for another, the more time will be available for an adjustment of the structure of production and the pattern of taste. Furthermore, the greater the rate of substitution of commodities in international trade, the smaller the significance of trade barriers. Quantitative restrictions represent a clear example of this. If A puts a quantitative limit on its wheat imports from B, then a change in the terms of trade between A and B cannot possibly lead to an increase in the quantitative demand for B's wheat. Hence the price elasticity of the wheat imports in A will be equal to zero as a result of the quantitative restriction. High tariffs levied on a specific basis will have the same effect. If a ton of wheat at the place of production in B costs $100 and if a fixed tariff rate of $200 per ton is levied on it by A, then a 50 per cent (to $50) reduction of the price by the producers in B will reduce the price in A merely by 16⅔ per cent—namely, to $250. Hence stabilizing price fluctuations are damped by a specific tariff.

We began with the effects of a change in domestic expenditures on the balance of payments. In the following, the effects of *some other typical disturbances* will be examined.

Let us assume that certain inventions make it possible to increase productivity in all industries of A by 10 per cent. In a closed economy, the cost of production will then decrease by 10 per cent and, if competition is effective, the price of the commodities will fall correspondingly. However, if A trades with B, the fact that commodity prices in A decrease relative to commodity prices in B will be particularly important. If the sum of the price elasticities of demand for imports in both countries is larger than one, the total expenditures for A's goods will rise, while *ceteris paribus* the expenditures for B's goods will drop by the same amount, so that the current account of A will improve. The smaller the marginal propensity of country B to save and to import, the more its rate of employment and income will fall. The income and rate of employment in A will rise for the same reasons, and, as before, will do so the more, the smaller the aforementioned marginal propensities in A. If the sum of the price elasticities of demand for imports in A and B is sufficiently large and A's marginal propensity to save is sufficiently small, it is possible that, as a result of the improvement in A's current account, all workers who have been set free by technical progress will find new employment. Developments will, however, be different if the marginal productivity of labor in B reacts sharply to a change in the rate of employment. Commodity prices in B will decrease very rapidly as a result of the substitution of goods of A for goods of B, and the terms of trade between A and B will not change much, so that employment, income, and the current account will not be much affected by secondary repercussions.

The next disturbance to be analyzed is a change in the pattern of taste. Let us assume that, at a given income, consumers suddenly take a liking to commodities of A and accordingly buy less of B's commodities. In a neutral economy, this increase in the demand for products of A will cause inflation in that country, while a deflationary process will start in B as a result of a reduction in the demand for its products. According to multiplier theory, the strength of these two changes is inversely proportional to the height of the propensity to save in both countries.[4] The direct effect of the shift in demand on the current account will be similar to the original reduction of expenditures for goods of country B. However, the residents of A will spend part of their additional income—in an amount determined by their marginal propensity to import—on the consumption of commodities from country B. At the same time, the residents of B will reduce their consumption of A's commodities in an amount corresponding to their income, which

[4] Here, as well as in what follows, we mean by "propensity to save" the marginal propensity to save, including the marginal rate of taxation, since the "neutral" economy also includes the public sectors. Our conception of propensity to save therefore corresponds to "home leakage" in the usual terminology of multiplier theory.

has been, in turn, reduced by their propensity to import. For both of these reasons, the current account of country A will be less favorable than could be expected on the basis of the primary effect alone. If the sum of the price elasticities of demand for imports in both countries exceeds one, the price effects will in addition also neutralize the primary effect of the shift in demand on the current account.

The effects of an autonomous increase in the transfer of payments from A to B constitute a further example of a spontaneous disturbance. It can be manifested, for instance, in an increasing preference by capitalists of country A for stocks and bonds of B. Since it has been assumed that the interest rates are constant and we abstract from a functional relationship between the liquidity—i.e., the composition of liquid assets— and the level of expenditures (wealth-spending relation), the demand for commodities will not be affected by this sort of disturbance in the financial sector. The balance of payments of A will become passive to the amount of the additional export of capital, and the balance of B will become active to the same amount. Secondary effects do not occur; income, rate of employment, current account, and terms of trade are not affected.

Let us assume that new, profitable investment projects show up as the result of an invention or the opening-up of new areas in country A. If the disturbance consists only of increased expenditures in country A, then the same income and price effects will manifest themselves as in the first, extensively discussed, case of a spontaneous change in expenditures. But a disturbance of this type is often accompanied by other spontaneous changes—for instance, as is very likely, by a spontaneous increase in capital exports from B to A. The way the balance of payments then develops depends on the extent to which outside capital is attracted by the new opportunities to invest in country A.

Finally, the imposition of an import duty by, for instance, the authorities of A will have direct effects on the external position of both countries. The quantity imported by A will decrease, and consequently so will the amount spent by the consumers in A on imports after deducting the revenues from the duty. If A uses the additional revenues from the duty for an increase of government expenditures and/or a reduction of taxes, then the duty will not cause a direct change in domestic expenditures for goods or services at factor costs. However, if the additional customs revenue manifests itself only in a more favorable balance of A's budget, then the expenditures of the consumers in A on commodities of that country will decrease to the amount of the additional proceeds from the duty. The shift in the demand for commodities of B to those of A that is induced by the duty will lead to an expanding tendency in A and a deflationary tendency in B. In the first instance, the current account of country A will become active. As a result of an increase in the budget surplus (or a reduction in the budget deficit) the imports of country A will decrease further. Among other things, it will depend on the elasticity of the demand for imports in country A whether the inflationary influence of the substitution of domestic commodities for imports on A's current account will be stronger than the deflationary effect of the increased budget surplus. If the elasticity of the demand for imports in A is low, then the value of the imports of A will decrease only slightly. This implies, first, that the substitution of commodities of A for those of B will not be strong; and, second, that the additional proceeds from the duty of country A and, correspondingly, the reduction in A's domestic expenditures will be relatively large. However, if the price elasticity of the demand for imports in A is high, there will also be a considerable rise in income in A.

2. THE POLICY OF INTERNAL AND EXTERNAL STABILIZATION

We have examined how spontaneous changes affect the balance of payments and have shown that these disturbances often lead to external disequilibrium. To what extent are the *measures* directed toward reestablishment of external equilibrium in agreement with a policy directed toward realizing internal equilibrium?[5]

In the neutral economy model, the following assumptions are usually made: government expenditures, tax rates, interest rates, money wages, and exchange rates are assumed to be constant and induced changes in foreign trade policy are neglected. Yet the first three assumptions will be dropped in what follows, since we will examine the means by which the government of a country could, by monetary and fiscal measures, neutralize the destabilizing internal and external impacts of a spontaneous disturbance on employment and the balance of payments. Fiscal and monetary policies are combined in the following under the concept of financial policy. Moreover, it is assumed that monetary policy restricts itself to changes in the quantity of money and the interest rate. Financial policy aimed at *internal* stability is defined as controls on domestic expenditures by fiscal or monetary measures directed toward the realization of that form of stability that corresponds to optimum employment from the domestic point of view. The optimum level of employment is generally taken to be the same as full employment. Financial policy directed toward *external* stability is aimed at controlling domestic expenditures in order to prevent a surplus or a deficit in the balance of payments.

The governments of both A and B can then pursue five stabilization programs. The authorities of country A can try to realize internal stability by fiscal or by monetary measures, and external stability by fiscal or by monetary measures. In addition to this, a "do-nothing" policy can be pursued. The government of country B has the same possibilities at its command. Hence, there are twenty-five conceivable policy constellations.

As we have already pointed out, their general feature is that there are *possibilities of conflict* between the objectives of internal and external stability. There are also situations in which

[5] Cf. also N. Kaldor, "Employment Policies and the Problem of International Balance," *The Review of Economic Studies* (1951/52), pp. 42ff.

both objectives will require the same measures. For example, let us assume that domestic expenditures in A are reduced spontaneously. The national income of the country will drop as a consequence, while the balance of payments will improve. In this case, internal stability would require a policy of expansion in A as well as in B. Moreover, if a balance-of-payments surplus has to be prevented in A, expenditures should also be increased for reasons of external stability. Hence, there is no conflict between both objectives in A, but there is one in B. In the latter, internal stability requires a policy of expansion, whereas external stability requires deflationary measures.

A case is also conceivable in which both countries face such a conflict. If we assume, for instance, that the demand for A's goods decreases while the demand for B's goods increases, deflationary tendencies will appear in A, but inflationary tendencies will occur in B and its balance of payments will improve. If A wishes to restore full employment, total demand has to be increased, while elimination of the balance-of-payments deficit requires a policy of deflation in A. Such a policy would also be necessary in B to safeguard its internal stability, while the elimination of its balance-of-payments surplus requires a policy of inflation. If both countries pursue financial policies directed toward external stability, unemployment will rise in A, while inflation will become more acute in B. But if both countries strive for internal stability, they will move still further away from equilibrium in the balance of payments. Hence, every country must consider the effects of its own policy on the situation in the outside world. In addition to the two criteria mentioned above, a third must also be considered: the effect of the financial program of every country on the internal stability of the others. As Meade has shown, there is not a single situation in which the governments of several countries could satisfy these three criteria simultaneously and could independently follow a consistent policy, as defined here.[6]

Still other assumptions of the model of the neutral economy

[6] J. E. Meade, op.cit., page 116.

must therefore be dropped: money wages and exchange rates will be regarded as variable in the following.[7]

If the money wages in B and therewith the prices of its commodities are decreased, or the money wages and therewith the prices of commodities of A are increased, or if the currency of B is devalued relative to the currency of A, then the price of commodities of B will be reduced relative to the price of commodities of A, if both prices are expressed in the same currency. This change in the terms of trade has the effects mentioned before: if the sum of the price elasticities of the demand for imports in both countries is greater than one, B's current account will improve. However, if this sum is smaller than one, the current account of B will deteriorate because of the fall in the prices of commodities of B in relation to those of A. As we have done up to now, the first case will be regarded as the normal one.[8] On the basis of the new assumptions, the shift in demand caused by the relative decrease in commodity prices in country B will then have three effects: (1) the current account of B will improve; (2) inflationary effects will manifest themselves in B as a result of the increase in the rate of employment; and (3) deflationary symptoms will appear in A as a result of the reduction in the rate of employment.

In order to examine the impact of flexible money wages or exchange rates, we will now reintroduce some of the earlier assumptions: government expenditures, taxes, and interest rates are again held constant. On the other hand, we will assume that the relative price and cost levels of both A and B

[7] Cf. also S. Laursen and L. A. Metzler, "Flexible Exchange Rates and the Theory of Employment," *The Review of Economics and Statistics* (1950), pp. 281ff.

[8] In this respect, cf. Guy H. Orcutt, "Measurement of the Price Elasticities in International Trade," *ibid.*, pp. 117ff. It can be concluded from Orcutt's explanation that, though the price elasticity of the demand for imports of a single country is often smaller than one, the sum of the elasticities is generally larger than one. Various reasons for mistakes in the measurements have to be taken into account: shifts in the demand function, errors of observation, index number problems, the relationship between short-term and long-term price elasticities, discontinuities in the demand function, etc.

cannot be influenced either by policy measures (a fall or rise in money wages dictated by the authorities) or by a variation in the rates of exchange between the two countries. How must the two parameters of action be changed if a disequilibrium is to be eliminated and at the same time the three criteria are to be satisfied? An internal and/or external disequilibrium can appear in country A as well as in B. It can be shown that varying the money wages or the exchange rates eliminates the disequilibrium in some but not in all instances. As mentioned, only in some cases will financial measures produce consistent results with respect to the elimination of disequilibrium situations. However, Meade has shown that it is possible in all conceivable situations to realize an internal equilibrium simultaneously in both countries and to bring the balance of payments between the two countries into equilibrium by a combination of financial and wage or of financial and foreign exchange measures.[9]

The following examples may clarify the way in which such a combination of measures functions. We will start with a situation of general, world-wide depression. Let one of the two depressed countries have a surplus in its balance of payments, and the other a deficit. Now the government of the surplus country must pursue a policy of expansion, while that of the deficit country must reduce the relative prices of commodities by devaluing its currency or by decreasing money wages. This price reduction will improve the balance of payments of the deficit country and at the same time raise the rate of employment. On the other hand, the policy of expansion will decrease the surplus in the balance of payments of the surplus country and increase its rate of employment. Let us now examine the opposite situation of an inflation in both countries, combined with an external disequilibrium. The deficit country has to pursue a deflationary financial policy in this case, while the authorities of the surplus country have to raise the relative prices of commodities by a revaluation or a wage increase. An ex-

9 J. E. Meade, *op.cit.*, page 155.

ternal equilibrium will be attained and the inflationary tendencies will be checked in the deficit country by these actions. However, the rise of prices in the surplus country will lead to a shift of demand to the commodities of the deficit country, whereby the surplus will be reduced and at the same time the forces causing inflation will be weakened. The third of the four possibilities is represented by inflation in the deficit country and depression in the surplus country. In this case, neither wage- nor exchange-rate adjustments will be necessary. The rate of employment and the demand for imports will be increased by an expansion of domestic demand in the surplus country. If the deficit country pursues a deflationary financial policy, its current and capital accounts will improve and this impulse will also eliminate overemployment. There now remains the case in which the surplus country experiences inflation, while there is unemployment in the deficit country. Financial measures will then have no effect. The shift in demand from the commodities of the surplus country to those of the deficit country, which can be accomplished by a change in relative prices, will, however, satisfy all three criteria: the disequilibrium in the balances of payments will be removed, the inflationary tendencies in the surplus country weakened, and the deflationary disturbances in the deficit country eliminated.

From what has been said, it follows that under these assumptions, the implications of which will be analyzed later, it is possible to attain internal and external equilibrium in several countries simultaneously. It is conceivable that fiscal and monetary policies would serve the purpose of external equilibrium, and the wage- and exchange-rate policies serve the purpose of internal equilibrium. However, in the following, we will start from the more usual opposite situation and will examine the problem of external stabilization in the framework of a policy of adjustment of commodity prices, and assume that internal stability will be realized by financial policy. We will deal first with the method of *varying the exchange rate*. The balance of payments of country B shows a deficit. The government of B pursues a policy of achieving external equilibrium by price adjustment and consequently devalues its currency. This change in the exchange rate can be carried out in two ways.

First, it is possible that there is a completely *free foreign exchange market* in B. Numerous foreign exchange dealers, in competition with each other, deal in both the currency of country A (foreign exchange) and the currency of country B. Every dealer has certain amounts of both currencies and for a commission sells the currency of A, for which he accepts currency of B, to every resident of country B who wishes to make a payment to a resident of A, and vice versa. Now, if there is a deficit in B's balance of payments, then greater amounts of B-currency than A-currency will be offered to the foreign exchange dealers of this country at the prevailing rate of exchange. Hence, the amounts of A-currency in the hands of the foreign exchange dealers will decrease and the amounts of B-currency will increase. In order to bring the cash balance of A-currency back to its original position, the foreign exchange dealers have to ask for each currency unit of country A more units of B-currency than before. The deficit in the balance of payments of B has therefore led to a devaluation of its currency.

Second, it is possible that the rate of exchange between the currencies of A and B may be officially fixed and that this fixed rate will be *changed from time to time* by official decree. This arrangement corresponds more or less to the rules of the International Monetary Fund (IMF). Let us assume that the monetary authorities of B buy and sell unlimited amounts of an international means of payment that we will call gold in the following. The price at which the monetary authorities of B buy gold—for which they pay newly issued banknotes in B-currency, or the purchase of which creates sight deposits in the banks—is possibly somewhat lower than the price at which the monetary authorities sell gold. The value of B-currency is thereby linked to a certain amount of gold, fixed between the limits of the purchase and the sales price set for gold in B. The gold price can therefore not rise above the sales price stipulated by the monetary authorities of B—expressed in currency units of B—for the following reason: If the price on the free market rose above this level, gold could be obtained from the monetary authorities at a lower price. Accordingly, the gold price, expressed in B-currency, cannot fall below the purchase price set by the monetary authorities of B.

By this mechanism, the value of the B-currency is pegged to units of gold. If the monetary authorities of A set fixed prices for the purchase and sale of gold in A-currency, there is also a constant relationship between the prices of A-currency and B-currency—i.e., the exchange rate is fixed in an indirect way. Now, if the balance of payments of B shows a deficit under these conditions, B-currency will not automatically be devalued, apart from the small fluctuations of the exchange rate between the two gold points. A resident of B who needs A-currency in order to pay a resident of A can obtain this foreign exchange by buying gold from the monetary authorities of B, for which he pays B-currency, and selling this gold to the monetary authorities of A in exchange for A-currency. The foreign exchange dealers in B will therefore not ask a higher price for A-currency than that at which A-currency can be bought in exchange for B-currency via the monetary authorities of both countries. Hence, the rate of exchange between both currencies remains fixed between narrow limits so long as the two currencies are firmly pegged to gold. These limits could, however, be shifted by the monetary authorities. If, for instance, the A-currency retains its value in gold while the monetary authorities of B raise by 20 per cent the purchase and sales prices of gold, expressed in units of B-currency, then B-currency is devalued by 20 per cent in relation to A-currency. In a "world economy" which consists of only two countries, the same effect could be obtained by a reduction of the purchase and sales prices of gold by 20 per cent in country A, while at the same time the gold value of B-currency is kept constant—

i.e., by a revaluation of A-currency. In what follows we will call these two methods of altering the exchange rate by an official change of the purchase and sales prices of gold the "system of the International Monetary Fund," or, the "IMF system." Until further notice, the following exposition will be related to both systems of adjusting the exchange rates.

We return now to our original problem: Let there be internal equilibrium in country B while its balance of payments shows a deficit. We will assume that, by one of the aforementioned mechanisms, the excess demand for A-currency leads to a devaluation of B-currency. What will be the effect of a devaluation of 1 per cent? If we first assume that the price of B-products, expressed in B-currency, and the price of A-products, expressed in A-currency, remain unchanged, the terms of trade will shift in exactly the same way as the exchange rate. (We abstract from induced income effects in A and B, and from changes in the prices of the commodities of both countries, each expressed in its own currency.) The devaluation of B-currency will under these circumstances lead to an improvement of the current account of B, if the sum of the price elasticities of the demand for imports of both countries is greater than one. What modifications must now be considered if we take into account, first, that total expenditures in A or in B change and, second, that the price levels in both countries change as a result of the devaluation? Let us first examine the internal reactions in country B. The current account of B will improve as a result of the expansion of its exports and contraction of its imports which both take place as a result of the devaluation. Since national income is composed of domestic expenditures and the balance on current account, this change will increase the income of B; in other words, the monetary demand for the products of B will increase. This inflationary tendency will menace the internal equilibrium of B and, since we have assumed that the authorities pursue a policy directed toward internal stability, we must now consider deflationary measures to counteract the inflationary tendencies.

128

The price level of commodities of country B, expressed in B-currency, will probably therefore change under the assumptions that were made, while the inflationary trend, originating in the improvement of the current account, will be compensated by deflationary action. Restrictive measures in country B will, however, decrease the demand of B's consumers for commodities of country A. For these reasons, it may be assumed that B's balance of payments will become more active as a result of the simultaneous policy of internal stability, to a degree proportionate to the improvement in the balance of payments which results from a devaluation without simultaneous internal stabilization.

However, we must also examine the reactions which will probably occur in A. These depend completely on the economic policy of this country. If the authorities of A also pursue a policy of internal stability, there is the more reason to assume that the devaluation of B-currency will activate the current account of B to a greater degree than can be assumed on the basis of the immediate effects. However, if the government of A does not pursue a stabilization policy, the activation of B's current account as a result of devaluation will be less pronounced. The improvement of B's current account—a direct result of the devaluation of B-currency, if the sum of the elasticities of the demand for imports is greater than one—corresponds to a deterioration of A's current account. Hence, deflationary tendencies will appear in A and, if the government does not pursue a stabilization policy, production, employment, and income will fall. The general price level of A's commodities, expressed in A-currency, will also drop and in fact will do so the more, the more the marginal productivity of labor varies with a change in the rate of employment. Both factors will tend to weaken the improvement of B's current account.

However, if the authorities of A pursue a stabilization policy, not only will these two negative effects on B's current account be avoided, but a new positive influence on B's current account will make itself felt. In this case, the government of A will stimulate domestic expenditures in order to eliminate the deflationary effect resulting from the deterioration of A's current account. This increase of demand in A will also increase the expenditures for imports from B. Hence, B's current account will increase even more than it already would without this measure.

So far we have examined only the effect of devaluation on the current account, while, in real life, the capital account determines the matter of external equilibrium. Assuming a financial policy of internal stability in both countries, the positive effect of a devaluation of B-currency will be stronger than the effect on the current account for three reasons: First, internal stability in B requires a reduction of domestic expenditures in order to neutralize the inflationary effects which emanate from the improvement of the current account. If this deflationary policy is pursued by monetary means, then it involves a reduction of the money supply and a rise in the interest rates in B as well. The higher interest rates induce an increase of capital exports from A to B and consequently an activation of the capital account of B. Second, maintenance of internal equilibrium in A requires an expanding financial policy. If this is pursued by means of monetary policy, the interest rates in A will fall and this will further stimulate the export of capital from A to B. Third, it is possible that capital has regularly been transferred between A and B before the devaluation. Since internal equilibrium has been preserved in A as well as in B, there is, apart from the just-mentioned changes in the interest rates, no reason to assume that there will be a change in the propensity of the savers in B to invest their savings, measured in B-currency, in country A and in the propensity of the savers in A to invest their savings, measured in A-currency, in country B. But the devaluation of B-currency then means that the capital exports by the savers in B, expressed in A-currency, will decrease and this will lead to a further improvement of B's balance of payments if the latter is calculated in A-currency. However, if the government of A pursues a neutral policy, these three effects on B's balance of payments will be less strong.

It follows from all these considerations that it is advantageous to supplement the method of eliminating a balance-of-payments disequilibrium by altering the exchange rate through a financial policy of internal stabilization in all countries. Not only are unwanted internal reactions to the policy of external stabilization thereby avoided, but also the desired effects of devaluation on the external balance are brought about. The preservation of internal equilibrium in A as well as B will reinforce the direct effect of devaluation on the current account in the desired direction, and also exert a favorable influence on capital movements between A and B. Consequently, a given improvement of B's current account can, *ceteris paribus*, be attained by a smaller change in the terms of trade if a policy of internal stabilization is pursued in both countries.

So far we have adhered to the assumption that external stability has been striven for by changing the exchange rate and that internal stability has been sought by financial measures. In the following we will assume that country B, in its endeavor to attain external stability by financial policy, gets into an internal disequilibrium involving a high rate of unemployment. In order to attain full employment, a policy of expansion must then be launched at the prevailing money wages. By hypothesis, however, such actions are not taken, since they would lead to a deterioration of B's current account. In this situation, what would be the effect of a lowering of money wages in B combined with a financial policy directed toward external stability? We define this method of striving for internal stability as the *method of wage flexibility*. Money wages are flexible, when they fall, as soon as the demand for labor is smaller than its supply. If there is competition in country B, then the reduction of money wages will lead to a fall in the supply prices of B-products. So long as the prices of B-products are higher than marginal production costs, the volume of output will increase—i.e., the goods and services of B will become cheaper at a given demand. If we assume that prices and costs in A have remained constant, the terms of trade between A and B will change and there will be a shift of demand from commodities of country A to those of B. B's current account will then improve. However, external equilibrium in B is no longer preserved in this case and, since the government is pursuing a financial policy of external stability, total expenditures have to be increased so long as the effect of the wage decreases on the current account has been offset. The primary increase in the demand for B's commodities (induced by the drop in wages as well as by the expansion initiated by financial policy) will increase the demand for B's products and also increase its rate of employment. However, the reactions in A have to be taken into account. If there are no capital movements between A and B, there will be no repercussions in A from the fall in wages in B, provided no financial measures toward internal stability are adopted in A or a neutral policy is pursued. The reduction of expenditures on A-commodities which threatened as a result of the fall in prices of B-commodities will be exactly offset by the increase in demand for A-products that is evoked in B in order to secure external equilibrium.

In general, it can be concluded that a fall in money wages in B will lead to an increase in its rate of employment, if the government of the country tries to attain the goal of external stability by financial measures. The reduction in the prices of B-commodities relative to those of A-commodities will activate B's current account: this makes it possible for the government of B to expand the market for B-commodities by increasing domestic demand.

This mechanism implies, of course, that there will be a change in the terms of trade in favor of country A, since the whole argument is based on a reduction of the prices of B-commodities relative to those of A-commodities. This change in the terms of trade to the detriment of B will be small, provided that, first, the elasticities of the demand for imports in A and B are large; in this case, a given reduction of prices of

B-commodities induces a strong increase in the demand for these goods and hence a pronounced improvement in B's current account; this calls for a strong expansion of domestic demand in B for the purpose of external stabilization. Second, the change in the terms of trade will be small if the marginal propensity to import in B is small, since a very strong expansion of the demand for B-commodities must then take place in order to preserve external equilibrium. These conclusions apply to the case in which A does not pursue a neutral policy or a financial policy directed toward internal stability. The result is less determinable if country A also pursues a financial policy directed toward external stability.

3. THE ROLE OF CURRENCY SYSTEMS

The currency system that corresponds to the method of wage flexibility is the *gold standard*. The term "gold standard" is applied to numerous international currency systems, and we will examine in the following the way in which internal and external equilibrium could be maintained simultaneously in two countries if their governments abided by the rules of a common international currency system. Such a currency system could also be based on a silver or wheat standard or an international raw material; an abstract international accounting unit, created for the purpose, is also conceivable. For instance, an international authority could issue banknotes or claims whereby all notes would be issued in the same accounting unit (e.g., "Unitas" or "Bancor,"[10] as proposed in the White and Keynes plans).

The rules of the gold standard which must be adhered to by all participating central banks are the following: (1) The monetary authorities of each country must fix the gold value of the national currency. (2) Every gold standard country must per-

[10] Cf. Roy F. Harrod, *The Life of John Maynard Keynes*, London, 1952, pp. 562ff.; as well as E. A. G. Robinson, "John Maynard Keynes," *Politik und Wirtschaft, Ausgewählte Abhandlungen von John Maynard Keynes*, Tübingen-Zürich, 1956, page 56.

mit the free import and export of gold. (3) Every monetary authority must see to it that the supply of national currency increases more or less automatically if gold continues to come in, and that the money supply decreases more or less automatically if continuous gold losses are registered.

These three rules suffice to secure external equilibrium among the gold standard countries. In order to guarantee internal stability as well, a fourth rule must be adhered to: (4) Money wages must be flexible in every gold standard country.

Rule 1 demands that the monetary authorities of each country that is on the gold standard take steps to stabilize, within narrow limits, the value of gold in terms of their own currency. This can be achieved in three ways:

(1) Under the gold-specie standard, legal tender takes the form of gold coins with a fixed gold content. The national mint can then always transform a certain amount of gold into gold coin and, by melting it, gold coin can be transformed back into gold bullion. The gold value of the quantity of money thus cannot rise above or drop below the value of the coin.

(2) Under the gold-bullion standard, there are no gold coins in circulation; at least, they are not put into circulation by the monetary authorities. But the monetary authorities supply a certain amount of gold bullion in exchange for a unit of national currency and also purchase gold for a unit of national currency.

(3) Under the gold-exchange standard, no gold coins are in circulation, and no gold is bought or sold by the monetary authorities in exchange for notes of the country concerned. But they buy and sell currency of another country that is on the gold-specie or on the gold-bullion standard. If we assume, for instance, that the monetary authorities of country B will always buy four dollars for one pound or sell four dollars for one pound, and that the monetary authorities of country A abide by the rules of a gold-specie or a gold-bullion standard, then a pound is always valued at four dollars and four dollars corresponds to a given quantity of gold. The value of a pound

is therefore indirectly pegged to gold and an owner of pounds could always obtain the equivalent quantity of gold by buying four dollars in B in exchange for one pound and then acquiring the gold in A for four dollars.[11]

If the authorities of both countries peg their currency to gold by one of these three methods, and if free imports and exports of gold are possible in both countries, a relationship has thereby been established between the value of A-currency and that of B-currency. If the same value of gold is exchanged for one pound in B as for four dollars in A, then the par-exchange rate is "four dollars = one pound."

Now let us assume that the balance of payments of country B has a deficit. The residents of B will then buy more dollars in exchange for pounds in order to pay their creditors in A than the residents of A buy pounds in exchange for dollars to pay their creditors in B. The dollar rate, measured in pounds, will therefore have a tendency to rise in the foreign exchange market. However, this rise cannot go very far. It is always possible for the residents of B to buy gold from their monetary authorities for one pound, export this gold to A, and sell it to the monetary authorities of A in exchange for four dollars. However, this transaction involves certain costs—smelting, sales, insurance, and transport costs, and loss of interest. Let us assume that all costs amount to 5 cents per $4 gold value. Then it pays to exchange dollars for pounds in B's foreign exchange market so long as it is possible to obtain for one pound more than $3.95. If the dollar becomes more expensive in that market—i.e., if one obtains less than $3.95 in exchange for one pound—it pays to export gold to A. Under these circumstances, $3.95 per pound is B's gold export point and A's gold import point. Similarly, $4.05 per pound is A's gold export point and B's gold import point. The exchange rate will not fluctuate outside these narrow limits. The balance of payments will be settled by gold movements as soon as the exchange rate tends

[11] Cf. George N. Halm, *Geld, Aussenhandel und Beschäftigung*, Munich, 1951, pp. 94ff.

to go beyond these two points. Hence, the exchange rate between gold standard countries can be fixed inside the gold points by virtue of rules 1 and 2.

Rule 3 will, in the simplest case, be fulfilled by a gold reserve of 100 per cent. An example of this is a gold-specie standard in which gold can be freely minted and melted and gold coins are, moreover, the only form of money (other forms of 100 per cent money are also conceivable). However, 100 per cent money is not customary. In all modern states, only a fraction of the total quantity of money is backed up by gold or other internationally acceptable forms of payment. Two means of fractional backing can be distinguished. The first involves what Meade calls the "fiduciary issue principle," in which only a fraction of the total quantity of money is backed up by gold, but each change in the stock of gold leads to an exactly equal change in the total quantity of money. If we assume that the monetary authorities in country A issue banknotes to the value of one million dollars which are backed up by claims on firms or by treasury bills, additional money in the form of notes can be issued, according to the fiduciary issue principle, only if there is gold to back it up. If there is a stock of gold worth $500 million, then the total quantity of money (in the form of banknotes) amounts to $1,500 million. Hence, only one third of the notes in circulation are backed up by gold. But a change in the stock of gold by only one dollar would change the money quantity by this amount. The system functions without disturbances in the case of gold imports. But if gold is lost, limits are set to the fiduciary issue principle. If, for instance, in the case just dealt with, external equilibrium demands a reduction in the total quantity of money in A from $1,500 million to $900 million and if the monetary authorities do not want the stock of gold to fall below $200 million, a gold loss to the amount of $300 million must lead to a contraction of the total quantity of money by $600 million. Thus, 100 per cent money is the only sure method of preserving the fiduciary issue principle.

On the other hand, the total quantity of money as well as marginal changes in money supply are only partly backed up by gold in the second method of observing rule 3—using the "percentage reserve principle," as it is called by Meade. In reality, the national bank systems do not accord exactly with either the first or the second principle, since their structure is much more complicated. For instance, the stock of gold could be manipulated by the central bank with respect to deposits in a different way than with respect to banknotes, and the commercial banks could hold their reserves in the central bank partly in the form of notes and partly in the form of deposits. Moreover, they could apply different reserve principles to their own liabilities; and, finally, the people can hold a larger or smaller part of their liquid assets in the form of banknotes or of deposits (the coverage of which is different from that of banknotes). At any rate, all possible systems belong fundamentally to one of the following three categories: (1) The gold reserve is equal to the total quantity of money and 100 per cent of the money is backed up by gold. (2) The gold reserve is smaller than the total quantity of money, but changes are the same in both gold and money (fiduciary issue principle). (3) The gold reserve is smaller than the total quantity of money and changes in the quantity of money correspond to smaller changes in the quantity of gold (percentage reserve principle). The third system is the customary one.

Apart from the technical aspects already discussed, what are the *differences* between the gold standard and a system of fluctuating exchange rates? The *gold standard* means in reality that the participating countries pursue a financial policy directed toward external equilibrium and a wage policy directed toward internal equilibrium. On the other hand, the *method of fluctuating exchange rates* can be combined with policies aimed at safeguarding internal stability. Both systems pursue objectives of internal and external equilibrium by a combination of two measures: first, by a financial policy aimed toward expansion or contraction of domestic demand; and, second, by a change in the terms of trade between the participating countries. In the case of the gold standard, this change is achieved by a decrease in money wages and prices in the deficit country and an increase of money wages and prices in the surplus country. In the case of fluctuating exchange rates, it is achieved by a devaluation of the currency of the deficit country relative to that of the surplus country.

Let us assume that countries A and B are originally in equilibrium internally as well as externally, and that a disturbance in the external equilibrium then appears. We must now determine how equilibrium is restored under both systems. In the first case, both countries abide by the rules of the gold standard; in the second case, A as well as B influences total expenditures by financial measures aimed at safeguarding internal equilibrium, while external equilibrium is sought by causing fluctuations in the exchange rate. Let the disturbance consist of a spontaneous increase in the export of capital from A to B.

Under the gold standard, the loss of gold by the central bank of A and the gain of gold by the central bank of B lead, first, to an increase in the interest rate in A and a decrease in the interest rate in B. Consequently, the export of capital from B to A will rise and the volume of transfers from A to B will decrease. This is the first compensating effect counteracting the disturbance of external equilibrium. The rise in interest rates in A and their fall in B will at the same time release deflationary tendencies in the first country and inflationary tendencies in the second. Since the imports are a function of income, this will lead to a decrease in demand for imports in A and to an increase in demand for imports in B. This change represents the second compensating effect on the balance of payments. The deflation of total expenditures in A and the inflation of total expenditures in B will usually lead to a fall in prices and money wages in A and to a rise in prices and money wages in B. Hence, the terms of trade between the two countries change and a shift in demand results. If the sum of the price elasticities of demand for import in both countries is greater than one, the value of the imports of A will decrease and the value of the imports of B will increase. This is the third compensating effect. The income and price effects and, in addition, changes in the capital account, under the gold standard, counteract a spontaneous disturbance in the balance of payments. It should be observed that these developments do not necessarily take place in a chronological sequence. We argue a static case in which all these effects occur theoretically at the same time.

This applies also to responses to spontaneous disturbance in the case of fluctuating exchange rates. The additional export of capital from A to B leads first to a devaluation of the currency in A and to a revaluation in B. This change in the terms of trade reduces the demand for imports in A and raises it in B. If the sum of the import elasticities in both countries is larger than one, the value of the imports of A will fall and the value of the imports of B will rise. This is the first compensating reaction to the disturbance of external equilibrium. The increase of A's exports and the decrease of B's exports will raise the interest rate in A relative to that in B. This change induces a decrease in A's capital export and an increase in B's capital export. A's balance of payments will improve accordingly. The rise of the interest rate in A and the fall of the interest rate in B, however, will also affect incomes—a change which ultimately is manifested in a reduction in the demand for imports in A and a rise in the demand for imports in B. The deflation of domestic expenditures in A and the expansion of domestic expenditures in B will redress the internal equilibrium in both countries. Hence, compensating price and income effects and a compensating change in the capital account can be observed in this case also as reactions to a spontaneous disturbance of external equilibrium.

If we abstract for a moment from certain complicating factors (for instance, the effect of deflation on nominally fixed debts and of a change in the exchange rates on speculative movements of capital, or of a difference in flexibility of money wages, on the one hand, and exchange rates, on the other), both mechanisms achieve essentially the same results.

These complicating factors will now be examined. They can be reduced to *differences in the conditions* which have to be fulfilled for the gold standard, on the one hand, and for the system of fluctuating exchange rates, on the other.

Under the gold standard, the general level of money wages has to fall or rise so long as there is an excess supply or an excess demand on the labor market. This flexibility of money wages presupposes either that there is no monopoly on the supply side of the labor market or that such a monopoly position is not being exploited. If *money* wages are not sufficiently flexible to satisfy the requirements of the gold standard, another method of price adjustment must take their place. (The flexibility of money wages is a prerequisite not only for reasons of international adjustment. If national income is to be maximized, wage rates in the various sectors must be flexible. The flexibility of relative wage rates, however, corresponds to the flexibility of the general wage level.) On the other hand, under the system of fluctuating exchange rates, *real* wages have to be flexible. For the elimination of the disequilibrium that results from a spontaneous disturbance, a change in the terms of trade which generally influence real wages is required. For instance, the cost of living will rise if the price of import commodities rises, and this reduction of real wages must take place under a system of fluctuating exchange rates. Under the gold standard, on the other hand, the necessary adjustment of real wages results in part from a reduction in the demand for labor and in part from an increase in the cost of living. The reduction in money wages is accompanied by a proportionate fall in commodity prices in the deficit country. The drop in real wages is therefore only a consequence of the rise in the prices of imported goods; if the wage earners did not consume imported commodities, there would be no change in real wages. Under fluctuating exchange rates, real wages would fall as a result of imports becoming dearer. On the other hand, money wages and commodity prices in the deficit country remain unchanged.[12]

Hence, for the mechanism of fluctuating exchange rates to function properly, real wages must be flexible. Every increase in money wages in the deficit country resulting from an increase in the cost of living—based, for instance, on an institutionally sanctioned constant relationship between money wages and cost of living (i.e., "sliding wage scales")—would prevent a change in the terms of trade and consequently remove the incentive for shifting demand from commodities of the surplus country to commodities of the deficit country. It is, however, conceivable that with a system of fluctuating exchange rates in the deficit country, the functional distribution of income would also change, in the sense that the earnings of productive factors other than labor would drop. However, the adjustment would not go very far, since labor income represents a large share of national income in modern economies.

It therefore follows that an effective preservation of the gold standard presupposes flexible money wages, while the method of price adjustment by a change in the exchange rates presupposes a sufficient dependency between the fluctuations in the cost of living index and in money wage rates.

So far we have neglected the problem of how the deficit and surplus countries share the *burden of adjustment*.[13] We take as our starting point a spontaneous deterioration in B's current account which requires a change of 10 per cent in the terms of trade in order to ensure internal and external equilibrium. If the money wages and prices in A remain constant,

---

[12] Cf. also S. Laursen and L. A. Metzler, *op.cit.*, pp. 283ff.

[13] This question held Keynes' attention during various periods of his life and it ultimately became an essential part of the Keynes Plan that, where existing exchange rates and price relationships did not provide a basis for equilibrium, the responsibility for part of the adjustment should be laid on the creditors as well as on the debtors in order to lessen the pressure on the debtor in the form of deflation and a lowering of the rate of employment and income. Suggestions for such a regulation can already be found in *A Tract on Monetary Reform*, London, 1923.

the money wages in B have to be reduced by 10 per cent under the gold standard system; or, if the money wages and prices in B remain constant, they must rise in A by 10 per cent. However, it would be possible and even desirable to lower the money wages and prices by 5 per cent in B and to raise them by 5 per cent in A. If the price adjustment is distributed over both countries, the absolute change in the prices required for the elimination of the disequilibrium is considerably reduced. Another condition which would smooth the functioning of the system is that the deficit countries as well as the surplus countries are on the gold standard and take part in the necessary price adjustment. The consequences of this postulate are: First, both countries must comply with the requirement of flexible money wages. Second, the monetary authorities of both countries must abide by the third rule of the gold standard—i.e., that neither a neutralization of the losses of gold nor a sterilization of the gains of gold should be aimed at. This policy is always possible if the foreign exchange reserves are sufficiently large. If, however, the monetary authorities of either country infringe rule 3 by neutralization or sterilization, the burden of adjustment to be carried by the other country will be heavier. Similar conditions apply under the mechanism of fluctuating exchange rates. The authorities of the surplus country adopt financial measures to prevent domestic money wages, prices, and money expenditures from falling. It is of vital importance under this system for the necessary adjustments of the exchange rates to be kept within narrow limits, and consequently the monetary authorities of the surplus country have to stabilize expenditures in terms of their own currency. In the same way, an increase in total demand has to be prevented in the deficit country. (What has been said applies fully to two countries under a free foreign exchange system as well as under the IMF system. However, if the relationships among more than two countries are examined, one arrives at the conclusion that it is necessary for more than reasons of sharing the adjustment burden that surplus countries revalue and deficit countries devalue in order to eliminate the deficit.)

Of course, an adjustment of prices and costs can be carried out more easily if sufficient time is available. In this connection, the monetary authorities of the deficit country must have a sufficient stock of gold or other internationally acceptable means of payment in order to finance the balance-of-payments deficit during the period of necessary price adjustments. As for the gold standard, the requirement for sufficient foreign exchange reserves is closely connected with the distinction between a percentage reserve system and a 100 per cent money system. Under the latter, an annual balance-of-payments deficit of $100 million will lead to a $100 million annual loss of gold and a $100 million annual contraction of the total quantity of money. However, if only 10 per cent of a nation's total quantity of money is backed up by gold and if the balance-of-payments deficit is annually financed by the export of $100 million of gold, the total quantity of money must be reduced annually by one billion dollars—unless the reserve ratio is modified. The deflation of money wages and prices will therefore not be carried out nearly so rapidly under the 100 per cent reserve system as under the system of fractional gold coverage.

Let the quantity of money in B amount to $10 billion; furthermore, let the balance of payments have an annual deficit of $100 million. Let us assume that, to restore external equilibrium, the total supply of B-money, money wages, and prices have to be reduced by 20 per cent. If 100 per cent of the $10 billion is covered by gold, B can lose gold to the amount of $100 million annually and, after a period of twenty years, will reach a new situation of external equilibrium with a total money quantity of $8 billion. The total quantity of money in B has therefore annually been reduced by $100 million or 1 per cent. (We are neglecting the effect of an annual contraction of the quantity of money on the balance-of-payments deficit. The further the deflation process has proceeded, the

143

more this would have diminished.) If, however, only a $1 billion gold reserve covers a money quantity of $10 billion, the adjustment cannot take place at such a leisurely tempo. Similarly, if gold reserves are lost to the amount of $100 million annually and the quantity of money decreases annually by $100 million, the gold reserve will be exhausted after ten years, even though B's quantity of money has only been reduced to $9 billion instead of to $8 billion. B's central bank must also speed up its deflation policy and, indeed, the tempo of deflation must be ten times as fast in case of a gold backing of 10 per cent as in the case of a 100 per cent gold backing. For B's total quantity of money has to be reduced every year by an amount ten times greater than the loss of gold that year (i.e., by the amount of the balance-of-payments deficit of that year). While a 20 per cent lowering of the money wages could possibly be achieved in a period of twenty years, this would be impossible to accomplish in two years.

The greater the share of a country's money that is backed by gold, the more time is available to the monetary authorities for eliminating deficits in the balance of payments. Since a rapid reduction of prices and wages could prove infeasible, the system of the gold standard requires that potential deficit countries be equipped with high reserves of gold or other currency.

Roughly the same results are engendered by the mechanism of fluctuating exchange rates. Let us assume that a disequilibrium could be eliminated by devaluing B's currency by 20 per cent. If the devaluation is carried out immediately and *in one move*, the real wages of B will be sharply reduced as a result of the pronounced rise in import prices. However, if the adjustment can be spread over a period of twenty years and carried out in annual steps of 1 per cent, the possibility exists that the only "lowering" of real wages will manifest itself in a reduction of the annual rate of growth from, let us say, 2 per cent to 1 per cent. But to spread the devaluation over the longer period would, of course, mean that B's balance-of-payments deficit would also continue for a longer time. Gold reserves would therefore be necessary to finance it.

Still another argument can be advanced in support of the necessity of higher currency reserves in deficit countries. There is reason to assume that the demand for imports reacts more strongly to long-term changes in relative prices than to short-term changes. If the prices of products of B decrease and those of A increase, consumers of A's commodities will shift over to those of B; as a matter of fact, the more conscious they are of the price difference and the more they find out about the possibilities for substitution, the more their demand will shift. The same applies to the suppliers who can rearrange their production facilities on a long-term basis better than on a short-term basis. This rearrangement may be necessary if the producers use B-commodities rather than A-commodities. In addition, it is even possible that within a very short period the sum of the price elasticities of the demand for imports will be smaller than one, even when the sum will be considerably larger than one in the long run. A devaluation of B's currency would therefore in the short run cause the balance of payments of this country to deteriorate. In such cases, the monetary authorities of the deficit country should have a suitable quantity of gold in reserve, for it is possible that the price adjustment mechanism will not function in the short run.

As we have already shown, the price adjustment method is the more effective, the higher the *elasticities of the demand for imports* in the partner countries are; and the higher these elasticities, the smaller the change in the terms of trade, in money wages, and in the exchange rates necessary to eliminate a balance-of-payments deficit by a shift of demand. One of the factors that has a bearing on the height of these elasticities is commercial policy. The price elasticities of demand for imports could be drastically reduced by international trade barriers which prevent demand from shifting from the products of one country to those of another country. Commercial controls may take various forms: import restrictions which make it impossible for the importers of country A to import more goods from B if the relative prices of the latter fall; or a high specific import duty in A which reduces the effect of a fall in costs in B on the sales price of B-commodities in A; or an international agreement concerning raw materials that limits by quota the export of a certain commodity from country B independent of the height of its production costs; or a cartel agreement among the producers of a commodity which effectively prevents the increase of exports from B; or a government monopoly in A which fixes the import quantities or the sources of origin of the imports independent of price changes; or laws which require that commodities must be transported, independent of costs, in vessels of a particular country; or production and export subsidies in A or import duties in A which are continuously changed in such a way that cost and price changes which threaten the production of A are neutralized. All these measures prevent the consumers from turning away from the commodities of country A and increasing their purchases of the cheaper product of B. International adjustments by way of changes in prices and costs or in exchange rates will therefore proceed with the less disturbance, the fewer restrictions are imposed on foreign trade.

4. FOREIGN EXCHANGE SPECULATION WITH STABILIZING OR DESTABILIZING EFFECTS

Some important items in the balance of payments which can act as disturbing as well as stabilizing factors have up to now been neglected. Extensive purchases and sales of foreign exchange for speculative purposes can be conducted in a free foreign exchange market. These transactions will now be examined.[14]

The mechanism of foreign exchange speculation can be illustrated by the following example. Let us assume that the

[14] Cf. *ibid.*, pp. 74ff.

foreign exchange dealers estimate the movements of the pound, the currency-unit of country B, optimistically. Stated otherwise, they expect a rise in the pound rate measured in dollars. Let the dollar be the currency unit of country A. Let the present rate be $2 for £1 and anticipate that next year the rate will be $3 for £1. Hence, the foreign exchange dealer expects that next year he can get $300 for the pounds which he now buys for $200. If developments accord with this expectation, the dealer can make a profit of 50 per cent on his capital. If the change takes only four months instead of a year, the annual profit rate rises as high as 150 per cent.

This sort of speculation can take various forms. First, foreign exchange dealers can speculate; but it is also possible that the importers and exporters of commodities will try to make foreign exchange profits. Importers in A who have to make a payment to a creditor in B, or exporters in B who have received dollars, can anticipate the exchange of the currencies concerned if they expect speculative profits to come from it. The importer in A will immediately exchange dollars for pounds instead of doing so at a later point of time; the exporter in B will convert the received dollars at once instead of later. These temporary shifts in the financing of foreign trade based on such expectations arise from the same cause and have the same effect as foreign exchange speculation proper.

Several factors, however, limit the extent of these speculative transactions. (1) If the interest rate which a debtor must pay in the money market of A is considerably higher than the interest rate which a creditor in B can get, speculative capital movements will be discouraged. However, this factor is less important if considerable profits are expected from speculation. (2) The second factor which limits speculative transactions results from inherent uncertainty. It is impossible to forecast future developments with certainty. The extent to which speculators will speculate in one direction is therefore limited; they will never stake all their funds on a single transaction. (3) A third factor is of the utmost importance. Let us assume that the present rate of exchange is $2 for £1 and the expected rate of exchange is $3 for £1. These expectations will induce conversions of dollars into pounds with the intention of changing the pounds back into dollars when the revaluation of the pound has actually taken place. This speculative movement itself, however, will immediately lead to a rise in the rate of the pound. If the speculators find that they and their competitors are keeping extraordinarily large amounts in the form of pounds, all of which are later to be changed back into dollars, they will revise their expectations regarding the value of the pound. The foreign exchange dealers will debate in their minds whether the expected movement from pounds into dollars will reduce the future demand for pounds so that the revaluation will in fact be less pronounced than it would be without speculation. The immediate revaluation of the pound as a result of the speculation and the reduction of the expected devaluation will therefore limit the extent of speculation against the dollar.

This shrinkage of the margin between the present and the expected rate of the pound leads to three important results: (1) It tends to prevent profit from speculation; if the future movement of the pound is anticipated correctly and if there is perfect competition in the foreign exchange market, profit from speculation may even be completely eliminated. (2) Speculation along the lines we have described will smooth out price fluctuations. Let us say that, without speculation, this year's rate would be $2 for £1 and next year's $3 for £1. As a result of speculation, the dollar value of the pound goes to $2.25 this year and to $2.75 next year. This stabilization of the exchange rate over time can greatly ease the wage policy of the country concerned by, for instance, causing a less abrupt reduction of real wages in the case of a devaluation. (3) Speculation will support the price adjustment mechanism as described before. If A and B are internally and externally in equilibrium at an exchange rate of $4 for £1 and a disturbance requires B-currency to be devalued, it is possible that a devaluation to $3 for £1 would be sufficient in the long run. However, since the elasticities of demand are greater in the long run than in the short run, an immediate devaluation to $2 for £1 might be necessary to restore equilibrium in the balance of payments. If there were no speculation, the ratio between the value of the dollar and the pound would pass through, say, the following three stages: 4:1, 2:1, 3:1. The most difficult stage is the middle one. The difficulties can, however, be alleviated by speculation. When the speculators recognize that the exchange rate has to be 3:1 to afford equilibrium, they have a speculative incentive, if the rate is lower, to change their dollars into pounds and consequently speculate against the dollar. The pounds can then later be changed into dollars, which would at first put the new equilibrium rate under some pressure. (Hence, the pound might first drop to $2.8; it would then, however, rise to only $2.9, since the previous exchange of pounds into dollars would force the new rate below the equilibrium rate in the long run.) However, the pound would never fall below $2.8; hence, the rate fluctuations would be damped by the speculation. Moreover, B's balance-of-payments problem would in the critical period also be eased by the speculation, for B's dollar reserves would increase as a result of the exchange of dollars into pounds. The surplus on current account should therefore be smaller in this case than it would be without speculation. A part of the burden of adjustment would be carried by the capital account.

What has been said so far was based on the assumption that foreign exchange dealers and other speculators anticipate more or less correctly the future movement of the exchange rate. On the other hand, speculation would aggravate the balance-of-payments problem in two cases. The first case is called "perverse" speculation, since the speculators appraise the movement of the foreign exchange rate incorrectly. In the second case, speculation is "grossly excessive"—the direction of the movement in the exchange rate has been correctly forecast but too great a change has been expected.

Let a spontaneous disturbance cause a deficit in B's balance of payments. The rate of the pound would fall without speculation in the first year from $4 to $2, and let the long-term equilibrium rate be $3 for £1. Now, if the original devaluation to $2 makes the speculators feel pessimistic, so that they expect a further deterioration instead of an improvement to $3, they will exchange pounds into dollars instead of the other way around and the exchange rate will temporarily drop to $1.5. When the speculators have recognized their mistake, the equilibrium rate (3:1) will ultimately be reached under these assumptions. But here speculation has enlarged the range of fluctuations and aggravated the balance-of-payments deficit.

Putting speculative expectations too high will have the same effect. If, again, a spontaneous disturbance causes B's balance of payments to deteriorate and a drop in the rate of the pound is necessary (with an ultimate equilibrium rate of $3), and if the speculators are overoptimistic about the future movements of the pound after devaluation has begun, the balance-of-payments deficit will be financed for some time by speculative transactions. For example, an exchange rate of 3.9:1 becomes effective in the first instance rather than one of 2:1. There will then be no price adjustment to speak of and no change in the current account. Since the excessively favorable pound rate of 3.9 can be maintained only by a continuous exchange of dollars into pounds, the speculators must recognize their mistake sooner or later. The speculative transactions will be broken off and the exchange rate will drop abruptly to $2—the rate which is temporarily necessary to introduce a price adjustment. Since the expectations have been false, it is unlikely that the foreign exchange dealers will support the pound rate at 2:1 by further exchanges of dollars into pounds; on the contrary, it is likely that from now on pounds will be exchanged into dollars, which will put a further strain on the pound. The fluctuation of the exchange rate is thereby again intensified and extra pressure is put on the balance of payments of the deficit country at the most dangerous moment.

Such harmful speculation could be checked by placing a control on international capital movements, but we have assumed that there was a free foreign exchange market. In the framework of this system, the movement of private capital could be neutralized by operations of the monetary authorities. If, as in the case of "perverse" speculation described above, pounds are changed into dollars instead of dollars into pounds, the monetary authorities could eliminate the undesirable effects by changing dollars into pounds. By these measures, they could try to obtain step by step the result that would be achieved in a free foreign exchange market with perfect competition. For this purpose, the monetary authorities need only appraise the future movement of the exchange rate more correctly than the private speculators. In addition, they can try to give more stability to the exchange rate than would be possible with perfect competition and correct expectations. If, under these conditions, the dollar value of the pound on the foreign exchange market fell from 4 to 2.8, then rose to 2.9 and finally to 3, the monetary authorities could make it their objective to eliminate every fall in the rate below $3 by purchasing at this rate all pounds that are offered for sale and continuing to do so until the new equilibrium rate has established itself. The greater stability in the cost of living which would result from such a policy would, among other things, ease the problem of a wage policy.

If official transactions of this sort are to be carried out, an *exchange equalization fund* must be maintained. This fund must be endowed with a stock of the currency of country A as well as with that of B. If, for instance, the rate of B-currency has to be stabilized with the help of this fund, currency of A must flow toward the foreign exchange market in exchange for the B-currency that is offered there. A part of the fund's stock of A-currency would thus be replaced by B-currency. The fund could be nationally organized—i.e., A and B could each independently maintain an exchange equalization fund. However, an international exchange equalization fund which, for instance, was manipulated by a supranational authority would have numerous advantages over a conglomerate of separate national funds.

A national fund incurs the risk of running short of foreign exchange. On the other hand, with a *supranationally organized fund*, if the currency of A has to be supported, it is possible for the government of B to offer B-currency for sale in the market, so that the additional quantity of money is obtained by creation of money. The same applies to the monetary authorities of country A when the B-currency has to be supported—i.e., for such a fund, there is no limit to the supply of any given currency. On the other hand, if B-currency has to be supported by an exchange equalization fund of B alone, this is possible only so long as that fund has A-currency at its command. B's banking system, however, cannot create additional amounts of A-currency. Moreover, a national exchange equalization fund runs the danger of misuse. It is possible that a national government will use its fund as an instrument of a "beggar-my-neighbor" policy and will try to sustain internal stability by an artificial export boom rather than by financial policy. The rate of employment of a country would then be raised at the expense of the rate of employment of another country. A supranational authority could prevent such misuse. However, a clear decision must be made beforehand about the level of the exchange rate that has to be stabilized.

Besides an exchange equalization fund, there is still another institution by which excessive fluctuations in the exchange rate could be counteracted—namely, a futures market in foreign exchange. To be sure, the disadvantages of speculation based on incorrect expectations cannot be eliminated thereby, but its effect on the importers and exporters can be avoided, since a futures market in foreign exchange serves to remove currency risks in international trade.

So far we have examined the speculation problem under the

assumption of a free foreign exchange market. Speculation has quite another character under the IMF system. If we again assume that there is a spontaneous deterioration in the external position of country B which makes it necessary to devalue the pound from $4 to $3, there will be a strong incentive for speculators to change pounds into dollars so long as the exchange rate does not change. The foreign exchange dealers will conclude from a permanent deficit in B's balance of payments that sooner or later a fall in the dollar value of the pound will be inevitable. The exchange of pounds into dollars—i.e., the export of capital by the speculators—will, however, not change the exchange rate under the IMF system. Moreover, neither will the exchange rate be influenced by changing dollars back into pounds after the devaluation has been accomplished. Hence, the profit which the speculators make out of the expected adjustment of the exchange rate is not only certain but unlimited. Consequently, strong capital movements from B to A will set in. These will not serve an economically useful purpose, since they cannot influence the exchange rate under the IMF system. In this case, the result of the speculation would only be that the speculators realize unlimited profits at the expense of official currency reserves. When the speculators change pounds into dollars, the monetary authorities of B must buy the pounds and pay with dollars in order to stabilize the rate of the B-currency; when the devaluation has been carried out, the monetary authorities have to repurchase the dollars at the higher rate. The IMF system can be maintained only if it is supplemented in one form or another by direct controls on speculative international capital movements. Such controls are not effective unless they involve the entire financial sector and the payments in the non-financial sector; moreover, they present great administrative difficulties, since speculative transactions cannot easily be distinguished from other transactions.

In the case of the gold standard, the exchange rate is absolutely stabilized in the range between the two gold points.

There are possibilities between these two points for a moderate speculation of the kind we have described. But under the gold standard the adjustment by definition must take place not through a change in the exchange rate but in money wages and prices.

Speculation under the IMF system is definitely harmful and therefore quite different from the free foreign exchange market, where the private interest of the speculator coincides with the interest of society. Hence a free foreign exchange market, coupled with a futures market in foreign exchange and supplemented by an exchange equalization fund, would constitute an optimum currency system.

5. SPECIAL FEATURES OF REGIONAL ADJUSTMENT OF THE BALANCE OF PAYMENTS

In what way do the problems of the balance of payments between two countries differ from the problems of the balance of payments between two *regions*? First, there are institutional factors which distinguish interregional from international trade.[15]

The regions of a country normally have the same money and banking system. At any one time, the national supply of money has a certain magnitude and the money is fully convertible within the regions. An interregional payment will therefore not change the national quantity of money. The mechanism of payments between the regions of a national economy is like a system of 100 per cent money (with certain important exceptions, to be noted below). As we have shown, such a system eases adjustments by allowing a longer period of adaptation than a system of fractional backing. The fact that the individual regions of a country, or possibly of an economic union, have a common currency therefore implies that

[15] Cf. also T. Scitovsky, "The Theory of the Balance of Payments and the Problem of Common European Currency," *Kyklos* (1957), pp. 18ff.

in the event of a disequilibrium in the interregional balance of payments the necessary adjustments could be carried out in a continuous sequence. But this does not mean that adjustments in relative prices and incomes would be smaller because of a common currency.

Another difference between the mechanisms of interregional and international adjustment touches on the degree of the required adjustment. While national governments restrict international trade by commercial policies, interregional trade can proceed undisturbed. This means that, between nations, the elasticity of the demand for imports is in general smaller than it is between regions. The elimination of interregional disequilibrium by way of price adjustments should therefore function better than the removal of international disequilibrium in the balance of payments. (On the other hand, it is of course impossible in an interregional domain to resort to controls employed in restoring external equilibrium.)

There is a further difference when it comes to financial policy. Differences in financial policy are probably greater between individual countries than between regions of the same country. The same applies to other institutional aspects. Thus, regional labor markets within a country will have a similar organization. It is possible, for instance, that one country will pursue a neutral economic policy with constant money wage rates, while another country will give free play to the mechanism of the gold standard; such differences are hardly conceivable between regions of a single country.

A third distinctive feature to which much importance is traditionally attached is the difference between interregional and international mobility of the factors of production—a problem with which we will deal more extensively later on. It was for this reason that the classical economists developed a special theory of international trade. They assumed that capital and labor were entirely mobile interregionally, but entirely immobile internationally. However, the question we must turn to is whether or not a higher mobility of productive factors between regions than between nations makes it easier to restore external equilibrium after a given disturbance.

We will assume that there is free trade between countries A and B; that internal equilibrium has been established in both by means of monetary policy and that external equilibrium between the two countries is maintained by means of fluctuating exchange rates or the gold standard. First, we will examine the significance of movements of capital which take place as a result of international differences in the interest rate, and which in turn result from a spontaneous disturbance of external equilibrium. As we remember, the method of price adjustment after a spontaneous disturbance normally requires a relative reduction of prices in the deficit country. No generalizations can be made as to the influence of international mobility of *capital*. The answer to our question depends on the type of spontaneous disturbance. In the case discussed, capital movements can have disturbing, neutral, or stabilizing effects.

Let us assume that the spontaneous disturbance consists of a reduction of domestic expenditures in country A. The immediate result of this change is deflationary. The government of A then adopts a cheap-money policy to restore internal equilibrium. If capital is not mobile internationally, the interest rate in country A will be lowered until full employment is restored. Since domestic expenditures will then again be as high as before, the balance of payments will return to equilibrium and the only change will be that the interest rate in A has fallen. However, if capital is mobile between A and B, the cheap-money policy will induce an increase in the export of capital from A to B. Consequently B's balance of payments will improve and B's currency will be devalued. If the sum of the import elasticities of A and B are greater than one, the demand for commodities of B will shift to those of A until the balance of payments is again in equilibrium. In any case, this tendency for the balance of payments to deteriorate initiates a deflationary tendency in country B and an opposite tendency in A. In order to eliminate these tendencies, the interest rate in B has to fall and that in A to rise, upon which the demand in B will rise via investments, income, and consumption function and the demand in A will fall. These changes in demand will lead to an activation of A's current account to the extent necessary to neutralize the capital export from A to B. Consequently, a deterioration in the terms of trade of A must take place in the event of this type of original disturbance in order to restore the balance-of-payments equilibrium despite a flow of capital from A to B. However, if capital is immobile internationally, the terms of trade need not change.

Now let us assume a disturbance which consists of a spontaneous shift of the demand for commodities of country A to those of B. The currency of B will then be devalued to such an extent that consumption expenditures are redistributed over the commodities of both countries in the same proportion as before. The external equilibrium is then restored and neither A nor B will be subject to inflationary or deflationary pressure. The interest rate will therefore remain constant in both countries; and it is irrelevant whether capital is mobile or not.

Let the third disturbance consist of a reparation payment by A to B. The governments in both countries employ fiscal policies so that total expenditures are not affected by this transaction. Country A then has a balance-of-payments deficit equal to the reparation payment and the currency of A is devalued as a result. If the sum of the import elasticities of A and B exceeds one, the devaluation will cause A's current account to become active by the amount of the reparation payment. However, at the same time, the fact that the currency account has become active induces inflationary forces in A's economy and deflationary forces in B's economy. The authorities in A raise the interest rate and the authorities in B lower it in order to maintain internal equilibrium. If capital is immobile, this change in interest rates will have no direct effect on external equilibrium. However, if capital is mobile, it will flow from B to A, and A's current account need gain less in order to eliminate the deficit in the transfer account than would

be the case if capital were immobile. Hence, the adjustment
to this type of disturbance would be eased by capital movements. As a result of the deterioration in A's balance of payments, the terms of trade of country A will develop favorably
in all three of the cases we have described.

On the other hand, if *labor* were mobile, the change in the
terms of trade would also be less detrimental to A in all three
cases.

The deterioration in the terms of trade of country A means
that the real wages in A drop in comparison with those in B.
Since there is full employment in both countries as before,
the volume of production and the rate of employment have not
changed and the marginal productivity of labor has therefore
remained constant. Hence, the workers in A receive a wage
which, measured in A-commodities, has not changed and the
wages of the workers in B will have the same purchasing
power in B as before. But because from now on fewer commodities of B can be bought for a unit of commodities of A,
the prices of goods imported by A will rise and the prices of
goods imported by B will fall. That is why real wages in A
will drop in relation to real wages in B and, if labor is mobile,
workers will move from A to B. Henceforth, internal equilibrium in A implies a smaller number of persons employed and
a smaller volume of domestic demand: the reverse will happen
in country B. At the same time, expenditures on imports will
decrease in A and increase in B. The movement of workers
from A to B as such will therefore cause an improvement of
A's current account and, consequently, the terms of trade will
not change as much as would be the case if labor had been
immobile. Labor mobility will make it easier to restore external equilibrium in all three cases described. If labor mobility were perfect (i.e., if the workers moved from A to B
until the real wage had become the same in both countries),
no other adjustment mechanism would be necessary to restore
equilibrium in the balance of payments. So long as A's terms
of trade continued to deteriorate and the real wage was smaller
than in B, the demand for imports would fall in country A,

since workers would, under this condition, continue to move from A to B and exports to B would continue to increase. These effects would be solely attributable to the expansion of demand in B and the contraction of demand in A, in turn caused by a growing population in B and a declining one in A.

However, this analysis is fully correct only if the marginal productivities of labor in both countries do not vary with the change in the rate of employment—i.e., if the supply elasticity of commodities is infinite in both countries. An increase in employment in B will, however, normally lead to a drop in the marginal productivity of labor, while a decrease in employment in A will increase marginal labor productivity. Since the ratio of capital to labor rises in A while it falls in B, the real wages of workers will rise in A and drop in B so long as workers continue to migrate from A to B. The deterioration in A's terms of trade will therefore be partly neutralized and the income effects evoked by the movement need not be as strong as in the case of infinite supply elasticities.

It follows from what has been said that the mobility of labor accelerates the adjustment in the balance of payments in every case. If marginal labor productivity in both countries is only weakly correlated with the rate of employment, the adjustment will depend to a higher degree on the movement of workers from A to B. This migration will increase the demand for imports in B and decrease it in A and thereby make it possible to obtain the improvement in the balance of payments without a major change in the terms of trade. If, on the other hand, the supply elasticities are small, the balance of payments will be partly adjusted by a change in the terms of trade.

6. INTERNAL ADJUSTMENT
OF THE BALANCE OF PAYMENTS OF AN
ECONOMIC UNION

We will now proceed to consider possible modifications of a balance-of-payments adjustment in an economic union. The interregional mechanisms of adjustment which we discussed above are under certain conditions also applicable to an economic union. In other words, after the transition to an economic union, the problem of adjusting the balance of payments internationally is affected, first of all, by the removal of trade barriers and controls. It should be observed in this connection that all the means of control analyzed in the first chapter could also be used by the monetary authorities as instruments to adjust the balance of payments. They might be so applied if the method of price adjustment—i.e., the income and price effects—evoked by a spontaneous disturbance and reinforced by a monetary policy of price adjustment failed, for one reason or another, to restore external equilibrium—in this case, between the individual regions.

If one abstracts from controls over international trade, which do not prevail in an economic union, there remain essentially three methods of restoring interregional equilibrium in the union:[16] financial support of deficit countries by surplus countries, alternating inflation and deflation, and changing the exchange rate.

Financial support of the deficit countries by the surplus countries can take the form of direct grants, unlimited credits by the central banks of the surplus countries, or accumulation of claims of the surplus countries (i.e., debts of the deficit countries) at a central clearing agency such as the European Payments Union. Such a system is viable over the short run and has been applied, for instance, in the Marshall Plan and the credits of the International Monetary Fund. It is, however, politically inconceivable as a long-term solution for a permanent balance-of-payments problem. The financing of balance-of-payments deficits by surplus countries would stimulate inflation in the deficit countries. Every mechanism of adjustment would be suspended thereby and the country with the largest

[16] For the following, cf. J. E. Meade, *Problems of Economic Union*, as well as the German translation in Meade, *Probleme nationaler und internationaler Wirtschaftsordnung*, Vol. B: *Probleme der Wirtschaftsunion souveräner Staaten*, Zürich-Tübingen, 1955.

gap in its balance of payments, the strongest inflation, and the smallest quantity of exports would receive the most help. Hence, only the two other methods remain.

For the method of alternating inflation and deflation—according to the principle of the gold standard—it is of fundamental importance that the mechanism function undisturbed. The population of the surplus countries should not oppose inflation and the deficit countries must be reconciled to deflationary actions and even to unemployment. In this system, monetary policy serves the purpose of external stabilization.

In this era, however, the economic authorities of a union must stabilize total expenditures and hence the rate of employment inside the union. As we have demonstrated in dealing with institutional methods, the individual nations would hardly be willing to take part in an economic union unless there were an absolute guarantee that this condition would always be fulfilled. Whether the second method of restoring equilibrium in the balance of payments is applicable therefore depends, as we have shown, on the flexibility of costs—in particular, of money wages rates. At any one time, wages flexibility will the sooner restore internal equilibrium, (1) the smaller the spontaneous disturbances expected in the union, and (2) the smaller the change in costs and prices that is required in the individual regions to neutralize the disturbance. The first of these two conditions will probably not prevail in a modern economy. Sudden rearrangements in the structure of demand may occur for reasons of military strategy, and spontaneous disturbances may also be generated by rapid technological progress. On the other hand, in an economic union as opposed to a loose free trade area made up of sovereign states, one can be more optimistic about the presence of the second condition. Since trade barriers no longer exist, it is very probable that the price elasticity of demand for imports from other member countries will be higher in the union than it was before the union was concluded. Consequently,

161

the mechanism of price adjustment will function much better in restoring equilibrium between the individual regions of a union.

In addition, with greater labor mobility between the deficit and surplus countries, a given disequilibrium of the balance of payments can be eliminated by a smaller change in the relative prices of commodities than under pre-union conditions. When money wage rates in the deficit country fall and unemployment increases, while in the surplus country wages rise and an excess demand for labor exists, the movement of workers from the first to the second country will be induced by the disequilibrium in the balance of payments. The more workers move, the smaller will be the regional price and cost changes which are necessary to restore external balance.

But even when these conditions which make it easier for the method of price adjustment to function are taken into consideration, much time is required to adjust the balance of payments. Two delaying factors above all have to be taken into account. First, the delay with which consumers adjust the structure of their demand to the new structure of relative prices corresponds to the Robertson lag in macro-economic theory. Second, the delay in rearranging production facilities corresponds to Lundberg's period of plan changes. It will take some time before these two "lags" are overcome, and the contraction of the demand for imports in the deficit country will be small during this period. Credits to cover the balance-of-payments deficit in the transition period would therefore be a necessary supplement to a system with a higher elasticity over the long run than over the short run.

A *common currency* in the member countries of the union would be a special case of the gold standard mechanism. On this Meade writes, "As one can generally observe, in the various regions of a single country with a uniform currency and with a uniform banking system, there are never balance-of-payments crises that would require a control on the interregional commodity and payments transactions."[17] Would it therefore not also be possible to solve the balance-of-payments problem of an economic union by the use of a common currency? As Meade himself recognizes, appearances are deceptive in the case of interregional balances of payments. Though the specific symptoms of international surpluses and deficits cannot be observed in regions with a uniform currency and banking system, since a payment can be carried out with the same ease between all regions of the country, balance-of-payments crises are also possible interregionally. Regions can get into serious external trouble as a result of spontaneous disturbances. This could be seen clearly in the so-called "depressed areas" of Great Britain before World War II. When the demand for coal fell, the payments made to other regions by regions that specialized in coal production, such as South Wales, were higher than the payments made by the other regions to these depressed areas. Hence, capital flowed to the other regions. Incomes and relative commodity prices dropped in the depressed areas, while production costs and money wages could not be reduced without severe frictions. Profits consequently fell, production was reduced, and there was much unemployment. Losses of reserves—in this case, of national currency—deflation, a deterioration in the terms of trade, and mass unemployment all are symptoms which appear in the case of a continuous balance-of-payments deficit of a country under the gold standard. Consequently, a system of a common currency corresponds in reality to a system of separate national currencies which are linked to each other by constant exchange rates, free trade, and a free system of international payments.[18]

But a common currency nevertheless has certain advantages compared with the gold standard. As we have seen, the money system of a country under the gold standard is usually organ-

[17] J. E. Meade, *Probleme der Wirtschaftsunion souveräner Staaten*, page 158.
[18] *Ibid.*, pp. 158ff. Cf. also F. Lutz, "Die Konvertibilitätsdiskussion," A. Hunold, *Die Konvertibilität der europäischen Währungen*, Zürich, 1954.

ized according to the fractional reserve principle. The ratio between the quantity of money in a country and its currency reserves is therefore higher than one and may, for instance, amount to 10 per cent. If balance-of-payments deficits and surpluses are settled in gold or other internationally acceptable means of payment, the money supply under the system of the gold standard has to be changed by an amount greater than the deficit or the surplus. There is, however, no "multiplier" of this kind at work in a common currency system, and the adjustment process can therefore be more gradual (as has been shown in the analysis of the 100 per cent money system). The inflation or deflation need therefore be less pronounced.

Of course, the introduction of a common currency would interfere strongly with national sovereignty. This is obvious when banknotes and coins are brought into circulation. Less clear but perhaps still more important is the connection between common currency and bank deposits.

The development of cash deposits in the banking system of a country (and thus in the banking system of countries in an economic union) supplies further material for the analysis of mechanisms for adjusting balances of payments interregionally. Let us first assume that all residents of Basel-Stadt, and only these residents, have accounts with the Schweizerischen Bankverein and that all, and only, the residents of Zürich have accounts with the Schweizerischen Kreditanstalt. Let the proportion of the cash reserves of both banks to their short-term liabilities be 1:10. Now if Basel, struck by a depression, has a deficit in its balance of payments with Zürich, then checks, for instance, are issued in Basel for the benefit of citizens in Zürich. The deposits and reserves of the Bankverein decrease and those of the Kreditanstalt increase. The reserve ratio of the Bankverein decreases at the same time, since its deposits decrease in the same amount as its cash reserves and the reserve ratio of the Kreditanstalt increases. If the Bankverein wants to maintain its 10 per cent reserve ratio, it must, in addition to its original payments to the Kreditanstalt, contemplate a destruction of money amounting to ten times these payments; the Kreditanstalt must at the same time create additional money in the same amount. Hence, under these assumptions, the monetary situation is as unfavorable in the case of interregional balance-of-payments difficulties (i.e., common currency) as in the case of international balance-of-payments difficulties under the gold standard.

The continuous removal of interregional disequilibria in the balance of payments can therefore be attained in the case of a common currency only if one of two additional conditions is fulfilled: Either the currency system of the entire union must correspond in fact to 100 per cent money, in the sense that the banks keep 100 per cent cash reserves to back their cash deposits; or, if a fractional reserve system is followed, each bank must operate on a large scale throughout the union. Only then is it probable that residents of different regions will be customers of any particular credit bank. To realize one of these two conditions and therewith the potential advantages of a common currency would require far-reaching interventions. Regarding the second assumption, the Kreditanstalt could perhaps sustain an inflation in Basel to compensate for a deflation of the Bankverein if that region were also included in its area of operations. The income effects of monetary contraction in Basel would then be partly neutralized and one mechanism for adjusting the balance of payments between Zürich and Basel would thus be rendered inoperative. The external equilibrium of these two regions would therefore have to be restored by a change in the terms of trade and/or by moving productive factors.

From the standpoint of equilibrium in the balance of payments, one advantage of a common currency would be that the governments of the regions having a deficit could not do anything about the contraction of the regional quantity of money. Deflation would therefore continue in the deficit area so long as a deficit persisted. If the deficit region contracted a loan in order to fight the depression in the area, the rise in the interest rate resulting from such a contract would make the deflation even more acute.

General depressions and inflations could be combatted by the central authorities of the economic union by means of monetary policy. By hypothesis, the economic union would have a central body to supervise the supply of means of payments in the union. This authority could vary the quantity of money by way of changes which were general rather than limited to a region. However, monetary measures would have to be supplemented by fiscal policy, and it therefore follows that the fiscal policies of the member nations should be controlled by a union authority. Otherwise, the fiscal policy of the member countries could not be synchronized with the monetary policy of the union.

The success of the third method, the restoration of external equilibrium by changes of the exchange rates, also depends on the long-term elasticities which we have mentioned. If these are too small, the method of flexible exchange rates must also be dropped and recourse be had to direct control of foreign trade. Yet we have seen that, by eliminating all interregional trade controls, the formation of an economic union increases the price elasticity of the demand for imports.

The advantages of price adjustment by way of changing the exchange rate are quite clear. First, the exchange rate can be changed more easily than money wages; second, the change in the exchange rate can be combined with stabilization of internal equilibrium. If a common currency could not be put into practice, the objective of internal stabilization would inevitably require that the balances of payments in the economic union be brought into equilibrium by exchange rate variations combined, in the ideal case, with the principle of 100 per cent money. The method of changing exchange rates is often objected to on the ground that it adds an element of uncertainty to international trade, at least in the case of a free foreign exchange market. We have already shown, however, that importers could ensure against this currency risk in the futures markets for foreign exchange. Under the IMF system, such uncertainty is a problem only when a change of exchange rates is expected.

7. EXTERNAL ADJUSTMENT
OF THE BALANCE OF PAYMENTS OF AN
ECONOMIC UNION

In our search for the optimum currency policy, we have abstracted from all trade and payments relationships of a union with the outside world. In the following we will deal with these relationships and clarify their significance for balance-of-payments equilibrium.[19] We will assume that countries A and B form an economic union and that both maintain trade relations with the outside world. We will simplify the problem, in the sense that we will treat the outside world as an area with a uniform currency. This would be the case, for instance, if the outside world consisted of one country only, or if all foreign currencies were fully and freely convertible into one another, or finally if, in the case of incomplete convertibility, A and B felt strong enough to behave as hard currency countries and demand from third countries that all their bilateral balances be settled completely in gold or convertible currency. (This would impede trade with soft currency countries, but the assumption makes it possible for us to deal with the outside world as an area with a uniform currency.)

Each bilateral deficit of country A with country B can, under these conditions, be eliminated in a way which leaves all balances of payments in equilibrium, if and only if A has a surplus in the trade with the outside world which is equal to its deficit in the trade with B, and if B has a deficit with the outside world which is equal to its surplus in the trade with A. In this case, A earns a surplus of foreign currency which it can use for settling its debt with B and this receipt of foreign exchange is just sufficient to finance B's deficit with the outside

---

[19] Cf. J. E. Meade, *The Theory of Customs Unions*, pp. 18ff.

world. Such a situation exists automatically when A as well as B shows a *multilateral equilibrium in its balance of payments*. For, in this case, A's deficit with B must have a counterpart of the same magnitude in a surplus with the outside world; and similarly B's surplus with A must have a counterpart of the same magnitude in a deficit with the outside world.

This result can be obtained in two ways: by way of the "national method" and by way of the "method of economic union." Both methods lead to exactly the same result, if each is completely effective. But since it is senseless to hope for an economic policy that will be 100 per cent effective in the actual world—the more so if policy depends on estimates (which can only be inexact) of the quantitative effects of any action and also on the cooperation of sovereign governments—in a particular case, one method may be preferable to the other.

The *national method* requires that every country pursue a financial policy which keeps its multilateral balance of payments in equilibrium. For instance, A has to pursue a policy of deflation or inflation of its prices, costs, and incomes depending on whether its multilateral balance of payments has a deficit or a surplus; B has to act similarly. If both series of actions are successful, A will automatically obtain a surplus with the outside world which enables it to finance its deficit with B, while B has a deficit with the outside world which it can entirely finance by its surplus with A.

Thus far we have neglected the fact that the economic union of A and B could solve its balance-of-payments problems by a direct control over payments to the outside world. It is always possible to improve a combined balance of payments with the outside world by imposing more stringent restrictions on imports from or payments to foreign countries. (The technical aspects of these controls were discussed in Chapter I, section 3.) Let us assume that more stringent restrictions are placed on payments. The multilateral balance of payments of both states would then tend to improve. Each country must therefore stimulate inflation or retard deflation in order to preserve equilibrium in its multilateral balance of payments. Stated differently: A and B must effect inflation or deflation in relation to one another in order to keep their balance of payments in equilibrium. But whether this must be done mainly by inflation in the country with a relatively favorable multilateral balance of payments or by deflation in the country with a relatively unfavorable balance of payments is a question which must be answered in the light of the union's internal financial requirements. If there is a general tendency toward inflation in the union as a whole, restrictions on imports from the outside world could be reduced, in which event financial measures of a more restrictive nature would have to be taken inside the union for reasons of external equilibrium. If unemployment and deflation threaten the union, a more restrictive joint policy with respect to import controls can be pursued, so that in each country a more expansive policy can be combined with external equilibrium.

It can easily be seen how conflicts of interest could develop in the application of these common instruments of control. If one of the member states is threatened by inflation and the other by deflation, the former will stress the importance of a liberal joint-import policy in conjunction with domestic financial measures of a more restrictive nature, while the latter will prefer a less liberal union import policy in conjunction with financial measures of a more expansive nature. Moreover, imports from the outside world can be of more importance to one of the member states than to the other, so that the former will prefer a liberal joint-import policy, while the latter prefers the preservation of a more expansive financial policy within the union. Finally, a joint policy with respect to payments control has numerous aspects: controls on capital movements, on tourist expenditures and other invisible items in the current account; controls on imports of agricultural products, raw materials, machinery, textiles, etc.; and possibly special measures to encourage or discourage various export industries.

The *method of economic union* stresses the importance of

169

joint action by the union authorities. Both governments would in this case agree on the following: first, to coordinate their independent financial policies in the interest of maintaining internal equilibrium inside the union—i.e., to prevent general pressures toward inflation or deflation which threaten to lead to undesirable price rises or to stagnation and unemployment within the union; and, second, to adopt a joint program of balance-of-payments controls in order to maintain the balance of payments of the union as a whole in equilibrium. Hence, they would jointly practice inflation or deflation in conformity with what the position of the entire union requires, and they would make their joint controls on the external balance of payments less or more stringent, depending on whether the combined balance of payments of A and B with the outside world shows a surplus or a deficit. If this object is achieved, each deficit that B might have with the outside world would be compensated by a surplus of the same size in A's trade with the outside world. A would then earn the foreign exchange necessary to cover B's deficit. But a complete balance-of-payments equilibrium would not be attained under all circumstances.

Let us assume that B's surplus with A is smaller than its deficit with the outside world (and consequently also smaller than A's surplus with the outside world, so long as the union as a whole is in external equilibrium). In this case, B would have a multilateral balance-of-payments deficit and A would have a multilateral balance-of-payments surplus of the same magnitude. Since direct controls between the member states are excluded, this situation can be corrected only by a deflation in B or an inflation in A. In other words: in order to preserve full employment, A and B have to coordinate their financial policy not only to attain the desired level of total demand in the entire union, but also to achieve this position by appropriate relative inflation or deflation in both countries. If, for instance, a total expansion of monetary demand is necessary in the union to prevent an increase of unemployment, but at the same time B runs into a multilateral balance-of-payments deficit and A into a multilateral balance-of-payments surplus, the reflation in the union as a whole must be based on reflation in A without financial expansion in B.

We will now assume that A and B trade with *two areas with different currencies*, which we will call the dollar bloc and the sterling bloc, and that the dollar and pound are not fully convertible into one another. For instance, while dollars might be freely convertible into sterling, sterling might be inconvertible into dollars. In order to attain equilibrium in all balances of payments, it no longer suffices that the union's balance with the outside world is in over-all equilibrium. There is now the additional requirement that the joint balance of payments of the union with respect to the dollar area should run no deficit, since this could not be financed by a surplus with the sterling area. If this condition is fulfilled, as well as those previously discussed, the balances of payments will be in equilibrium.

However, several modifications must now be introduced in both systems of adjustment. Discrimination must be practiced in the joint union controls on foreign trade and payments so that the union as a whole runs no deficit with the dollar bloc or surplus with the sterling bloc.

Thus far we have introduced conditions whose fulfillment guarantees that A will always have a stock of foreign exchange which is *in total* just sufficient to settle its bilateral balance with B and that the composition of that stock also meets B's requirements for settling its balance of payments. In fact, only when this condition is fulfilled can an arrangement be made that fully satisfies both partners and is in agreement with maintaining complete freedom of trade and payments in the union. In that case, it no longer matters which of the following two methods is actually adopted:

(1) In settling its bilateral balance with B, country A can be obliged to make its payments to B in the foreign exchange which B needs to settle its own balance of payments with the outside world. (2) In order to settle its bilateral surplus with A, B can be obliged to accept such foreign exchange as A has

obtained from the outside world; B will use this foreign exchange to settle its balance of payments with the outside world.

But, even when both sides have the best intentions of giving the national method or the union method every possible chance, an exact annual compensation will in reality never be attained. One compromise or another between the two techniques of settlement must therefore be found.

Thus far we have assumed that the rate of exchange between the national currencies is fixed and constant. By doing so we have eliminated one of the most effective and smoothest forms of price adjustment. Let us now assume that the rate of exchange between the currencies of A and B is fixed, but that the rate of exchange between these currencies and those of the outside world can be changed. In this event, both partners could consider a combined change in the outer value of their currencies as an alternative to a change in their joint policy of restrictions on imports and payments. In many cases, this will make the adjustments easier to carry out. For instance, a serious drop in the economic activities of the outside world could call for stringent import restrictions, employing either the national method or the method of economic union, if the member countries want to preserve equilibrium in their balances of payments without taking action of a deflationary nature. Instead they could let the outer value of their currencies drop.

Now let us assume that the outer value of A's and B's currencies can be changed separately. It will then be possible to bring the balance of payments of one partner into equilibrium with that of the other by a change in the exchange rate as well as by inflation and deflation in the two countries.

It is an essential attribute of the union that the balance of payments between A and B cannot be settled by direct controls, since this would involve the imposition of restrictions or compensating payments. If the exchange rates are fixed, equilibrium can be attained only by inflation or deflation in A in relation to B. For these reasons, in the cases described here,

A and B have to adapt their financial policy to external requirements and are not free to use financial policy for the purpose
of internal stabilization. But if the exchange rate between their
currencies can be changed, this freedom has been restored.
Each member country can then adopt the financial policy that
best suits its own needs and settle its balance of payments with
its partner by changing the exchange rate. This makes it possible in an economic union to introduce a national method of
adjustment, allowing full freedom of trade and payments between the partners and yet real independence of the national
money systems.

8. STABILIZATION PROBLEMS IN A FREE TRADE AREA
AND IN THE COMMON MARKET
OF THE EUROPEAN ECONOMIC UNION

In the following, we will apply the conclusions with respect
to internal and external stabilization that we derived from the
general model to the institutional facts and some of the possible
regulations of the planned European Free Trade Area and the
European Economic Union. As our starting-point, we will re-
consider the question: in what way can the member countries
of one of the two planned preference systems achieve the joint
objectives of internal stabilization and a balance-of-payments
equilibrium?

The point of departure for the analysis is the previously derived conclusion that balance-of-payments problems of the
member countries of a Free Trade Area can be avoided if each
of the partner countries maintains external equilibrium. If we
assume that the balance of payments of France with the non-
French world is in equilibrium, it does not matter, so far as
the external stabilization of the regional preference system is
concerned, whether France can also attain external equilibrium
with respect to the other members of the Free Trade Area.
The French balance of payments with third countries might
be active under these assumptions and France could use the

173

resulting surplus of foreign exchange to cover its deficit with the partner countries. The foreign exchange of third countries which France supplies will be needed, under the assumed conditions, by the other members of the Free Trade Area to pay off their deficits with third countries. For, if the French balance of payments with the area is passive, the regional balance of other countries—for instance, Germany—will be active to the same extent, since according to our assumption Germany, too, is in multilateral external equilibrium.

The history of the Benelux Customs Union provides numerous examples of the multilateral principle. The usual situation in the Benelux area is characterized by a bilateral deficit of the Netherlands with the Economic Union of Belgium-Luxembourg. In addition to this, the over-all Dutch balance of payments showed a deficit during the first years after World War II. Under these circumstances, the problem of intraregional (bilateral) payments settlements could be solved only by Dutch restrictions on imports from the other two union countries. After 1951 the Netherlands attained multilateral external equilibrium; hence, it could use the surpluses obtained from its trade with third countries to cover the deficit with Belgium and Luxembourg.

But is the method of equilibrium in the over-all balance of payments of the individual member countries of a preference system the only possible solution of the intraregional balance-of-payments problem? The experience of the Benelux countries almost makes us answer this question in the affirmative. An alternative to this solution would be, for instance, that every member country settled only the balance of payments with respect to the other member countries. Without intraregional restrictions in the Benelux countries, this result could have been attained only if Belgium inflated its price and cost level or if the Belgian franc had been revalued. This would have stimulated Belgian imports from the Netherlands. But another unfavorable consequence of this method would have been the danger of a multilaterial balance-of-payments deficit on the part of Belgium. Belgium would then have had to impose restrictions on imports from third countries. However, if, instead of a Belgian policy of price adjustment, the Netherlands pursued a policy of deflation, the Dutch multilateral balance would have become active—with no guarantee that a Belgian deficit with all other countries (including the Netherlands) would have corresponded to the Dutch global surplus with the outside world. Under the most probable condition of intraregional payments disequilibrium within a preference system, the principle of multilateral external equilibrium of each partner country is therefore the only sound one.

The usefulness of this principle must be tested under an additional condition: the fact that all currencies are not mutually convertible must be taken into consideration. If the Netherlands as well as Belgium has attained multilateral external equilibrium, and if the Netherlands has acquired a surplus of hard currency in its trade with third countries, this surplus could be used without difficulty to pay off the Dutch deficit with Belgium; and Belgium could employ the hard currency thus obtained to settle its deficit with third countries.

But, though the Benelux countries as a union are in external equilibrium, difficulties arise when this balance is composed of a surplus in soft currency and a deficit in hard currency. Belgium then cannot exchange the surplus put at her disposal by the Netherlands for the hard currency she needs.

In the Free Trade Area, this case is relevant for two reasons. First, it is possible that the Free Trade Area may acquire a surplus in a currency which is not freely convertible with respect to the currencies of third countries, but which can be freely exchanged for the currency of a member country. The overseas member countries of the sterling area are an example of this situation. Let us assume that, in the Free Trade Area, Germany has a deficit with the United States and France has a deficit with Germany, while the French balance with Australia is active. The Australian pound is freely convertible into the British pound—though, contrary to Great Britain, Australia is not a member of the Free Trade Area. But if the British pound is not convertible into the dollar, then France cannot put the currency at Germany's disposal which the latter needs to cover its dollar gap. The problem can be solved only when the whole sterling area is in external equilibrium. The principle must therefore be modified, in the sense that every member country of the preference system must try to attain external equilibrium in the whole monetary area to which it belongs (and in the domain of which there is convertibility).

Second, an essentially similar problem poses itself when the Free Trade Area in its totality has a deficit with the dollar area, but a surplus in a currency such as the Brazilian *cruzeiro* which is not convertible into the currency of a third country (for instance, dollars) or into that of a member country (for instance, pounds). This problem can be solved by common action by the European countries. If no European central bank is willing to exchange Brazilian currency for its own currency, then the European exporters will have to demand payment from the Brazilian importers either in the currency of the exporting country or in some hard currency. The authorities in Brazil will then be forced to limit the value of Brazilian imports to the level of its receipts of convertible foreign exchange. Contrary to the period immediately after World War II, during which the European countries tried to master this sort of situation by bilateral agreements, a multilateral settlement of the Brazilian balances in European trade now takes place within the framework of the "Hague Club." The "Paris Club" fulfills this function for commercial relations with Argentina. Hence, if one member country of a European preference system runs a surplus in trading with Brazil, this will not mean that the entire preference group has a surplus of soft Brazilian currency.

Therefore, the principle that every member of the preference system must endeavor to attain multilateral external equilibrium is also valid under the aforementioned special conditions. We will now explore the methods which can lead to external stabilization in concrete situations. The institutional relationships under which the planned preference systems should operate must now be spelled out further than they were in earlier sections. The five methods distinguished by Meade prove useful in this connection.[20]

We will denote the first method as the *method of increasing reserves*. This method is aimed at increasing the liquid assets of the countries which have a deficit in their over-all balance of payments so that they can enjoy a breathing spell. However, a permanent solution of the balance-of-payments problem is impossible by this means. But the necessary essential steps, which with some delay will make a start toward correcting the situation, as we have shown, could be taken during the transition period. The method of increasing reserves cannot be left out of consideration during the present period of low levels in the reserves of some West European countries. Would it be possible to achieve this objective of increasing foreign exchange reserves within the framework of the European Payments Union? The EPU automatically provides the deficit member countries with credits from the EPU members that have a surplus. But many objections can be raised to such a system. First, we must consider the situation in which the whole European Free Trade Area runs a deficit with the outside world. In this event, it would no longer be possible to compensate deficits of member countries by surpluses of other members. A world-wide monetary organization like the International Monetary Fund could render good service in this case. In the situation described, the Fund should help every European country, regardless of its position in the preference system, to obtain a higher degree of international liquidity. Over-all balance-of-payments problems of the member countries of a preference system could be solved in this way during the transition period.

If this procedure should fail for one of the reasons we have

[20] Cf. J. E. Meade, "The Balance-of-Payments Problems of a European Free Trade Area," *The Economic Journal* (1957), pp. 379ff.

examined in our exposition of universal as opposed to regional integration, a system must be formulated that requires the European surplus countries to put temporary credits at the command of the deficit countries. According to its present regulations, the European Payments Union cannot be regarded as the proper institution for this purpose. If country A runs a surplus of dollars and a deficit of the same size with an EPU partner, country B, it should be possible for the dollar-surplus country, A, to put at the command of the dollar-deficit country, the bilateral creditor B, the dollars that the latter needs. However, under the EPU system, the dollar-surplus country would, *ceteris paribus*, increase its dollar reserves *and* at the same time obtain an EPU partner that has a dollar gap in its balance of payments. The dollar-deficit country, however, must settle its deficit, *ceteris paribus*, with gold or dollars, while its assets in the EPU partly consist of claims on the Payments Union. If 100 per cent of the balances inside the European Payments Union had to be settled in gold, this problem would be solved; but in this case the payments system of "regional multilateralism" would no longer serve its purpose, which consists of providing over-all deficit countries with credits from over-all credit countries.

It is, of course, conceivable that the European countries might make arrangements that would not have this deficiency. For instance, the authorities of the Exchange Stabilization Fund could come to an understanding that the over-all surplus countries should maintain more currency of the over-all deficit countries than usual. The proposed European Monetary Fund, to which all countries would contribute a certain quota of their own currency (and eventually gold and dollars as well) and which would permit deficit countries to incur temporary debts, would have similar consequences. The most radical method would consist of pooling all gold and dollar reserves of the member countries in one common fund. Payments between member countries could then be settled by claims on this pool, and payments to third countries by actual transfers of foreign exchange from the Fund.

The method of increasing reserves would serve to overcome external disequilibrium situations directly and on a short-term basis. However, a permanent restoration of external equilibrium is possible only by the means indicated earlier (Chapter IV, section 3). As the analysis has shown, the way in which balances of payments are settled under the gold standard is a dangerous one. It requires that the member countries pursue a financial policy aimed at external stabilization and leave internal stabilization to other mechanisms which will undoubtedly be less effective, under the present assumptions. According to the rules of the gold standard, Germany would be obliged, so long as it has an over-all surplus in its balance of payments, to let the inflation of its national income and its price and cost levels range at will. But the German parties, bound as they are to a policy of price stabilization, are not in a position to abide by this rule of the game. Recent experience has shown that the surpluses of foreign exchange can to a very great extent be kept away from the money and capital market by a policy of sterilization; in addition, the expansive income effect of a high export volume can be limited by a restrictive financial policy. This means that for quite some time it is possible for a country to run surpluses and to neutralize the inflationary effect simultaneously. To that extent, the mechanism of the gold standard suffers from an "inherent tendency towards deflation."[21]

The consequence of this state of affairs is that a potential deficit member country of a European preference system—for instance, France—has to carry most of the burden of price adjustment—in this case, of a deflation of money income, price, and cost levels. Contrary to the situation in which a surplus country finds itself, the position of a deficit country under the gold standard is characterized by the fact that there is no anti-

[21] Cf. Joan Robinson, "The International Currency Proposals," *ibid.* (1943), page 161.

deflationary parallel to the policy of sterilization and that an adjustment cannot therefore be permanently postponed. Hence, under the gold standard, the deficit country could be forced to give up an expansive financial policy at the very moment that such a policy, as a consequence of difficulties in adjusting to new relationships in foreign trade, would be most urgent for reasons of internal stabilization. For political reasons, such a compulsion would nowadays be tantamount to the end of a regional system of preferences.

At this phase of the argument, a *common currency* of the European preference system seems the most obvious and most successful method of restoring external equilibrium. Still, the implications of this proposal are far-reaching. Though the advantages of interregional settlement of balance-of-payments differences appear obvious, we must not neglect the assumptions under which such a mechanism functions. In an area where balance-of-payments settlements take place interregionally and not internationally, and are therefore characterized by a common currency, there is free trade as well as complete mobility of capital and labor. Hence, a common commodity, capital, and labor market must accompany a common currency in order to make it meaningful. Restoration of an interregional equilibrium inside the preference system would no doubt be eased thereby. But the regions which at the moment share a common currency also belong to a common banking system. However, the banking system in the individual European economies is subordinated to a fractional reserve system of the central banks. If the reserve ratio between the stock of gold plus foreign exchange and the national quantity of money is low, then the transfer of internationally acceptable means of payment will entail a relatively greater change of the national quantity of money than the transfer of national currency within a national banking system whose contraction and expansion effects are not multiplied by a fractional reserve system. This drawback could be overcome by 100 per cent backing of the total quantity of money that is in circulation in the national economy.

Otherwise the common currency system should be combined with the replacement of the national central banks by a single supranational central bank.

The financial policy in the areas which are at the moment linked together by a common currency is, by and large, uniform and national. This, too, eases the settling of the balance of payments. Consequently, in order to benefit by the present interregional external stabilization, the financial policy of internal stabilization should also be transferred to a supranational authority when the change-over to a common currency is accomplished. But the difficulties that lie in the way of a common budget policy have been discussed elsewhere.

Moreover, the economic authorities of the national economies, i.e., the regions which are now linked by a common currency, have the power to impose uniform restrictions on the common or national imports in the case of an over-all deficit in the common currency area. Accordingly, in the event of complete economic integration, a European supranational authority should be created which would set up a single import authority for the whole preference system. So far as foreign trade policy is concerned, this supplement to a common currency would not be compatible with the principle of a Free Trade Area—that is, with the principle of national sovereignty in the realm of commercial policy with respect to third countries.

Finally, it is possible for national governments to come to the assistance of a region that has been hurt by the restoration of external equilibrium. In the Free Trade Area, no corresponding supranational authority would have this competence. The treaty of the European Economic Union, signed by the six states forming what is called "Little Europe," is more favorable in this respect, since the treaty provides for a European Investment Bank.[22]

Hence, in order to preserve in a preference system all the advantages which are at present enjoyed by *national* common

[22] Cf. Articles 129 and 130 of the Treaty of the European Economic Union.

currency areas regarding the settlement of interregional balances of payments, a common currency not only must be accompanied by a common commodity, labor, and capital market, but also requires a very extensive transfer of sovereign powers to a supranational authority. Since the problem of finding politically feasible methods of external stabilization presents itself at the moment, the objective of a common currency, which is desirable in the long run, must be postponed for the time being.

Other methods have therefore to be found. The balance of payments can also be brought into equilibrium by *direct controls*.[23] True, this system is in essence compatible with internal stabilization, but, used against partner countries in a preference system, it infringes the important principle of coordination. Such a procedure is strictly forbidden by the treaty of the European Economic Union.[24] In the first place, the method of direct controls would have a deterrent effect on potential investors; but their willingness to assume risks is an essential prerequisite to the realization of specialized mass production, which among other things actually justifies economic coordination. As Meade points out, "The mass production of motor cars in Detroit in the United States involves the investment of huge sums of capital in plant and equipment in Detroit, which is undertaken because the producer knows for certain that the whole United States market will always be freely open to him."[25]

The absence of commercial controls requires as a logical corollary an absence of payments controls in commercial dealings. However, this does not imply simultaneous freedom of international capital movements among the member countries, at least not theoretically (and perhaps also not from a practical administrative viewpoint). Complete freedom of capital to settle where it likes in France and Germany would, for in-

---

[23] Cf. Chapter I, section 3. [24] Cf. Articles 12, 13, 32, 33, and 34.
[25] J. E. Meade, "The Balance-of-Payments Problems of a European Free Trade Area," *op.cit.*, page 388.

182

stance, enable French residents to obtain German marks for current payments as well as for export of capital. If we assume that the foreign exchange authorities of France prohibit the exchange of French francs into dollars but that Germany allows an exchange of D-marks into dollars, French restrictions on the mobility of capital become meaningless. French financiers could then export capital to the United States via Germany. From this it follows that the application of controls on capital dealings in a preference system requires a harmonization of the foreign exchange controls of all member countries if freedom of capital movements exists within the preference system. If such harmonization proves to be too difficult to establish, freedom to export or import capital is for the time being still impossible in a preference system, since there is still no over-all equilibrium in the balance of payments of the member countries and their currencies are still not freely convertible into the hard currencies of third countries.

As for commercial controls, the question arises whether a deficit country that is a member of a preference system can restrict imports from third countries without controlling imports from its partner countries at the same time. The controls on imports from third countries could be maintained according to two methods: national and supranational. In the first case, each country controls its imports individually; in the second case, an over-all import quota for the preference system as a whole is set up by mutual arrangement. We will not consider the supranational method at the moment. Let us assume that Germany's over-all balance of payments is active and the French over-all balance passive, but that the deficit is larger than the surplus, so that the union as a whole has a deficit. A common program to control imports from third countries thus requires agreement on three points: First, to what extent must total imports be restricted? For instance, one country may mainly advocate monetary measures, while another country stresses the importance of import restrictions. Second, which imports will be restricted? Every country wishes to restrict the

183

imports that compete with its production. Third, what volume of import licenses should be granted to French and what to German importers? The experience of the Benelux countries has shown how difficult the supranational method is to put into practice.[26]

Let us now consider the case of a preference system which as a whole has a deficit with the outside world and which tries to overcome this disequilibrium exclusively by controlling imports from third countries. This commercial policy of discrimination would have only a limited success in Western Europe, since most West European countries acquire a large share of their total imports from countries which would possibly be partners in a preference system. In 1955, Great Britain imported 28 per cent of its total imports from West European countries; the corresponding figures for that year were 51 per cent for West Germany; 33 per cent for France; 46 per cent for Italy; and 59 per cent for Belgium-Luxembourg and Holland. Restrictions could therefore be applied to only a limited percentage of the total imports of the area. Moreover, European imports from third countries consist largely of raw materials and food, i.e. of "essentials" which are less easy to give up than the manufactured goods that are internationally traded in the European area.

The preservation of the method of import controls according to the national principle also encounters great difficulties in the framework of a preference system. We will start with the assumption that France restricts imports from the United States as a result of a dollar gap in its balance of payments, while Germany, being a dollar-surplus country, does not impose that sort of control. If, however, American products can be freely exported from Germany to France, according to the rules of the preference system, then the French controls become ineffective. (If the French controls are in the form of fiscal meas-

[26] Cf. J. E. Meade, *Negotiations for Benelux: An Annotated Chronicle, 1943-1956*, Princeton, 1957, pp. 48 and 69-71.

ures like duties, this will be taken care of in the Free Trade Area by certificates of origin.) In order to make the control system function, France must be authorized to restrict the import of American commodities no matter whether the latter are imported directly from the United States or imported from countries which are France's partners in the preference system. But even in this favorable situation, the result of the French restrictions could be that Germany increases its imports of the related American products and from now on sells more German substitute products in the French market. The national method is therefore in essence less effective than the supranational one. A common program of import controls eliminates the possibilities for substitution. The country which controls its imports from third countries by way of the national method will therefore be forced to rely on other methods for adjusting its balance of payments.

On the other hand, if all the member countries of a preference system simultaneously show a deficit in trade with third countries, then the national method will prove to be effective. Each country will then be forced to restrict its imports from third countries; the result therefore corresponds in this case largely to that obtained by the supranational method.

As has been shown previously, the drafting of a common import program requires unanimity among the partner countries at so many points that the supranational method has no prospect of success in the near future. It may therefore be necessary for the six countries united in the European Economic Union to maintain their import restrictions according to the national method.[27] For this reason, and quite apart from the escape clauses provided for balance-of-payments difficulties,[28] the members of the Common Market must in the future maintain a customs control at their common borders. This has the purpose of preventing imports of commodities from third coun-

[27] Cf. J. E. Meade, "The Balance-of-Payments Problems of a European Free Trade Area," *op.cit.*, page 391.
[28] Cf. Article 109 of the Treaty of the European Economic Union.

tries via partner countries if the import restrictions with respect to third countries are not maintained uniformly by all member states. However, the experience of the Benelux countries proves that, apart from this necessity, the members of a customs union have to maintain mutual customs controls so long as excise taxes, sales taxes, and measures for the support of agriculture are not harmonized.

Hence, there remains only one other method of restoring external equilibrium in a European preference system: the method of price adjustment by *variable exchange rates*. This procedure seems to be the only one that can be realized at the moment, if the national governments use fiscal policies to achieve internal stabilization and do not wish to extend import controls to imports from partner countries in the preference system—a course of action that would contradict the principle of regional free trade. Adjustment of exchange rates would be very desirable, of course, in the first stage of the functioning of a preference system. The alteration of the intra-European trade structure which can be expected to result from the removal of different national trade barriers will influence the external position of the member countries to a varying degree. Some countries will find that their balance of payments becomes active, while other countries will suffer a deficit.[29] It would probably require only a single adjustment of the exchange

[29] For this, cf. the exposition of the ECE, *Economic Survey of Europe in 1956*, ch. IV, page 27: "The problems of adjustment of the industrial structures of member countries of the Common Market and the Free Trade Area which may arise have already been mentioned and it has been suggested that these may involve the appearance of balance-of-payments difficulties—possibly accompanied by some unemployment in certain member countries during the period of transition and adaptation to the new trading system. Such difficulties could result if the abolition of tariff-barriers to inter-member trade increased the flow of imports into a particular country more than its exports. It would, in fact, be surprising if such difficulties did not appear; in other words, it would be most remarkable if the pattern of exchange rates appropriate to the present tariff structure of western Europe proved to be appropriate also to the tariff structures of the Common Market and the Free Trade Area, even after such adjustment of relative labour costs as may result from 'harmonization' measures."

rates to correct this structural disturbance at the start—a measure which, however, cannot replace later variations of the exchange rates for the purpose of preserving external equilibrium. According to the exposition regarding the distribution of the adjustment burden (cf. Chapter IV, section 3), the system of variable exchange rates requires that countries which have a persistent surplus of foreign exchange revalue their currency and that countries with a permanent deficit devalue.

We have described elsewhere the dangers that are connected with this method, too—for instance, destabilizing speculation. The danger of inflation involved in the stabilization of real wages in the event of devaluation will be considerably less if the governments pursue a policy of internal stabilization. The method of varying the exchange rates can therefore by no means be considered a substitute for an effective financial policy. But at present the greatest danger generally arises not from a demand inflation, which can be combated by financial policies, but from the permanent tendency toward cost inflation. "Present-day institutional and political conditions make it more difficult than ever before, in some countries, to preserve the purchasing power of money and maintain approximately balanced international accounts. If the inflationary pressure had its source only in the tendency of investment to outrun savings, monetary and budgetary policies could cope with it. But when it is partly due to cost inflation caused by too rapid a rise in wage rates the authorities may have to choose between sacrificing the stability of the value of money and risking a certain amount of unemployment. This dilemma is not only one of the main factors making for chronic inflation in the world, but, as institutional arrangements and trade union policy vary from country to country, it also makes for different rates of inflation as between countries and therefore helps to bring about disequilibria in international accounts. The dilemma can be resolved only if wage increases in each individual country are kept within the limits set by the rise in average productivity in the country's economy as a whole."[30] A destabilizing speculation as well could be prevented only under these assumptions. A regional preference system, in which external equilibrium would be safeguarded by variable exchange rates, therefore requires in this sense, and only in this, a certain harmonization of wage *policy*.

Under the present assumptions, the problem of costs inflation can be tackled only within a national framework, since unions are national organizations and the methods of wage determination and collective bargaining differ from country to country. But even when the national governments finally obtained positive results from their wage policy, the annual rates of increase of European prices and costs in the various countries would differ accordingly. These differences would lead to situations of external disequilibrium if they continued from year to year. From this, in the case of free trade, results inevitably the necessity of a certain flexibility in exchange rates.

However, a change in the exchange rate is not to be regarded as synonymous with devaluation. Rather, the burdens of adjustment must be shared by the various countries concerned.

In examining speculative transactions, we came to the conclusion that, once internal stability is safeguarded, the principle of variable exchange rates would best be realized in a free foreign exchange market. Under certain additional assumptions, this institution need not cause sharp fluctuations in the exchange rates. These assumptions include international stabilization and a futures market for foreign exchange. The European Economic Union merely contemplates general directives so far as internal stabilization and exchange rates are concerned. Coordination is secured by provisions of a consultative character only with respect to the important objective of internal stabilization.[31]

Now the question arises as to the purpose of foreign ex-

[30] Bank for International Settlements, *Twenty-seventh Annual Report* (*April 1, 1956–March 31, 1957*), Basle, June 3, 1957, p. 22.
[31] Cf. Articles 104-109 of the Treaty of the European Economic Union.

change reserves in an international preference system supplemented by a free foreign exchange market. Every country can use its foreign exchange reserves under the direction of an exchange stabilization fund, an institution that should neutralize speculative disturbances. The instrument of official counterspeculation can, of course, be misused for the purpose of a "beggar-my-neighbor" policy. For this reason also, a European Monetary Fund would be desirable. Every member would contribute a particular quota of its national currency to this Fund. The Fund would operate along supranational lines, i.e., it would serve the purpose of stabilizing the external situation of the member countries. This would also create at the same time a coordination forum for national monetary policy. The possibility may then arise that the European Monetary Fund could be regarded as a forerunner of a common currency. As European integration progresses, the member countries of the preference system could deposit increasing quotas in the Fund; moreover, the Fund could be extended to a pool of national currency reserves,[32] so that it would become a substitute for the national exchange equalization fund. The necessary variations of the exchange rates would become smaller and smaller with increasing coordination of national economic policies, until finally the conditions of a common currency would virtually be fulfilled.

[32] Cf. F. Hartog, "European Economic Integration: A Realistic Conception," *Weltwirtschaftliches Archiv* (1953), pp. 165ff.

CHAPTER V

FISCAL POLICY

1. THE INFLUENCE OF FISCAL POLICY
ON THE INTERNATIONAL
MAXIMIZATION OF WELFARE

OUR ARGUMENT that free trade, via the mechanisms of optimization of trade and maximization of production, leads welfare to be maximized was based on the assumption that no divergences exist in the trading countries between the marginal utility of the commodities produced by the factors of production and the marginal disutility of employing these factors (cf. Chapter I, section 1). Now, in practice all forms of taxation, whether direct or indirect, create such divergences. The effect of an income tax is that the marginal product of the income earner is greater than his net remuneration; that of an indirect tax is that the marginal utility of a product is greater than its marginal costs.

What is the effect on trade of these divergences arising from the various systems of taxation, and can one find in each case criteria for an optimal tax system? Let us assume that a general income tax makes it possible for a government to use its revenues in such a way that economic welfare in each of the trading countries is disturbed as little as possible. There is then no reason to abandon a free trade policy simply because such a tax leads to divergences in the individual countries between remuneration and the marginal product of productive factors. General income taxes do not cause differences between the prices which consumers have to pay in countries A and B for a particular product: in other words, they do not upset optimization of trade. Moreover, general income taxes do not prevent maximization of world production either, assuming that there is factor mobility within the individual countries.[1] The tax

[1] Throughout this chapter, it is assumed that there is no international factor mobility.

applies to a given portion of income, no matter in which industry the factor is employed. If there is free trade between A and B, then the price of suits is the same in A and B and so is the price of butter. In the case of a uniform income tax in A, the net incomes (after taxes) from the production and sale of a suit will be lower in A than in B, and the net incomes from the production and sale of a barrel of butter will also be proportionately lower in A than in B. The ratio between the marginal costs of producing a suit and a barrel of butter will be the same in A as in B, and consequently world production will remain maximized. The same argument applies in the case of a government raising revenue from a general taxation of domestic production (no matter whether the commodities are consumed in the country or exported) or from a general taxation of domestic consumption (including imports). In a closed economy, a tax of 10 per cent on all purchased finished products must amount to the same as a tax of 10 per cent on all sold finished products, and this again is the same as a tax of 10 per cent on all income from the production and sale of the real social product. If the sale of intermediate products were also taxed, this would certainly lead to disturbances.

The state of affairs is not so clear in an open economy. Let us assume that in one country a tax of 10 per cent is levied on all income; this amounts to a tax of 10 per cent on all commodities and services. To the extent that the commodities are produced in the country for domestic consumption, it does not matter whether the tax is placed on production or on consumption. But when international trade is taken into consideration, the 10 per cent tax on production (which, as we have seen, is the same as a 10 per cent tax on income) implies that the commodities which are produced in the country and then exported are also taxed, and that commodities imported from abroad for consumption are not subject to duty.

Let us assume that the 10 per cent tax on production is transformed into a 10 per cent tax on consumption. To the extent that commodities are manufactured inside the country for domestic consumption, nothing has changed. In the case of commodities traded internationally, however, the 10 per cent tax on the export of domestic commodities has to be compensated by a 10 per cent duty on imports. The substitution of an import duty of 10 per cent for an export tax of the same size is without meaning from a realistic standpoint, but it will have a definite monetary effect. In the case of an export duty, the prices of the exported commodities will be the same in both countries, but the price of imported goods will be higher in the country that levies the duty than in the rest of the world. The transition from a *general* export duty to a *general* import duty must therefore be accompanied by an inflation of all prices and costs in the taxing country, a deflation of all prices and costs in the rest of the world, and a revaluation of the currency of the country that levies the duty. If this occurs, then the price relationships, the volume of production, and the current account will not change.

This proves, therefore, that neither a general 10 per cent tax on production nor a general 10 per cent tax on consumption will upset optimization of trade or—if factor mobility exists—maximization of production. The levying of a general 10 per cent tax on production does not cause the price which consumers have to pay for suits or butter in the taxing country A to differ from the price in the rest of the world, B; but since the price of each product in A is lower by the same proportion than in B, there is no interference with maximization of production. The same result also holds, *mutatis mutandis*, for a general tax on consumption.

The situation is completely different if the tax is not levied on the production or consumption of all finished products, but only on the production or consumption of a single commodity. In general, it can be stated that the levying of a tax on the production of a single commodity in a single country prevents maximization of world production, but not optimization of trade. On the other hand, a tax on the consumption of a single commodity interferes with optimization of trade, but not with maximization of production. Let us say that A levies a tax on the production of suits, irrespective of whether they are used domestically or exported. The price which the consumers have to pay will be the same in A and B, and when all other prices in the two countries remain the same, trade is optimized. But the price received by the producers will be lower in A than in B, and when all other prices remain constant, production cannot be maximized. If A levies a tax on the consumption of suits, the price which the consumers have to pay for a suit will be higher in A than in B to the amount of the tax and trade will not be optimized. However, the prices received by the producers will remain the same and production will be maximized. The argument in regard to an imported product, *mutatis mutandis*, follows the same lines.

If A's government secures its revenue merely by taxing butter produced in A, this is a pure production tax. The government can keep its revenue at the same level by slightly reducing the tax rate on domestic butter and covering the decline in receipts by a tax on butter imported from B. If this process is continued until the tax on A's butter has fallen so far and that on butter imported from B has risen so far that they have attained the same level, we have a pure consumption tax. If the tax on A's butter is decreased further and that on butter imported from B increased further until only the latter is taxed, the result is a pure trade tax.

Now the question arises, at what point in this shift of the tax away from domestic products to imports is the greatest possible welfare attained? In the following, only the effects of the various tax systems on world productivity will be examined. We will assume that the marginal utility of income is the same for all inhabitants of the world. (This simplifying assumption is unrealistic if country A levies a tax for its own purposes, and the outcome of the analysis must therefore be modified when the effects on the terms of trade are also taken into consideration.) We will assume furthermore that, apart from the divergence between the marginal utility of the products and the marginal costs of the employed factors of production that arises as a result of the tax under consideration, no further divergences will show up. (This, too, is an unrealistic assumption.) It is clear that only a second-best solution can be expected. The ideal solution would undoubtedly be abolition of the tax. However, if a government has no other sources of income, it will not be possible to avoid this divergence.

Two points must now be considered.

(1) Whether the shift of the tax from a production to a consumption basis is useful or harmful depends on whether it is more important to maintain maximization of production or optimization of trade in the product in question. For instance, if one is dealing with a product that requires for its manufacture factors which, as a result of specialization, cannot easily be transferred to another job and if the product can at the same time easily be replaced by other products so far as consumption is concerned, then the shift from a production tax to a consumption tax will have harmful effects. A production tax will not greatly impede the employment of the productive factors; the consumption tax, however, will disturb and decrease the desired volume of trade.

(2) If country A changes a production tax of 10 per cent on butter into a consumption tax, this does not mean that a tax of 10 per cent on imported butter will have to be paid in addition to a 10 per cent tax on domestic butter. The whole point is to keep government revenue constant, so that the tax rate can be reduced when the basis on which it is calculated is broadened. We must therefore compare a tax of 10 per cent on the domestic production of butter, on the one hand, and a tax of 5 per cent on the domestic production of butter and a tax of the same height on imported butter, on the other hand. If a divergence of 5 per cent is created in the imports and at the same time the divergence is reduced from 10 per cent to 5 per cent in the domestic supply, welfare will rise more than it will if a 10 per cent production tax is added to a 10 per cent tax on imports. The decline in import demand will be smaller

in the first case, and the demand for domestic butter will increase to the extent that the production tax is lowered. It can always be expected that the broadest basis of the tax will be the most favorable, since in that case a lower tax rate applies uniformly to a larger number of transactions.

Since in the case of the imported commodity, butter, consumption is larger than either domestic production or the amount imported, we will start with the assumption that a consumption tax is the most advantageous. Let us assume that a tax of 5 per cent is placed on the consumption of imported butter. If the tax rate on the import is slightly reduced (by 1 per cent, for instance) and the tax on domestic production is raised as much as is required to stabilize the revenue of the government, will world welfare rise or fall?

The import of butter from A will probably rise as the result of the reduction of the tax on this import and butter production in A will decrease, since the tax increase will be detrimental to the incentive to buy and produce. Now, if the supply elasticity of butter is low in A and high in B, the increase in imports will be greater than the decrease in domestic production in A. The extent to which the increase in imports will exceed the decrease in domestic production depends on the elasticity of demand for butter in A. On the basis of our assumptions, the price which the consumers have to pay for butter will fall in A. The fall in the price of imported butter which results from lowering the income tax will not immediately be compensated by a rise in the costs of imported butter if the supply elasticity in B is very high. To be sure, imposing the tax on domestic output will have a tendency to raise the butter price, but this rise will soon be compensated by a decrease in cost as a result of the drop in butter production if the supply elasticity in A is very low. Now, if the elasticity of demand for butter in A is zero, consumption will not increase despite the price fall, and the increase in imports would in this case be exactly equal to the decrease in domestic output. On the other hand, if the demand elasticity is high, consumption will increase sharply and in this case imports must increase much more than domestic production decreases.

Hence, a shift of the tax from imports to domestic production will increase economic welfare if, as a result of this measure, imports rise much more than domestic output falls. This will occur under the following conditions: (1) The supply elasticity of B's exports is high. (2) The supply elasticity in A is low. (3) The demand elasticity in A is high. But, if the process of reducing the tax on imports and raising the tax on domestic production is continued, the gain will become smaller and smaller and finally turn into a loss. This will be the case when the divergence between domestic output and imports becomes so great that the loss of welfare in domestic production exceeds the increase in welfare from increased imports. Therefore, in order to maximize welfare, the tax on domestic production should be higher than that on imports (i.e., a changeover should be made from a consumption to a production tax), if the supply elasticity inside A is lower than the supply elasticity of B's export. The best ratio between the tax rate on domestic production and the rate on imports will therefore be the higher, (1) the higher the elasticity of supply of export goods in B; (2) the lower the supply elasticity of the same goods in A; and (3) the higher the demand elasticity in A. In the same way, it can be shown that the tax on the imported commodity should be higher than that on the domestically produced commodity, if the elasticity of supply of exports in country B is smaller than the supply elasticity of domestic production.

Hence, if one starts with a consumption tax on an import commodity, one should change over to a production tax to the extent that the elasticity of supply inside the country in question is lower than the elasticity of supply of export commodities in the foreign country. And, conversely, one should levy a trade tax if the elasticity of supply inside the country in question is higher than the elasticity of supply of export commodities in the foreign country. The special circumstances of the product

196

in question must be known in advance. However, it can generally be stated that it is better to tax domestic production more heavily than imports, for the supply elasticity of domestic production depends on the ease with which productive factors can be used for the manufacture of alternative products if a particular commodity is taxed. However, the elasticity of supply of export commodities in the foreign country does not depend on this circumstance alone, but also on the ease with which other commodities can be substituted for the product in question. The statement that the tax on imports in A should be lower than the tax on domestic production is based on the assumption that the government of A wishes to maximize world welfare, although it can only tax production or consumption in A. If A's government or a supranational government could, for revenue purposes, tax B's butter production irrespective of whether the butter is consumed in B or exported, there would be no reason to tax butter more heavily in A than in B.

The argument is similar when an export commodity is taxed.

This analysis suggests that it is advantageous to change over to a certain extent from a trade tax to a production tax when an import commodity is concerned, and to a consumption tax when an export product is concerned. However, this conclusion must be modified for particular cases, since it is based on very restrictive assumptions.

(1) If the elasticity of foreign supply of an import commodity or of foreign demand for an export commodity is extremely low, a trade tax is preferable.

(2) It may be possible to increase welfare by a redistribution of income to the benefit of the inhabitants of the country that levies the tax and at the expense of the inhabitants of the other country. In this case, there would be reason to change over to a trade tax; in the reverse case, however, there would be a still more compelling reason to change over from a trade tax to a production tax in dealing with an import commodity, and to a consumption tax in dealing with an export commodity.

(3) If the tax-levying government has the right to impose

taxes in the foreign country as well, the presumption against the taxation of foreign production or consumption disappears.

(4) The analysis has to be modified if we drop the assumption that there are no other divergences between the marginal utility of the products and the marginal costs of the productive factors that are employed. If the objective is to raise the price of a particular commodity by taxation in order to make leisure less attractive (for instance, if leisure is demanded complementarily with butter), indirect secondary effects have to be considered, too.

No hard and fast rules can therefore be given as to the best means of indirectly taxing production, consumption, and international trade to provide government revenues. In every case, the increase in welfare has to be weighed against the decrease.

By the method used above, it is also possible to examine the effects of subsidies or of a combination of taxes and subsidies.

Some of the modifications that are necessary as soon as the assumption of international mobility of productive factors is abandoned will be reserved for the following chapter.

2. TAX PROBLEMS OF INTEGRATION

A *customs union* is characterized by, among other things, abolition of import and export duties within the union and by fiscal autonomy of the member states. However, it cannot be assumed that for this reason trade-distorting motives are no longer at work inside the union, since national tax systems continue to influence the flow of international trade. The more trade barriers are removed, the more important will be the disturbing effects that result from general and special consumption taxes and, under certain circumstances, from income taxes as well.[2]

The impact of taxation on national production varies in the

[2] Cf. Carl S. Shoup, "Taxation Aspects of International Economic Integration," *Aspects Financiers et Fiscaux de l'Intégration Economique Internationale*, Travaux de l'Institut International de Finances Publiques, The Hague, 1953, pp. 89ff.

six states of the European Economic Union,[3] as can be seen in Table 3.

TABLE 3

Burden of Taxation on National Production in the Member
States of the European Economic Union

(taxes in per cent of gross national product at market prices)	
Belgium	17.1
France	21.8
Federal Republic of Germany	26.6
Italy	19.6
Luxembourg	23.6
Netherlands	22.9

Source: *Schnellberichte zur Finanzwirtschaft des Auslandes*, published by the German Treasury, No. 36, March 1, 1957, page 65; OEEC, *Statistical Bulletin* (1957), No. 1, pp. 104ff.

According to this table, the impact of taxation in France amounts to 82.3 per cent of the impact in West Germany, and in Belgium to only 64.3 per cent. The revenue from individual taxes, as part of the total tax revenues, also varies from state to state (see Table 4).

Hence, in Luxembourg, the Netherlands, the Federal Re-

TABLE 4

Impact of Tax Categories as Percentage of Total Tax Impact
in the Member States of the European Economic Union

	Taxes on Income and Property	Turn-over Taxes	Consumption Taxes
Belgium	50.7	26.5	22.8
France	38.4	41.5	20.1
Federal Republic of Germany	52.4	26.9	20.7
Italy	32.3	21.1	46.6
Luxembourg	66.4	15.4	18.2
Netherlands	60.0	20.1	19.9

Source: *Schnellberichte zur Finanzwirtschaft des Auslandes*, op.cit., page 66.

[3] Cf. Europäische Wirtschaftsgemeinschaft und Steuerpolitik, Institut *Finanzen und Steuern*, Vol. 52, Bonn, 1957, pp. 14ff.

public of Germany, and Belgium the main emphasis lies on income and property taxes. Contrary to this, more than 60 per cent of the total tax revenues in France and Italy is collected in the form of turnover taxes and consumption taxes.

The techniques of taxation employed in the area of the Economic Union also show important differences. This holds for income taxes as well as for turnover taxes. In the states which levy a cumulative tax on more than one stage of production, one usually also encounters taxes on one production stage as well as taxes in the form of a lump sum at a certain stage of production. Consumption tax systems differ most from one another. The practice of taxation, as prescribed by law and applied by tax officials, is also not uniform in the individual states.

The impact of these differences on integration will now be examined.

Taxes can be levied according to two principles: the principle of the country of destination (destination principle), and the principle of the country of origin (origin principle). According to the first, commodities with the same place of destination are taxed with the same tax rate regardless of their place of origin. Hence if country A levies a *general turnover tax* of 2 per cent and country B a corresponding tax of 4 per cent, an export from A to B will be exempted from the 2 per cent rate and taxed by the 4 per cent rate, according to the principle of the country of destination, so that the A-export in country B is neither discriminated against nor favored in comparison with the commodities of country B. According to the principle of the country of origin, however, commodities with the same place of origin are subject to the same tax, regardless of their place of destination. An export from A to B would accordingly be taxed with the 2 per cent tax of A, but exempted from the 4 per cent tax of country B. Hence, the A-commodities in B will be favored in comparison with the commodities produced in B, if they are taxed according to the principle of the country of origin. Conclusions regarding the necessity of unifying taxes in a customs union or other regional preference systems can be drawn from an examination of the effects of both principles in the case of a general turnover tax, special consumption taxes on single commodities, corporation taxes, and payroll taxes.

By "turnover taxes," we mean here production and consumption taxes, irrespective of whether they are levied on the value added, or cumulatively at various stages of production (cascade tax); these taxes have in common that they bear on all commodities and services rendered or, in other words, a large part of the total production. The problem of turnover taxes has been dealt with by a committee of experts of the European Coal and Steel Community, which assembled under the chairmanship of Jan Tinbergen.[4] The following remarks on turnover taxes restate the generalizations derived by Carl S. Shoup from the report of the Tinbergen Committee. The conclusions based on the sector integration of the Coal and Steel Community are generalized to the case of over-all integration within the framework of a customs union.

We will begin with a simple though unrealistic case. Two countries both levy a general turnover tax, the rates of which differ. Let the tax rate in one country be zero, i.e., it levies practically no turnover tax. Countries A and B have the same national income and their population is the same. Their tax systems consist only of an income tax. Each country exports half of its products to the other. Let the balance of payments be equal to the current account and in equilibrium. The currency unit of country A is the A-unit, that of B the B-unit. Let the exchange rate be at par. Now, let country B be compelled to put a larger share of its total production at the disposal of the government sector. A production tax of 10 per cent is levied in B to achieve this purpose. Country A does not levy such a tax, i.e. the tax rate in A remains zero.

[4] Cf. Europäische Gemeinschaft für Kohle und Stahl, *Bericht über die durch die Umsatzsteuer aufgeworfenen Probleme auf dem Gemeinsamen Markt,* Luxembourg, 1953; as well as H. Mendershausen, "First Tests of the Schuman Plan," *The Review of Economics and Statistics* (1953), pp. 278ff.

Now should the principle of the country of destination or the principle of the country of origin be adopted? According to the destination principle, the exports from B to A will not be taxed; on the contrary, a compensating import tax will be levied in B on the imports from A. (A compensating import tax is, in essence, also levied in A, but the tax rate is in this case zero.) According to the origin principle, on the other hand, exports from B are subject to a 10 per cent tax, while the imports of country B are exempted from the tax. Hence, B levies a 10 per cent tax on all imports according to the destination principle, while B taxes all exports by 10 per cent, according to the origin principle. As has already been explained, the transition from the destination principle to the origin principle—i.e., in this case, the transition from a general import tax to a general export tax—requires only a change in the exchange rate of the two currencies. If the B-currency is devalued with respect to the A-currency from 100:100 to 110:100, then A-commodities and B-commodities will remain equally expensive in both markets after the devaluation. The Tinbergen Report says at this point: "With respect to static equilibrium, in the long run the only difference between systems a (destination principle) and b (origin principle) will lie in the exchange rate."[5] This statement holds under the assumption that at the start—i.e., while the destination principle is still being followed—the exports from B to A are equal to the imports, and furthermore it is assumed that capital transfers will not take place. If then the origin principle is followed instead of the destination principle and the B-unit is devalued as stated, the export receipts of the exporters in B, expressed in B-units, after deduction of the tax will be equal to the export receipts under the destination principle. Under these simplifying assumptions, which also imply that the shifts in the demand and supply functions induced by the devaluation are disregarded, a general import and a general export tax are equivalent. If, on

[5] Cf. *Bericht über die durch die Umsatzsteuer aufgeworfenen Probleme auf dem Gemeinsamen Markt*, page 24.

the other hand, the situation at the start is characterized by a deficit or a surplus, this equivalence no longer prevails.

In practice, neither the destination principle nor the origin principle can be adopted in a pure form. Technical difficulties occur when tax exemption or restitution is granted, or when compensating import taxes are levied. Tax resistances become very great when tax rates are high or when there are considerable differences between them. The difficulties which show up in following the destination principle will be described first.

It is hardly possible to determine precisely exemption, restitution, and import compensation, even if both countries levy a turnover tax of the same kind—for instance, a cascade tax. An example will illustrate this.

We will assume that countries A and B impose the same type of turnover tax, but apply different tax rates. A 2 per cent cascade tax is levied in country A and a 4 per cent one in B. The commodities are sold three times on their way to the consumers: by manufacturers to wholesalers, by wholesalers to retailers, and by retailers to consumers. Let the price of the commodities, expressed in a third currency (for instance, dollars), be the same in both countries before the tax is levied. Let the sales price of the manufacturer be $100, the price of the wholesaler be $125, and the retail price be $200. The destination principle is followed. Now let us examine the case in which a wholesale dealer sells to a foreign retail dealer. We can distinguish four categories of commodities:

(1) Commodities produced in A and sold by the wholesaler in A and by the retailer in B:

Tax of country A on the sale by the producer to the wholesaler, 2 per cent of $100 $ 2

Compensating tax on the import by the retailer in B from the wholesaler in A, 4 per cent of $125 $ 5

Tax of country B on the turnover by the retailer, 4 per cent of $200 $ 8
                                                                                                                        ——————
Total amount of tax of both countries on exports from A to B $ 15

(2) Commodities produced in B and sold in the retail trade of B:

$4 + $5 + $8 = $ 17

(3) Commodities produced in B and turned over in the wholesale trade of B and in the retail trade of A:

Tax of country B on the sale by the producer, 4 per cent of $100 $ 4

Compensating tax of country A on the import by the retailer, 2 per cent of $125 $ 2.50

Tax of country A on the turnover by the retailer, 2 per cent of $200 $ 4

Total amount of tax of both countries on export from B to A $ 10.50

(4) Commodities produced in A and sold in the retail trade of A: $ 8.50

Under our assumptions, the commodities produced in A (the country with the lower tax rate) have a tax benefit of $2 compared with the commodities of B, regardless of whether these commodities are sold in A or in B. This discrimination does not result from following the destination principle, but springs from the technical difficulty that complete restitution of the tax to the exporters is counteracted by a compensating import tax. Ideally, country A would, in the first case, not only exempt the products in the wholesale trade from the tax, but also restitute the $2 which the producer has paid; country B would levy a compensating import tax which must, however, consist of two parts: the $5 mentioned in the first case, plus a 4 per cent tax on the sales price of the manufacturer—i.e., a further compensation tax of $4. A corresponding practice in country A would also remove the difference in the prices of the imports from B.

Of course, in this simple example it would be easy to restitute the $2 to the manufacturer when the wholesaler exports the products in question. It is in reality very difficult to estimate for this sort of transaction how much turnover tax is contained in a particular export commodity, since the production process and the organization of trade are much more complicated than is described in our example. If one strives for absolute exactness, then one must take into account tax payments that were made far in the past; in the production of textiles for export, for instance, steel has been used that in turn was produced in taxed production facilities, etc. But it is difficult enough to arrive at even a moderate approximation of the amount to be restituted.

Similar problems present themselves if the importing country wishes to levy a compensating tax. One general principle holds if at various stages of the transaction countries levy general turnover taxes at various rates: the nearer the exporter is to the manufacturer, the more exactly can the restitution and the compensating import tax be defined. It is also easier to ascertain exports of manufacturers to wholesalers than exports of wholesalers to retail dealers.

In all these questions, no assumptions have been made about the incidence of taxes and the possibilities of shifting the tax burden. The technique of following the destination principle does not depend on who is burdened by the tax differential of $2.

We will now assume that both countries levy a tax at one stage of production only, but that this stage is not the same for both countries. Country A levies a 15 per cent tax on the turnover of the manufacturers (production tax), while country B taxes the turnover of the retail trade by 7.5 per cent. A manufacturer in country A who exports to B is, according to the destination principle, exempted from the 15 per cent tax and the commodity in question is only taxed by the 7.5 per cent tax of B. No compensating tax is required in B if country A does not sell directly to the consumers in B; in the latter case, a compensating tax should in principle be levied on the consumers. Goods produced in B and exported to A have to be subjected in A to a compensating import tax of 15 per cent of the value of production, since country B does not impose a tax on retail trade.

The administration of a tax at one stage of production is also the easier, the nearer the manufacturer is to the dealer who exports the commodity. Moreover, in the case of the single-stage tax, a general principle applies to the technique of taxation: the difficulties which arise in connection with tax restitution or exemption and with the compensating import tax will be minimized if the exporting as well as the importing country levies the turnover tax on the transactions of the retail trade. Exports are then automatically exempted from the tax, except when the retail dealers export (e.g., sell to tourists); on the other hand, all imports are caught in the retail trade net, unless the importing is done by the consumers themselves. These rules apply only when turnover taxes are levied according to the destination principle. From this, the conclusion can be drawn that a mere harmonization of the turnover tax practices of the members does not suffice for a European customs union. If all the members adopted the French system of a production tax (in the form either of a value-added tax or of a single-stage tax), great difficulties would arise in the future in determining the compensating import tax and the tax exemption, despite this harmonization. This applies in particular to goods which are exported by wholesalers to retail dealers. Though the difficulties would be somewhat smaller if the German system of taxing several stages of production were uniformly adopted, this method is also anything but ideal, because it entails discrimination against enterprises which are not vertically integrated. True, the levying of a sales tax on retail dealers has a disadvantage from the viewpoint of tax technique—the difficulty of controlling a large number of retailers. But from the standpoint of integration and the avoidance of tax diversions in international trade, this form of taxation is the best possible one.

In the ideal case, no customs control is needed in the trade between member states of a customs union. But how should the compensation tax be levied on imports, as is necessary if the destination principle is followed? The experience of the United States is useful in this connection. For our purposes, the individual states of the American federation can be regarded as members of a customs union which levy different sales taxes. The individual states have no customs control at their borders, but instead, if a sales tax constitutes part of the states' revenues, they levy a "use tax" on the importer or on the consumer. Most of them tax retail trade with a single-phase tax according to the destination principle. They therefore do not have to levy a compensating import tax on the importing wholesale or retail dealer. Instead, they employ a use tax, whose impact falls on the consumers. Exports of retailers to consumers in other states are accordingly exempted from the tax. In practice, this system is satisfactory only in the case of relatively expensive consumption goods like cars and refrigerators, and even then it does not always function perfectly since there are many possibilities for evasion.

What opportunities for tax evasion are open to a consumer who lives in state X, which levies a 3 per cent sales tax and borders upon state Y, which levies a 1 per cent sales tax? The consumer has the alternative of buying in X, where a tax evasion is impossible, or of trying to evade the tax by a purchase in Y. He can travel to Y, buy the desired article there without claiming the tax exemption and, in so doing, take the chance that state Y will not inform state X. Whether the taxpayer evades the tax in this way depends on the difference between the sales tax rates in the two states. If his action is successful, he saves taxes to the amount of 2 per cent of the sales price. On the other hand, the consumer can order the desired article in Y by letter or by phone. In this case, he need not pay the 1 per cent tax of state Y, but his chances of evading the 3 per cent tax of state X are smaller. Here the incentive to try to evade the tax does not depend on the difference between the sales tax rates, but on the tax rate of the state in which the consumer lives. If the article in question is difficult to transport, only the second method of tax evasion is open to him. Hence, the absolute level of the sales tax rates in the consumer's home state settles the matter in the case of commodities which are difficult to transport and the difference between the taxes has no meaning if the destination principle is followed. On the other hand, the difference between the tax rates is decisive in the case of consumption goods that have a high value and are easily transported.

The difference between the tax rates is, of course, never greater than the tax rate in the state of the consumer and always smaller than that rate if the tax rate in the neighboring state is higher than zero. For this reason, the tax rate in the consumer's home state has more weight than the tax differential. In the United States, the highest sales tax amounts to 3 per cent; therefore, the maximum difference between the tax rates of neighboring states can be no greater than that. Tax evasion is relatively unimportant at this ratio. On the other hand, if the absolute rates or differences between the rates amounted to 5 per cent or more, delinquencies would probably be more numerous.

If the turnover tax is levied at a stage prior to retail trade, the question arises of to what extent the retail or wholesale dealers who purchase goods from the foreign wholesalers or producers may be able to evade taxes. Since importers usually do not themselves transport the imported commodities, but have them shipped to their places of business, the absolute level of the tax in the country of the buyer is decisive for the intention to evade, and the difference between the tax rates of the exporting and importing countries plays no part. This holds under the assumption that the exporting country either completely exempts the export from the turnover tax or makes restitution of taxes that were paid before. On the other hand, if the exporting country does not practice restitution or exemption, the difference between the tax rates is decisive for the

incentive to commit tax evasion. Hence, a complete harmonization of turnover tax rates in the partner countries is, under
the destination principle, in general no great deterrent to tax
evasion. Rather, it is the absolute height of the tax rate in the
importing country that settles the matter. The formation of a
customs union will influence tax evasion mainly by virtue of
the fact that administrative control of imports will no longer
be as extensive as before. The administrative problems could
be very great in the case of a turnover tax which amounts to
18 per cent in the production stage, as in France, or to a 4 per
cent cumulative tax, as in Germany.

The difficulties in calculating the compensating import tax
or in complying with the export restitutions or exemptions
therefore need not in all cases lead to a unification of turnover taxes in a customs union that follows the destination
principle. However, taxing retail trade as well as low tax
rates would yield favorable results.

Now let us examine the difficulties which arise when the
origin principle is followed. It will not be easy to follow this
principle if the turnover tax is levied on a dealer who is near
the consumer. Let us assume that country B levies a tax on
the turnover of the retail trade and follows the origin principle, while no tax is levied in country A. Now, if a producer
or wholesale dealer in B exports goods to A, these exports are
tax exempt, despite the origin principle, since the sales tax is
levied in B on the retailer. And despite the purpose of this
principle, exports of A to the wholesale or retail dealer in B
will be subject to the sales tax of the latter country, unless B
adopts a rather complicated method of exempting those imports, at least so far as the import value is concerned. If A
levies its turnover tax on the producer at an earlier stage
than B, for instance, then the origin principle will virtually
lead to taxing the exports from A to B twice (production tax
in A, retail sales tax in B). To prevent this, B should introduce a production tax; for, as stated in the Tinbergen Report,

harmonization would not be guaranteed if A changed over to a retail sales tax.

Now, we will assume that A administers a general cumulative turnover tax and B levies a value-added tax on production. The tax in B is then calculated in such a way that the tax which has already been paid on the raw materials, etc., contained in the article in question can be deducted from the tax which has to be paid on the sales price of the article. A wire producer in A exports to a nail producer in B; nails are taxed in A with a cascade tax on account of the raw material they contain—i.e., wire—as well as with a sales tax on the sales price of the nails in B. The origin principle could indeed be followed to a limited extent, if B granted the nail producer a deduction for the cascade tax paid in A on wire. But the difficulty is that the turnover tax system also includes those stages of production which precede export. The reason for this lies not in the difference between the cascade and the value-added tax, but rather in the fact that the origin principle is difficult to follow even when both countries have the same tax system but levy the tax on a dealer who is close to the consumer. Many exports which should be taxed leave the country before they reach the tax stage, and imports which should be exempted will be taxed if no special measures are taken for their exemption.

However, under the origin principle, there is no incentive to evade taxes on additional imports since no compensating import tax is levied. To that extent, the origin principle ignores borders. A difference between the tax rates of two countries therefore causes no administrative complications according to this principle. Of course, the absolute level of taxation in a country is still important, since the higher the tax rate, the more difficult it becomes to administer the tax; but this problem does not result from the special character of the imports, since the latter are not subject to the domestic tax according to the origin principle. From this, it follows that a harmonization of turnover taxes is not necessary—at least, not for technical reasons.

On the other hand, differences in turnover taxes could possibly have far-reaching economic consequences. Export firms located in a country with a high tax rate are tempted, under the origin principle, to move to countries with lower tax rates. Such interference with maximization of production will not take place under the destination principle.

Now we turn from the general turnover tax, which falls uniformly on all commodities, to the effects of *consumption taxes on a few commodities only*. We assume that the revenues of country A stem entirely from a high tax on alcoholic beverages and that B draws its total tax revenue from a tax on tobacco. Up to now, tariffs have not prevented the import of alcoholic beverages by A or the import of tobacco by B. Now the two countries form a customs union, and consequently face the problem of which of the two principles they should follow in levying their consumption taxes.

The economic implications of the two principles are quite different. Under the origin principle, the producers of alcoholic beverages in A will have only a small market in both countries, since their products are subject to a high consumption tax, while their competitors in B are not burdened by such a tax. The tobacco manufacturers in B are ousted from the market in the same way under this principle. Hence, the production of alcoholic beverages in B and tobacco production in A will expand; this shift in the structure of production would not be attributable to differences in factor endowment but simply to differences in taxation. Following the origin principle would therefore discriminate against maximization of production.

Consequently, if A and B wish to maintain their own consumption taxes in a customs union, they will be forced to follow the destination principle. But this means that both countries must institute some sort of customs control to levy the compensating import tax; and, moreover, that the tax administration must provide for exemptions or grant restitutions on exports.

These difficulties could be avoided if B replaced its tobacco tax by a tax on alcoholic beverages, or A replaced its tax on alcoholic beverages by a tobacco tax, or if both countries decreased the rate of both taxes. The first method will not be feasible if the inhabitants of A consume large quantities of alcoholic beverages but not much tobacco, and when the pattern of tastes in country B is the opposite. (If, instead of alcoholic beverages and tobacco, the two commodities were coffee and tea, then the probability of such differences becomes even more clear.) But since these consumption taxes do not constitute the only source of income in any country and, moreover, the most important taxes are levied in all countries on a few commodities only, it is likely that geographic differences will continue to exist in a customs union. The destination principle is the only one that fits this situation.

Would it be possible to maintain the present very high rates of a few European consumption taxes in a customs union? It is doubtful, if no rigorous customs control is continued, whether tax evasion in international trade can be kept within reasonable bounds. This danger is illustrated by the experience of the American states which have much lower consumption tax rates. In an economic union, the authorities could continue to impose high consumption taxes on single commodities, but in a customs union a general lowering of consumption tax rates will probably be required for reasons of administration.

It is also conceivable that countries A and B both draw all their income from *taxing corporation profits*. The destination principle cannot be applied to this tax. It is very difficult to convert the profit tax into a tax on corporate sales and, if such a change is made, considerable differences show up among firms of the same industry and among various industries. Consequently, it is hardly possible to levy a compensating import tax which can be expressed as a percentage of the amount of the sale or to grant a corresponding restitution on imports.

The origin principle is therefore mainly used in taxing profits. It must, however, be modified in all cases of big enterprises which do business in both countries. The profits have to be distributed between the countries in which the firm in question operates. However, this distribution does not accord with the destination principle. Though distribution of the profits on the sales of a firm in two countries is generally practiced, still the origin principle is adopted everywhere.

Within the framework of a European customs union, very great differences can be expected between the rates and structure of payroll taxes which are levied by the individual countries to finance *social security*. The question of whether it is necessary to harmonize these burdens is, for political reasons, particularly vital at present. Does the mechanism of the customs union require that the social premiums which are handed over by the employers or employees be uniform in the various countries?

Through the agreement made by the future members of the Common Market with respect to a harmonization of their social security contributions, other adjustment measures should become superfluous during the transition period and long-term interferences in competition should be removed.[6] Such measures could really contribute to alleviating the transition difficulties in the balances of payments. Apart from that, there are no valid economic reasons for a permanent harmonization of this type of taxation within the Common Market or the Free Trade Area.

There are, of course, certain arguments for a harmonization of social policy for reasons of international mobility of productive factors (for instance, with respect to insurance against illness and unemployment as well as pensions). But what is usually advocated in favor of such harmonization—standardization of holidays, of the work week, of overtime pay, etc.—implies that differences in wage costs among the various countries which are attributable to these factors are incompatible

[6] Cf. ECE, *Economic Survey of Europe in 1956*, ch. IV, page 28.

with competition within a customs union or a free trade area. In fact, harmonization is actually necessary for these reasons only when there are differences in the social legislation or social security contributions within a particular country, and these differences are not matched by similar differences in the burden imposed on various industries in the other countries. Social security contributions which influence the general level of factor costs in a country, but not their relative structure, can be "harmonized" readily between countries by an adjustment of exchange rates. There is no reason why a country should increase its labor costs by taxing them simply because another country takes such a step for purposes of social policy, while it is demanded at the same time that differences in labor costs, resulting from a difference in factor endowment, should be eliminated by changing the exchange rate.[7] The necessity for a harmonization of social security contributions is therefore with good reason contested by numer-

[7] Cf. Report of the Leaders of the Delegations to the Government Committee Appointed for the Conference of Messina, *op.cit.*: "One often encounters the opinion that effective competition would be possible only if the main elements of the production costs have come closer to each other everywhere. But it is precisely on the basis of such differences that equilibrium can be established and trade develop. This applies, for instance, to differences in wage levels if they correspond to differences in labor productivity. . . . No attempt should therefore be made to change . . . the foundations of an economy, which reflect its natural resources, the degree of its productivity, and the size of public levies. So-called harmonization will therefore result partly from market developments, the interplay of economic forces, and the relationships of those who take part in market transactions. The procedure for realizing the conditions which must be fulfilled for the proper functioning of the Common Market seems therefore to be much more limited: it deals with the rectification or compensation of the consequences of special distortions which favor or discriminate against certain branches of the economy. . . . If two economies are united, regulations which do not create distortions within each economy may cause them as a result of differences between regulations in the countries concerned. If, for instance, in one country social security is financed by contributions based on wages, the burden weighs mainly on the labor-intensive industries. If, on the other hand, in another country social security is predominantly financed by the government—i.e., by taxes which are paid by the whole society—then the labor-intensive industries in the latter country are in a more favorable position than those in the former country."

ous economists.[8] As Meade has said, to argue for harmonization "means committing the mistake of applying absolute instead of comparative costs to international trade."[9] According to Kahn, "Such ideals are alien to the principles of free trade and it is reasonable to hope that their stupidity will gradually be recognized. But at the same time greater recognition is needed of the incompatibility of free trade with the present-day sanctity of exchange rates, which is almost worthy of the gold standard."[10] An American authority expresses himself similarly: "In general, it seems that a customs union should not be deemed impracticable merely because of large differences from country to country in payroll taxes for social security."[11]

What consequences does a customs union have for the *tax system as a whole?* Changes in the tax systems actually necessitated by the formation of a customs union are probably smaller than the changes which must take place in the hypothetical cases which we have examined. The economic disadvantages and administrative difficulties which were so great when, for instance, all revenues stemmed from a turnover tax or from a corporation tax, will be smaller for each type of tax when they form only a part of the tax system. The most severe conflicts between tax systems occur when the various national tax systems are not composed of numerous taxes, but each system consists of a special tax which is different in each country.

The following example makes this clear. Let us say that revenues of country A are mainly based on a production tax,

[8] Cf. ILO, *Social Aspects of European Economic Co-operation,* Chapters III and IV and Appendix II; also "Memorandum über die gesamtwirtschaftliche Integration," *op.cit.,* page 21.

[9] Cf. J. E. Meade, *Probleme der Wirtschaftsunion souveräner Staaten,* page 146.

[10] Cf. R. F. Kahn, "A Positive Contribution?" in *Bulletin of the Oxford University Institute of Statistics* (1957), pp. 64ff.

[11] Cf. C. S. Shoup, "Taxation Aspects of International Economic Integration," *op.cit.,* page 103; also F. Neumark, "Die budgetären und steuerlichen Aspekte einer wirtschaftlichen Integration," *ibid.,* page 45.

levied according to the destination principle; country B draws its income from a profit tax. According to the destination principle, commodities produced in A and exported to B are not subject to a turnover tax, and if they are imported by a retailer in B, these commodities do not contribute much to tax receipts in country B. (If the consumers in B themselves import the commodities, the A-exports are exempted from taxes in *both* countries.) But goods produced in B and exported to A are at least partly affected by the corporate income tax in B; in addition to this, they are burdened by the compensating turnover tax in A. A difference of this magnitude between the tax systems of the members of the union will give rise to so many complaints that tax unification becomes necessary. But the European countries do not differ that much in practice. To summarize, we can conclude that in the event of a customs union the adjustment has to be concentrated, at least in the case of numerous taxes, on the stage at which the tax is levied and on the level of the tax rate, rather than on the removal of differences in the types of taxes or in the tax rates themselves.

The results of the analysis of the tax policy aspects of a customs union can be carried over directly to the case of *sector integration*, as this is realized by the Coal and Steel Community. The specific tax policy problems of sector integration become apparent in the historic example of the so-called "tax battle" of the Coal and Steel Community.[12]

The tax battle was started by the German iron industry.[13] Its argument was something like this: Two kinds of turnover taxes were levied in France: a production tax, with a rate at

---

[12] Cf. the report cited earlier by the committee of experts for the study of the problems created by the turnover tax in the Common Market; also G. Schmölders, "Der Steuerstreit in der Montanunion," *Archiv des öffentlichen Rechts* (1953-54), pp. 91ff.; W. Albers, "Steuerprobleme in der Montanunion," *Die Weltwirtschaft*, Kiel, 1953, pp. 162ff.

[13] Cf. the detailed notes of R. Regul, "Wirtschaftsintegration und Steuersysteme (Der gegenwärtige Stand der Untersuchungen über das Steuerproblem in der Europäischen Gemeinschaft für Kohle und Stahl)," *Finanzarchiv* (1955), pp. 313ff.

that time (1953) of 15.35 per cent (for products of the steel industry), and a transaction tax, with a rate of 1 per cent. Both taxes were levied on the sales price, plus taxes. Hence, the tax on the domestic sales price, excluding previous taxes, actually amounted to 19.55 per cent. Imports were taxed with a compensating tax of 20 per cent of the price, plus transport costs; exports were exempted from the tax to the amount of $15.35 + 1 = 16.35$ per cent of the sales price, including previous taxes, or 19.55 per cent of the price without previous taxes. On the other hand, Germany levied a cumulative turnover tax with a rate of 4 per cent and a total height of 9.8 per cent of the sales price without tax; the compensating import tax amounted to 4 per cent for semi-manufactured products, and 6 per cent for finished rolling-mill products, of the price plus transport costs. The tax exemption in the case of exports amounted to 4.17 per cent of the price without tax, plus from 0.5 to 1.0 per cent export restitution. The total tax exemption was estimated as ranging from 4.68 and 5.1 to 9.1 per cent, respectively. From these comparisons it was concluded that in the free Common Market of the Coal and Steel Community, French steel could be offered 20 per cent cheaper in the German market than German steel in the French market—assuming equal production and transport costs. The apprehension felt by the German iron industry in regard to its exports caused the German government to make a frontal attack on the tax problem. How could different tax systems be combined with the existence of a sectoral Common Market and with the stipulations of the Schuman Treaty? In particular, how could the existing practice of the turnover tax—i.e., the export exemption and the compensating import tax—be combined with the functioning of a partially integrated market? At many though not at all points in the discussions, the view of the German government was directly opposite to that of the other countries—in particular, France.

The High Authority instructed a committee to report on these problems. This committee of experts, assembled under

Prof. Tinbergen, reached the conclusion that, so long as the rates and kinds of taxes differed, the destination principle and origin principle were equivalent only if the turnover taxes affected all products. It was therefore concluded in the report that a pure destination-principle system was not to be recommended for the iron and steel sector alone, since this principle held only approximately for all other products. Under these circumstances, its application would lead to distortions in the production structure. Furthermore, the committee of experts became convinced that a pure destination-principle system could not be generally applied for the previously stated reasons (difficulties of restitution, exemption, and compensation tax). On the contrary, it could be expected from such a practice that the governments would try to stimulate exports by allowing an unjustifiably high export preference. Hence, the committee favored a modified destination principle, the preservation of which would not cause too great difficulties. This recommendation was in agreement with the *status quo*. Shoup points out, in his critical examination of these conclusions, that the imperfections of the destination principle cause considerable distortions, particularly at the high rates of the relevant turnover tax. That these distortions have not had too disturbing an effect can only be attributed to the accident of the price changes which were made at the opening of the Common Market. The French steel producers increased their prices, while the German steel prices decreased. The question regarding the stimulation of exports by way of taxes was therefore pushed into the background, but the problem of how sector integration could be combined with autonomous fiscal measures by the participating states remained.[14]

We must now introduce the *concept of a confederation of states*. The executive of the confederation, the supranational government, does not levy taxes on its own behalf, but participates in the national tax revenues by contributions, i.e. "requi-

---

[14] Cf. Horst Mendershausen, "First Tests of the Schuman Plan," *op.cit.*, pp. 278ff.

sitions." The member countries meet these requisitions by increasing their own taxes, if the expenditures of the supranational authority are superimposed on those of the national and local bodies. It is clear that national and local taxes have to be changed if states which were heretofore independent are going to unite; this change can possibly be confined to tax rates. If the expenditures of the confederation replace previous expenditures of the national and local bodies, changes in the tax system may not be needed. However, it is unlikely that the new expenditures of the confederation will exactly balance tax requisitions from each state. In that event, tax changes will become necessary, depending mainly on the type of requisition which each state places at the disposal of the confederation.

The most primitive method of calculating the requisitions consists of fixing an amount per capita. This brings more pressure to bear on the tax system of the poorer members; and obviously these states would eventually be forced to introduce new taxes. This problem is minimized if national requisitions are calculated on the basis of national income per capita.

The confederation, of course, faces all the problems which we have already examined in the case of a customs union (how to deal with imports and exports inside the confederation under the turnover tax system, consumption taxes, etc.). What has been said there applies to this form of unification as well. Assuming that the method of calculating the requisitions complies with the stated criteria, it should be possible to make the transition to the confederation without great changes in existing tax systems, particularly if the expenditures of the supranational authorities are moderate.

By a *federation*, we mean in this connection the fusion of regional authorities into a supranational authority with financial autonomy. Considerable changes in the national tax systems are inevitable in this case.

A European federal government could not resort to any

tax not yet exploited by national or local governments. The formation of a federation would therefore create the problem that either national and local governments must give up the type of tax which the federal government adopts or they must rely far less on this type of tax than they previously have done. Otherwise, the combined rate of the national and federal tax (possibly also the taxes of other local authorities) would reach too high a level, in view of the imperfections of each type of tax. If, for instance, a European federal government levied a value-added production tax of 20 per cent, then a combined tax rate of, for instance, 38 per cent in France would be definitely too high, because investments can be taken only incompletely into consideration under the present method of incorporating the tax in the calculation of the value added. The French government would therefore have to lower the production tax rate drastically and increase another tax rate, if the supranational government did not waive additional expenditures and take over some expenditures which so far have been exclusively a national matter. Similar examples could be found in the area of income and consumption taxes.

The problem is especially acute in view of the fact that the tax burden has become greater and greater in the course of two world wars in the states that would form a federation. Some of these high tax rates must be considerably reduced if a federal tax is to be superimposed. In the United States, on the other hand, the federal government was established long before this century of high taxes and the existence of federal taxes made it impossible for the state and local authorities to increase their tax rates beyond a certain point. The procedure was therefore less painful in the United States than it would be in Europe, where the national taxes must necessarily be removed gradually. To the extent that the expenditures of the federal government are merely of the substitutive type, the switch of course becomes easier. But even then considerable changes in the tax systems must be taken into account. The adjustment of national and regional systems to that of a supranational one would be less difficult in a centrally oriented state than in a federation. There are already three tax authorities at different levels in Germany, so that great differences exist in the taxes of the individual *Länder* of the Federal Republic.

Apart from the relationship between national and supranational tax systems, there is in the event of federation also the question of how the national systems would be related to each other. The question has particular relevance for enterprises which operate in several countries. The incentive for national expansion would be still stronger in a federation than in a customs union. The imperfections existing in the system of distributing corporation profits in such a way that double taxing is avoided would therefore damage a larger number of firms, and it can be expected that heavy pressure will be brought to bear on the national governments in the federation to unify income taxes.

A federal tax has distinctive features with which the taxpayer in most of the member states would be unfamiliar. For instance, let us look at the income tax. The definition of taxable income in France differs from that in Germany. A federal income tax will probably be based on still another definition of taxable income, and even when the definition of a member country is taken over, the federal tax will be new for the inhabitants of the other states. There are also corresponding differences in the way taxes are levied in the individual countries—for instance, the ways deduction at the source, amnesties, assessment, and payment are regulated. The federal tax will therefore seem to many taxpayers to represent a fundamental change in the tax system. Resistance to the application of different income tax rules will induce the individual countries to set up a uniform definition of taxable income. But the experience of the United States does not make these prospects look very promising. Almost no single American state which taxes income has its tax technique geared to that of the federal government in order to reduce the technical difficulties that confront the taxpayer. Still, it might be possible for the European countries to adopt a relatively simple system of income tax, since in some of them the local income tax is calculated on a national basis. Likewise, the federal government could share certain taxes with the national governments, by restituting to the member countries a part of the revenue on the basis of its origin. The extent to which differences in any particular tax can be maintained in a federal tax system is astonishing. This is illustrated by the taxes on alcoholic beverages in the United States.

The forces which tend to a regional adjustment of financial matters are much stronger in a federation than in a confederation. There are great differences among geographical regions in income per capita and in property per inhabitant— i.e., in the sources of taxes, on the one hand, and in the need for government services, on the other. A heavily populated rural region with low income and wealth is, for instance, the opposite of a wealthy urban region with a completely different composition of population so far as age is concerned. Whole nations also differ in these characteristics, but there is no reason for rich nations to support the poorer ones, so long as no foreign policy interests are at stake, and it is improbable that the formation of a customs union would lead to such a financial adjustment. Even in a confederation, it can hardly be expected that the rich nations will automatically be willing to support their poorer partners. But the stronger feeling of political solidarity and the financial autonomy in a federation favor such a financial adjustment. The poorer states would therefore perhaps not be forced to raise their tax rates as much as would be necessary without such an adjustment. This adjustment process, too, requires reorganization of the tax system. In general, it will probably work toward a greater uniformity in taxation in the whole federal area. Every new federal tax represents a step in the direction of unification, and the less the poorer member countries are burdened, the sooner will they be in a position to forgo abnormally high tax rates.

In summary, we can state that a federation will lead to a profound reorganization of the tax system in most of, if not in all, the countries concerned. But though harmonization of the national tax systems is desirable, it can nevertheless be stated that the economic integration of Europe is feasible without sudden changes in present tax methods, even within the framework of a federation. "If economic integration fails, this failure will almost certainly be attributable to other factors than differences in taxation."[15]

[15] C. S. Shoup, "Taxation Aspects of International Economic Integration," *op.cit.*, page 111.

CHAPTER VI

FACTOR MOBILITY

1. THE MOBILITY OF PRODUCTIVE FACTORS IN EUROPE

ACCORDING TO MYRDAL, one of the main reasons why European integration does not make much progress is the lack of international freedom of factor movement and of factor mobility in general. Thus far, the governments of the European states and the executive bodies of the European organizations have devoted themselves exclusively to the liberalization of commercial and payments transactions, while the problem of the international mobility of productive factors has for the greater part been neglected. This state of affairs is easy to understand, since questions regarding commercial and payments transactions present themselves daily, while mobility of the factors of production is usually relevant only to long-term considerations. The classical theory of international trade still makes itself felt to a certain extent. It is based on the assumption that the factors of production are internationally immobile. Earlier, however, we offered the United States as an example of a common market; and we should not forget that the free mobility of commodities between individual American states is accompanied by an absence of political restrictions on the mobility of capital and labor.

If, like Myrdal, one sees the objective of economic integration as the realization of the "ideal of equality of opportunity," then mobility of productive factors is definitely a necessary correlate of the aforementioned measures aimed at integration. As we will show below, free commodity trade is only in a very limited sense a substitute for international mobility of productive factors insofar as international equalization of incomes for equal factors of production is concerned. At any rate, it cannot be expected that any form of liberalization of international commodity trade can eliminate the income differences which are an aspect of international economic disintegration.[1]

In discussions of a closer economic cooperation among the European states, free mobility of labor and capital has therefore been recognized as essential despite the relative concentration on a liberalization of commodity trade. For instance, in the OEEC treaty (April 1948) it was agreed that the obstacles to free *migration* between individual countries should be gradually removed. In its second annual report, the OEEC expressed itself on this topic as follows: "A reasonably free flow of labour between nations is a desirable accompaniment of the free flow of goods and services in a multilateral trading system. The freeing of intra-European trade, which is now one of the principal tasks of the Organisation, should therefore be accompanied by greater and freer movement of labour between participating countries. At the same time, in countries in which there is a surplus of manpower, the problem of adjustment to measures for the freeing of trade may be a particularly serious one."[2] Subsequently, most member countries of the OEEC have agreed to forbid foreigners from other member countries permission to work only if (a) an eligible native worker can fill the position in question; (b) the foreigner in question is not eligible; (c) special reasons of national economic policy can be given against the employment of foreigners; (d) the appointment of foreigners would result in unsatisfactory conditions (in the first instance, wages); or (e) labor peace would be jeopardized by granting such permission. However, the OEEC itself admits that no great results have been obtained with respect to eliminating the obstacles to international migration: "In this field, the restrictive spirit is still widespread."[3]

[1] G. Myrdal, *An International Economy*, page 2.
[2] OEEC Report for 1950: *European Recovery Programme*, page 213.
[3] OEEC Report for 1955: *From Recovery Towards Economic Strength*, Vol. I, page 19.

On the basis of Article 69 of the Schuman Treaty, the members of the European Coal and Steel Community undertook to guarantee free mobility of qualified workers of the coal and steel industry. This resolution was intended to contribute to economic expansion and to raise the standard of living in the member states, an objective that is in agreement with the general aim of the Community as specified in Articles 2, 3, 4, and 5 of the treaty. "As the High Authority has declared, it regards the agreement between the member states as a first step on the road to the realization of a 'common market' for workers. Such a market would be indispensable if favorable conditions for employment stability are to be created, on the one hand, and equality in the improvement of living and working conditions be attained, on the other."[4] However, it has been pointed out by the High Authority that the national governments have interpreted Article 69 of the treaty too restrictively.

According to a convention concluded in 1954 by the Scandinavian countries, the citizens of the signatory states no longer need a working permit in any of these countries. In practice, a common labor market has thereby been established and it has been generally recognized that this policy has proved advantageous.[5] In addition to this, steps have been taken to guarantee, on the basis of reciprocity, that workers from the other treaty states will receive equal treatment in respect to social security. While within the framework of the union of the Benelux countries such a formal agreement has not yet been concluded, there exists in practice an extraordinary freedom of settlement of labor inside the union, and even where a working permit is still required, there are forces at work which oppose the exclusion of or discrimination against foreign workers.

Labor migration in Europe since the end of World War II has fluctuated around one million workers (not counting refu-

[4] *Third Overall Report on the Activity of the Community*, 1955, page 171.

[5] ILO, *Social Aspects of European Economic Co-operation*, page 98.

gees) employed outside their country of origin. Migration gains were obtained by Belgium (particularly in coal production), France (where labor bottlenecks have been overcome mainly by the employment of workers from North Africa), Great Britain, Sweden, and Switzerland. By and large, it seems that the European countries which are for the most part industrialized have not suffered from a general scarcity of labor, though bottlenecks have occurred in individual sectors. To be sure, migration has not been very extensive: but it has proved very useful, especially in the coal and construction industries, as well as in agriculture. The size of the migration has not sufficed, however, to solve the problems of overpopulated regions in Southern Europe.

The *obstacles opposing migration* in Europe are of two kinds:[6] first, workers are little inclined to leave their home country and, second, there are restrictions on their employment abroad.

The inclination of West European workers to change their profession or place of work is notoriously small. The extent to which the objective of a full-employment policy is interpreted as assurance of employment in the same locality is surprising, particularly to American observers. It is not at all uncommon in Europe for employers to refuse to take on profitable business if this means an increase in the number of workers employed in the firm, for the employer considers himself as legally or morally responsible for the continued employment of the newly appointed employees. On the other hand, the unemployed European worker often waits patiently for a new

[6] Cf. R. Wagenführ, "Integration and europäische Sozialpolitik," *Mitteilungen der List-Gesellschaft* (1957), pp. 323 and 334; *Hindernisse für die Beweglichkeit der Arbeitskräfte und soziale Probleme der Anpassung,* Europäische Gemeinschaft für Kohle und Stahl, Studien und Dokumente, Luxembourg, 1956; Institut National d'Etudes Démographiques, *Les attitudes des mineurs du Centre-Midi et l'évolution de l'emploi,* Paris, 1957; A. Girard, *Développement économique et mobilité des travailleurs,* Paris, 1956; *Anpassung und Wiederbeschäftigung der Arbeiter,* Europäische Gemeinschaft für Kohle und Stahl, Studien und Dokumente, Luxembourg, 1956.

position in his old profession and locality and neglects the possibility of moving to a more promising area.[7]

But the resistance of domestic labor to the employment of foreigners is perhaps still more important. This resistance is largely due to antipathies arising from differences in language, religion, and background: the population of Europe is very heterogeneous. In addition to this, there is the fear that the assurance of employment will be endangered by the admission of foreign workers. Finally, it is assumed that immigration will lower the domestic level of wages. Moreover, the problem is complicated in many countries by housing scarcities.

The *present situation* seems in general to be characterized by the fact that an international agreement on immigration can be reached only with respect to those categories of workers in whom the industrial countries are directly interested over the short run and whose influx is not opposed by the domestic workers. In the countries with full employment and advanced industry, foreign workers are from time to time employed to overcome temporary and local bottlenecks, as well as to perform duties for which no domestic labor is available. In the first case, there is a short-term international immigration which often is not to the interest of the overpopulated country. In Switzerland, for instance, where many foreigners, particularly Italians, have been employed in times of increased labor demands, working permits have not been renewed when the demand decreased: "The immigrants come in last on the labor markets and they go out first."[8] The country of emigration is therefore in a favorable position only when its workers are employed in sectors which are shunned by the population in the country of immigration. The best examples are housekeeping and mining; the latter, in particular, is becoming less and less attractive to the workers of countries with advanced

[7] D. E. Christian, "Resistance to International Worker Mobility: A Barrier to European Unity," *Industrial and Labor Relations Review* (Cornell University, Ithaca, N.Y.), Vol. 8, No. 33 (April 1955); cited in ILO, *Social Aspects of European Economic Co-operation*, page 99.

[8] *Ibid.*, pp. 100ff.

industry. In some European countries (France, Luxembourg, and Switzerland), foreigners have also found employment in agriculture and construction.

International *capital transactions* can take numerous forms. For instance, exporters can grant short-term credits to importers. This is the normal way of financing international trade. On the other hand, short-term government credits serve the purpose of financing seasonal or other balance-of-payments deficits and surpluses. Long-term private capital transactions can take the form of "financial investments"—i.e., the transaction consists of the purchase, or the sale, of shares or bonds of foreign firms or governments—or of direct investment. Direct international investment takes place, for instance, when a firm sets up productive facilities abroad. Long-term government transactions, on the other hand, are highly significant, particularly for purposes of postwar reconstruction, the financing of armaments, and the development of underdeveloped areas.

The private export of capital in Europe has been narrowly limited since the breakdown of the international capital market in the beginning of the 1930's. A liberalization of the commodity trade might influence the direction and volume of private international investments. On one hand, the establishment of a common commodity market would stimulate such investments; the private export of capital would be promoted by reducing the risks of uncertain import restrictions. Moreover, if liberalization of trade could be supplemented by liberalization of payments transactions—thus eliminating the risks of repatriation of capital and the transfer of capital revenues— the pull of international investments could be further strengthened. The removal of protective measures in the capital-exporting country would also make some sectors less attractive for domestic investment, while other sectors with expanding export markets would absorb additional capital. In addition, the removal of trade barriers would eliminate some other obstacles to the export of capital which at present are still important.

Under a system of protection it sometimes pays to jump over national tariff barriers by an international investment. For instance, it has been observed that the considerable amounts of capital invested by American firms in West Europe after World War II had the purpose of coping with the dollar gap and the trade barriers resulting from it.

2. EQUALIZATION OF FACTOR PRICES

International trade has the function of increasing economic welfare. In the following, we will examine the question of whether free trade in commodities alone yields an absolute maximum of welfare or whether it needs to be supplemented by mobility of productive factors. As is well known, maximization of production and consequently, according to our criterion, maximization of welfare are characterized by the fact that, under free competition, the marginal productivity of a factor and hence its price are the same in all sectors and areas. Thus, if free trade leads to an absolute welfare maximum, equalization of factor prices would have to come about as a result of international commodity trade.

The influence of international trade on the relationship of international factor prices was first examined by Ohlin. His conclusions were the following: "A complete local adaptation of production through interregional factor movements and the resulting complete price equalization would make prices just the same as if there were only one region and no geographical distribution of the industrial agents. These would be used and combined just as is explained in the one-market theory. Space would be of no consequence. In such a state prices would be different from what they are when we have a number of isolated regions. Clearly, the state of prices, caused by interregional trade, . . . lies somewhere between these two extremes. The tendency is to push prices from the complete independence state to the complete equalization state, but it is not carried through. The price differences as regards the productive factors are reduced, but they do not disappear. Were the mobility of the productive factors between the regions free, then a leveling of their prices and a more effective combination of them could be brought about through a movement from the region where some of them are cheap to others where these factors are dearer. . . . There are, however, many more or less important obstacles to such movements and efficient combinations cannot be established in that way. There is nothing else to do but use them where they are and bring about a localization of production which suits the geographical distribution of factors as well as possible. In this indirect way a certain equalization of their prices and adjustment of their combinations take place through the interregional exchange of commodities. The total volume of production is increased. . . . Thus, the mobility of goods *to some extent* compensates the lack of interregional mobility of factors: or (what is really the same thing), trade mitigates the disadvantages of the unsuitable geographical distribution of the productive facilities. This is the cause of gain from interregional trade."[9]

Samuelson undertook to prove mathematically that Ohlin's thesis regarding the equalization of factor prices not only holds "to some extent" but also holds fully under certain conditions.[10]

Samuelson develops his antithesis to what he calls the "Oh-

[9] B. Ohlin, *Interregional and International Trade*, London-Cambridge, Mass., 1935, pp. 39-42 (italics added).
[10] P. A. Samuelson, "International Trade and the Equalisation of Factor Prices," *The Economic Journal* (1948), pp. 163ff., and "International Factor-Price Equalisation Once Again," *ibid.* (1949), pp. 181ff. A forerunner of Samuelson is A. P. Lerner; see his article written in 1933: "Factor Prices and International Trade," *Economica* (1952), pp. 1ff. See also B. Ohlin, *op.cit.*; J. Tinbergen, "The Equalization of Factor Prices between Free-Trade Areas," *Metroeconomica* (1949), pp. 39ff.; J. F. Pearce, "The Factor Price Equalization Myth," *The Review of Economic Studies* (1950-51), pp. 111ff.; E. Heckscher, "The Effect of Foreign Trade on the Distribution of Income," *Readings in the Theory of International Trade*, Philadelphia, 1949, pp. 272ff.; S. Laursen, "Production Functions and the Theory of International Trade," *The American Economic Review* (1952), pp. 240ff.; R. A. Mundell, "International Trade and Factor Mobility," *op.cit.*, pp. 321ff.

lin-Heckscher theorem" under the following assumptions: The same two commodities are produced in each of two countries; each of these commodities is manufactured with the same two productive factors (labor and land); the production functions are the same for both commodities in both countries; both production functions are linear-homogeneous—i.e., they are of the Cobb-Douglas type (if the employment of each of the two factors is increased by a certain percentage, the yield increases by the same percentage); the marginal productivities of both factors decrease with increasing production; the two commodities require different factor combinations, one commodity being land-intensive, the other labor-intensive; the quality of both factors is the same in both countries; both commodities are exchanged between both countries; there is mobility of commodities, but there is no factor mobility; there exist no trade barriers and transport costs are neglected; the price mechanism therefore works in such a way that, on the basis of the assumptions just mentioned and the assumption of free competition, the price ratios of both commodities are equal in both countries; finally, it is assumed that neither country specializes in the production of only one commodity.

From this set of data, Samuelson comes to the following conclusions: (1) So long as there is no specialization and each country produces both commodities, the prices of the factors in both countries will be absolutely and relatively equalized by international free trade. (2) Except when the factor endowment in the two countries differs too greatly, commodity mobility is, under the aforementioned assumptions, a perfect substitute for factor mobility. (3) Independent of the factor endowment of both countries and even when the labor factor is mobile, workers will have to migrate only to a limited extent. (4) To the extent that commodity exchange is a substitute for factor movement, world productivity is in a certain sense optimal; but marginal productivity of labor in one country and of land in the other country will be necessarily less than under a regime of national autarchy—and this both relatively and absolutely.

Under the condition of free trade without factor mobility, production normally reaches only a relative, but not an absolute, maximum. This means there are possible—and, as Samuelson himself admits, probable—situations in which the marginal product of a factor in one country is higher than in the other, so that full maximization of world production requires free factor mobility not only intranationally, but also internationally. Only when the earlier mentioned assumptions hold will complete immobility of the productive factors between the two countries not disturb maximization of production.

To illustrate this theorem by an example,[11] let us assume that suits and butter are manufactured in both countries, that transport costs can be neglected, that there is free trade in suits and butter (so that the price of these commodities is the same in both countries), and that suits are always labor-intensive, while butter is land-intensive. It is easy to see that free trade between countries A and B tends to equalize factor prices between A and B. Let us assume that A is provided with much land and few workers and B with many workers and little land, and, moreover, that the production of butter requires much land and little labor and the manufacture of suits much labor and little land. If the two countries do not trade with each other, the superfluous supply of land and the short supply of labor in A will cause rents to be low and wages high. The production of butter will therefore be cheap in A and that of suits expensive. The opposite holds, of course, for B— if the two countries start to trade, then B will import cheap butter from A and A will import cheap suits from B. This will lead to an increase in the demand for butter produced in A and to a decrease in the demand for suits produced in A; hence, the demand for land in A will be increased indirectly, while

[11] For this and the following, cf. J. E. Meade, *Trade and Welfare*, pp. 333ff.

the demand for labor will decrease, so that rents will rise and wages fall. The reverse process will occur in B, so that the differences in the factor prices of the two countries will tend to be equalized. Under the five conditions mentioned, this tendency will continue until the money wage rate and the nominal rent in A and B have each become equal.

Since we have assumed perfect competition and the production of both commodities in both countries, commodity prices will be equal to production costs. Since international exchange in the two commodities is free and costless, the price of butter and of suits in A will be the same as in B. From this it follows that the cost of a suit in A will be the same as in B, and similarly the cost of producing butter. If wage rates and rents in A and B were the same, the production costs of butter in A would be the same as in B, since production costs depend on factor prices only when the size of a firm and its place of establishment are irrelevant. Hence, if factor prices were the same, freer exchange of butter and suits between A and B could be combined with continued production of both commodities in both countries. But it is not enough to show that production costs are the same in both countries when factor prices in both countries are the same; it must also be proved that the factor prices in both countries *have to* be equal when product prices and thereby production costs are the same in both countries.

Let us start by assuming that wage rates and rents (and hence output costs) in A and B are at first the same, and that wages in A then rise and rents fall. If the rise in wages in A causes a greater increase in the production costs of labor-intensive suits than in the costs of land-intensive butter and when, as a result of the fall in rents, the production costs of land-intensive butter fall more than the costs of labor-intensive suits, this rise in wages and fall in rents will raise the costs of producing suits relative to the costs of producing butter.

But since the price of butter and suits in B has remained unchanged, the increase in the production costs of suits relative to those of butter will be incompatible with equilibrium in free trade. The demand will shift from suits of A to those of B and from butter of B to that of A—i.e., the forces which bring about the equalization of factor prices in both countries are actually the same. One can conclude from this that the marginal productivity of each factor will be the same in A and B, not only in the two special free-trade industries but in every industry that the two countries have in common. This also will occur in sectors which produce for the domestic market only. Even in those industries which exist in only one country, the marginal productivity of both factors, measured in products which are manufactured in only one of the two countries, will be the same. It should be noted that this result does not depend on the assumption that only two products are manufactured in only two countries, and that free trade is also related to other than these two products.

If one of the stated conditions is not fulfilled, a transfer of factors between the two countries becomes inevitable. First, we will examine how the thesis that free trade is a substitute for the movement of factors must be modified, if it is acknowledged that production costs are influenced by differences in production conditions and in output volume.

Let us assume that the conditions for production are in general more favorable in A than in B. A given quantity of land, labor, and capital will in this case yield more in A than in B. It is then significant in which country the factors are located. It is furthermore assumed that labor, land, and capital will be employed in the same ratio in every industry in A and B. The conditions for production being generally better in A, the productivity of each factor in each industry of A will be, let us say, 10 per cent above the productivity of the same factor in the corresponding sector of B. Under these conditions, prices and costs would be the same for each product in both countries. In contrast to the previous example, the real marginal productivity and therefore the real and money remuneration of each factor is 10 per cent higher in A than in B. However,

235

free trade is incompatible with a lasting surplus of marginal productivities in A. In order to guarantee maximization of production, factors must move from B to A.

However, the land factor cannot be shifted; if labor and capital move from A to B, the marginal productivity of land in B will become smaller and smaller—i.e., land becomes less and less scarce in relation to labor and capital. On the other hand, the marginal productivity of land in A will rise continuously. If the mobility of factors is completely free and costless, a new equilibrium will be attained if the marginal productivities of labor and capital have fallen somewhat below their original high level in B. But the result is that the original discrepancy between the rents of A and B will become still more pronounced, for the marginal productivity of land rises in A, where it was already higher at the start, and falls in B, where it was already lower. A further increase in world production could take place only if land were also mobile.

This extreme result is based on special assumptions. In reality, the superior conditions for production in A will not be general, but will be more favorable for *one* product or for the employment of *one* factor in one country than in the other. When the conditions for individual production processes and/or the employment of factors vary between two countries, maximization of world production always requires mobility of commodities as well as of factors.

Similar modifications occur when the production functions in the two countries differ. Let us assume that country A is larger than country B, in the sense that it is endowed with more land, labor, and capital and can therefore produce more than B; that the marginal revenues increase with increasing production in all industries, either because some of the employed factors are indivisible during certain intervals of the production function, or because mass production creates favorable conditions for production; finally, that the remuneration which each factor receives in the two countries equals the value of its social marginal product. The average productivity of factors will be higher in large country A than in small country B under these conditions: the yield per employed factor unit will be higher in A than in B. But it remains uncertain in which country the marginal productivity of the factors will be greater. If "increasing returns to scale" mean that large savings could be made by expanding the industry in B beyond the threshold of mass production, but all these savings have already been realized in A, since the industries there have already crossed the threshold, marginal factor productivity may be considerably higher in B than in A. The employment of small additional quantities of factors in B would result in considerable new savings by increasing the volume of output, so that the additional productivity of the additional factors can be very high, even when the average yield per factor is relatively low. On the other hand, if the advantages of mass production become effective only at the production volume that is usual in A (and that is considerably larger than in B), the average as well as the marginal productivity of the factors will be higher in A than in B. If the advantages of mass production are important, then it is purely accidental when the marginal productivity in the small country is as high as that in the big country.

Let us assume that free trade has led to the same price for butter and suits in both countries; the ratio of labor to land in A and B is the same in both the production of butter and that of suits. If, as a result of mass production relationships, the marginal productivity of the factors becomes higher in A than in B, the mobile factor of labor should move from B to A in order to increase world production: the ratio of labor to land will rise in A and drop in B, and the marginal productivity of labor will fall in A and rise in B. If the marginal productivities of the two countries are equal, no further movement of factors would be necessary.

Now, let us assume that transport costs are taken into account. Country A has much land, country B is amply provided with labor, the production of suits is labor-intensive and that of butter land-intensive, and both countries produce both commodities. In this case, either products or factors can be exchanged in order to increase productivity. Both movements incur costs. The costs of transporting commodities have to be weighed against the costs of transporting the factors of production when it comes to deciding whether commodity exchange or factor transfer would be the best solution.

Various elements play a part in the costs of migration: first, physical transportation involves costs. These can be converted into annual costs at the usual interest rate. If the transport costs amount to 1000 francs and the interest rate is 5 per cent, a burden of 50 francs per year results. If the interest rate is an exact measure of the marginal utility of capital, the transportation of labor absorbs means which would correspond to a future additional yield of 50 francs if they had been used instead to supplement the capital equipment of the country. This loss must be compared with the increase in wages in order to determine whether the increase in annual wages compensates for the annual interest costs of transportation.

In addition, there are less tangible migration costs, such as the discomforts of a change in environment, etc. These intangible costs could be determined only by examining the problem of what margin between net earnings in the new country and wages in the old country is necessary to induce the worker to move.

The matter of transport costs is more difficult to discuss with respect to international capital transfer. Since we continuously assume in this discussion that the balance of payments between countries A and B is kept in equilibrium by the measures previously described, and that full employment is assured in both countries (through the mechanism of the gold standard or variable exchange rates), B must have an export surplus in its trade with A during the period in which capital is transferred from B to A. Only in this way can country B maintain a surplus in its current account which will suffice to compensate the autonomous transfer of capital from B to A.

Hence there is a monetary and commercial aspect to international capital investment. Let us assume that an inhabitant of B invests capital in A instead of B. The monetary aspect then consists of the purchase of foreign currency by the saver in B in order to invest it in a foreign enterprise. If there are no foreign exchange controls or taxes on the transfer of capital, these transactions incur only very small real costs to pay for the services of the institutions concerned with international capital transfer. Of course, there are also certain intangible costs, but they are negligible in this case.

If we consider the real commercial aspect of international investment, problems of a quite different character arise. A real (in contrast to a purely financial) investment in A instead of in B means that the exports from B to A must exceed the imports of B from A to an amount which is equal to the value of the real investment. This does not always and in all circumstances mean that, for instance, an additional machine has to be transported from B to A. In this case, additional transport costs would occur. It is also possible that country A has exported machines to B in the past. The investment of capital for a machine in A instead of in B might mean in this case that A would export one machine less to B. Then the saving of transport costs as a result of the drop in the machine export of A would have to be taken into account. The balance-of-payments surplus of B might also mean that more consumption goods are exported to A and less of them imported by A, so that A can employ its factors in, for instance, constructing an airport instead of growing wheat. Transport costs are important here, too: if the surplus stems from a reduction of imports, there is a saving of transport charges; if it stems from an increase in exports, additional transport costs occur. In examining the costs of international capital movements, not only do the direct costs of the international transfer of capital have to be considered, but also the increase or decrease in capital costs which stems from an increased or decreased flow of commodities, the real basis of the capital transfer between A and B.

239

If we take into account the transport cost of products as well as of factors, we must for another reason make a distinction between international migration of labor and international movement of capital. Labor is not only a productive factor: economic welfare obtained from the enjoyment of goods and leisure is, after all, the objective of all economic policy. If workers migrate from B to A, not only a certain number of factor units have been shifted, but also a certain number of consumers. On the other hand, if a machine is assembled in A instead of in B, the owner of the machine can stay in B, where he is a consumer. The effect on the balance of payments will be different. If a worker moves from B to A, the current account need not always and under all circumstances change if he consumes his whole income before and after the migration. However, if capital has moved from B to A, the dividends are consumed in B although they have been earned in A. Hence, a surplus in A's current account will develop, the value of which must be equal to that of the dividends which are transferred from A to B. This means an increase in A's exports if the consumption of dividends consists of A's export products, or a decrease of B's exports if the consumption includes products which B exports. In the first case, additional transport costs occur for the export from A to B; in the second case, there is a saving in transport charges. As a result, there are significant differences between the theory of labor mobility and that of international capital movements.

To summarize the causes of migrations, (1) emigration of labor is justified only when this movement is required for maximizing production. (2) The cost of transporting products between two countries tends to increase the marginal productivity of labor in the country in which labor is a relatively scarce factor and to decrease it in the country in which it is relatively abundant. If the costs of migration are small, the movement of workers from the country with the lower marginal product to the country with the higher marginal product results in a private as well as a social advantage. (3) In considering the question of when migration costs prohibit migration, one has to take into account what part of the transport costs of products that cause the migration arose from the transport of products from A to B and what part from the transport of products from B to A; what part of the new incomes of the emigrants is sent back from A to B; to what extent the emigrant workers spend their income on products which are exported by A or by B. (4) If the workers who emigrate to A send the larger part of their income back to B, the desirability of migrating from B to A will be greatest when only a small share of the transport costs are incurred by land-intensive products which are exported from A to B and the labor-intensive products which B exports to A are burdened by high transport charges. If no money is remitted to B, it does not matter whether the transport costs, which are the heart of the whole problem, are incurred through the export of butter from A to B or through the export of suits from B to A. (5) To the extent that the workers do not send their income back to country B, the desirability of migration will be greater, the more of their income the workers spend in A on land-intensive products than on labor-intensive ones. The greater the share of their incomes which the workers remit to B, the less relevant this point becomes.

These conclusions also apply to international capital movements. But one additional factor must always be considered in the case of capital mobility. The transfer of wages and dividends which have been earned in A to country B for the purpose of consumption in B implies the creation of an export surplus in A's current account. We have previously shown that for this reason the transfer of a factor from B to A (in the form of labor emigration from B to A or an international investment) is the more desirable, the higher the transport costs of B's exports and the lower the transport costs of A's exports. The transfer of capital from B to A represents an effective transfer of real capital only if it is accompanied by an export surplus in B's current account, while the transfer of labor can take place without the creation of such a surplus. If the capital movement from B takes the form of an increase in the demand in A, and a decrease in the demand in B, for capital goods which are exported from A to B, then the surplus in B's current account stems from the reduction in imports of those commodities. If the transportation of such goods from A to B is costly, the capital movement implies a saving in transport costs and therefore becomes desirable.

The aspects so far discussed indicate the most important reasons why in the real world free trade without factor mobility does not suffice to maximize world production. Still to be discussed are the first two Samuelson conditions, wherein we assume that there are no differences in production conditions and production functions or in transport costs for the products in question. We assume furthermore that country A as well as B manufactures land-intensive butter and labor-intensive suits; that the labor and land factors are employed, and that the land-to-labor ratio is higher in A than in B; that A imports suits and B imports butter; and that the marginal productivities of land and labor in A and B, expressed in both products, are the same.

If, under these conditions, A expands the output of butter and B the manufacture of suits, the absence of a third productive factor has the result that the marginal productivity of land depends only on the ratio in which land and labor are used and is analogous to the marginal productivity of labor. (As we have already indicated, the marginal productivity of each factor is the same in each industry in A and B, if the land-to-labor ratio is the same in both industries in the two countries.) We now introduce into this model the third productive factor, capital, and assume that A has more capital than country B—i.e., that the capital-to-land and the capital-to-labor ratios are higher in A than in B. Furthermore, it is assumed that the capital intensity in producing butter and suits is about the same, in the sense that with given rents, wages, and interest, the share of the production costs that results from the use of capital is the same in both industries. More capital is used in A than in B, since capital is cheaper in A. The marginal productivity of capital is therefore low in both industries in A, while the marginal productivities of land and labor are high; the opposite holds for country B.

There is no reason to assume that the introduction of the capital factor in both economies does not affect, *ceteris paribus*, the cost of butter relative to that of suits. For instance, if capital plays a more important part in the manufacture of suits than of butter, taking each factor into account will considerably reduce the production costs of suits relative to those of butter in A. This effect will be less pronounced in B, where less capital is used. An adjustment cannot be obtained by free trade. The consumers in A will buy less butter and more suits, and those in B more butter and fewer suits. This implies an increase in demand for labor and a decrease in demand for land in country A, and consequently a rise in wages and a fall in rents. Since the reverse process will take place in B, prices and costs will become equal. The ultimate equilibrium is then characterized as follows: the wage rate will be higher in A than in B, since A has more capital at its disposal than B. This tendency is reinforced by expansion of the labor-intensive manufacture of suits in A (contraction in B). Rents will probably be somewhat higher in B for the same reason. This tendency is weakened, however, by the contraction of land-intensive butter production in A (expansion in B). The interest rate will be lower in A than in B, since the marginal productivity of capital in A is lower. This discrepancy exists despite a partial equalization by the expansion of the capital-intensive production of suits in A (contraction in B). But this effect is only weak, since much more labor than capital is used in the production of suits and much more land than capital in the production of butter. The interest rate therefore plays a less important part in the equalization process than wages and rents.

The situation changes profoundly if a third commodity—for instance, chemicals which are produced in both countries in highly capital-intensive industries—is exchanged between A and B. We will assume that the production of suits is definitely labor-intensive, that of butter definitely land-intensive, and that of chemicals definitely capital-intensive. Let the wages and rents in A be very much higher and the interest rates in A be very much lower than in B. Under these circumstances, free trade will lead to an expansion of chemical production and to a contraction of the production of suits and butter. This raises the demand for capital and lowers the demand for labor and land, so that the interest rate rises to the level of country B and wages and rents drop to the level of country B. The reverse process will take place in B. Then an equilibrium will establish itself in which all three products are manufactured in both countries with the same factor ratio in each industry and with the same marginal productivity of each factor in both countries. (Complications will show up if the complementarity and substitution relationships among factors are taken into consideration.)

Our argument up to now holds only when the relevant industries in both countries continue to exist. If complete specialization takes place, the problem will be different. Let us assume that country A is much smaller than B and has less land and labor. Let us further assume that consumers in A and in B spend a larger share of their incomes on butter than on suits. There are considerable differences between A and B in factor endowment; the land-to-labor ratio is higher in A than in B. At the first trading stage, A will export butter to B and B suits to A, and the previously described process tending toward equalization will begin. As a consequence of our assumptions, it is now possible, however, that country A may cease manufacturing suits before full equalization has become a fact. Since country B is very large, its manufacture of suits need expand only a little to satisfy the demand in A as well. The contraction of butter production in B will for the same reason be very small in comparison with the total butter production in B. Great disparities between the marginal productivities of A and B will also continue to exist when A has stopped the production of suits. Wages will fall very little in A and rise still less in B, and rents will rise little in A and fall still less in B. When A has stopped producing suits, free trade can no longer bring about an equalization of factor prices.

We have shown that no more than two commodities need be present for a complete equalization of factor prices in the case of two factors, provided that the exchange of these goods is completely free and without costs and that they are produced in both countries. Duties on other commodities are fully compatible with equalization of factor prices. The situation is different in the case of specialization; in that case, it really matters how many commodities are subject to free trade. The more commodities are taxed with duties, the sooner will there be specialization in those products which can be freely exchanged. It is difficult to predict which conditions have to be fulfilled so that, in the case of numerous products and factors, free trade will lead only to an equalization of the marginal productivity of each factor in each industry.

The following influences are the most important ones: (1) The smaller the difference in the original factor endowment of the two countries, the sooner will free trade lead to equality of marginal productivities. (2) The smaller the number of productive factors in each country, the sooner will free trade lead to equality of factor prices. (3) The larger the number of products that are produced in each country, the larger will be the number of channels through which free trade can make its equalizing influence felt. (4) The larger the number of products which are freely exchanged between the two countries, the larger will be the area in which factor prices are influenced by free trade. (5) The more difference there is in the ratios in which the various factors are employed in the production of single commodities, the stronger will be the influence of free trade on the relative demand for individual factors in both countries. (6) The more pronounced the labor-, land- and capital-intensity of the individual products, the sooner will free trade work toward equalization of factor prices in both countries.[12]

As we have already indicated in our examination of free commodity trade, numerous situations are conceivable in which there is some justification for departing from the principle of free trade. In the case of mobility of productive factors, similar situations exist. We will first discuss the extent to which a policy of income redistribution[13] undertaken by individual countries modifies the freedom of international factor movements and gives cause for *controls*. A country can influence its income distribution by a series of direct controls and interventions. It can, for instance, reduce the prices of essential commodities by subsidies and ration the supply available to the consumers in order to guarantee all citizens a fair share; moreover, it can limit the production volume of those goods which are consumed by the well-to-do strata of society. Such a system of controls is incompatible with equalization of prices and marginal utility—i.e., it encroaches upon the principles according to which a uniform, integrated, and free market should be organized.

The desired income and property distribution can, however, also be obtained by way of general fiscal policies. These may include a progressive income tax, progressive death duties

[12] An empirical examination of the equalization of factor prices—i.e., in this case, of real wages—has been conducted by the statistical department of the High Authority of the European Coal and Steel Community for industries with which it is concerned. The analysis gave the following result: "Gross wages rose from 1953 to the middle of 1956 in all industries and all countries of the Community; it was clear that this progress was to a large extent the same in the various countries—apart from some cases in Italy." This equalization was not due to interventions of the High Authority—which could, according to the treaty, exert at best only an indirect influence on wages, a power of which no use has been made up to now—but to the liberalization of commodity flows and to greater factor mobility. However, in the case of a merely partial integration, the assumptions are not the same as in the case of free trade, on which our examples were based. Compare *Die Arbeitereinkommen der Industrien der Gemeinschaft im Realvergleich*, Europäische Gemeinschaft für Kohle und Stahl, Studien und Dokumente, Luxembourg, 1956, page 149.

[13] Cf. J. E. Meade, *Problems of Economic Union*, pp. 56ff.

on property, and the payment of social security benefits, such as children's allowances, unemployment benefits, sickness benefits, etc. Such policies would be compatible with integration since they do not seriously change relative prices. Stated differently: neither optimization of trade nor maximization of production would be jeopardized.

However, if one country goes further with its income redistribution policy than another country, there can exist a strong incentive for factors of production to move in an uneconomic way between the countries. Let us assume that country A has a system of substantial redistribution, while country B has done little in this respect. The emigration of unskilled labor from A to B can then be prevented by the higher social security benefits paid in A, though the marginal revenue of labor is actually higher in B than in A. Highly paid specialists and property-owners could migrate from A to B and take their property with them to evade the high tax rates in A, though the marginal productivity of capital may be basically higher in A than in B.

Despite this effect, movements of labor and capital inside the economic union from the regions with lower productivity to the regions with higher productivity remain, of course, desirable. But it is possible that these regions may no longer be identical with the regions with higher and lower *net* earnings. Planned or supervised factor mobility inside the union may prove necessary under these circumstances. But, if such co-ordinated planning among states which have previously been independent creates undue difficulties, from an economic point of view it will be better in many cases to prevent the migration of factors altogether than to introduce complete freedom of movement for capital and labor. This must be done when there are such extreme differences in the social and economic policies directed toward redistribution of income and property that a migration of productive factors in the wrong direction would result.

The member states, therefore, must either keep pace with

one another with respect to redistribution measures or forgo the possibility of increasing their standard of living by the formation of a common market with free mobility of labor and capital. Hence, social redistribution measures could be a cause for considerable curtailment of internal freedom of action even in the case of complete economic unification.

It may also be necessary to control factor movements for reasons of stability. Difficulties arise here particularly from the mobility of capital. Let us assume that two partners of an economic union are threatened by inflation and both countries intend to combat the inflationary demand for goods and services by restricting investment expenditures. Country B tries to achieve this goal by monetary policy: it reduces the supply of available capital in the capital market and thereby raises the interest rate and the costs of contracting new loans. Country A, on the other hand, does not resort to this policy, so that the interest rate does not rise. Instead, A reduces expenditures for investments by way of direct controls—i.e., by requiring licenses for new construction, by fixing steel rations, etc. Under these circumstances, B's interest rate can rise far above that of A, while the actual productivity of capital in B can continue to be much lower than in A. In such cases, steps will be considered to prevent the flow of capital from A to B. But going too far on the road of direct controls on investment expenditures can thwart the recombinations of capital and labor that are required to maximize production.

Such difficulties not only arise from direct controls on investments, but could also result from other economic policies. Let us again assume that B combats inflationary pressure with a monetary measure while A takes fiscal action. The effect in B will be the same as in the last example. The interest rates in A, however, will remain the same. The authorities in A will acquire a large budget surplus as the result of the rise in tax rates. Individual consumers will therefore be forced to give up part of their consumption. Disinflation is not the result of a dear-money policy limiting investments, but of high tax rates restricting consumption and raising savings in the public sector. Under these circumstances, there can exist a strong, temporary incentive for capital to move from A, where interest rates are low, to B, where interest rates have risen. This capital movement need not be economical. Investment activity in B has been reduced and consequently the marginal productivity of capital has risen there. Country A has decided, contrary to country B, to combat inflation by increasing savings and, according to the laws of the international capital market, part of the high savings of A will be invested in B. In order to finance this export of capital, A needs a surplus in its current account, while B's current account must have a deficit. This can be brought about by an adjustment of the exchange rate between the two currencies, as we have discussed before. If the economic policies directed toward combating inflation in both countries were permanent, it would be desirable to adjust the current account as required. However, if these policies only manifest different methods of combating temporary inflationary pressure, it might prove necessary to subject capital movements between the two countries to a certain control.

A third argument in favor of controlling factor movements lies in the fact that neither the number of people in a country nor the supply of capital will remain constant in the long run.[14] Let us assume that country A eliminates the duties on certain products. This will result in an increase in demand for these products from B and the real income per capita of the original population in B will rise. How the increase manifests itself will depend, above all, on the policy of income redistribution in B. If there is an equal distribution of income, then all the inhabitants of B will experience an increase in real income. On the other hand, if factor incomes vary with marginal productivities, labor income could drop sharply, with the effect that elimination of the duties will result in a reduction in the

[14] Cf. J. E. Meade, *Trade and Welfare*, pp. 460ff.

demand for labor-intensive products of country B; the other factors would then enjoy higher incomes.

This effect depends furthermore on the way individual classes react to a change in their real income. An increase in the standard of living can lead either to population pressure, as Malthus has described, or—completely in contradiction to Malthus' prognosis, but in accordance with numerous historic examples—to a decline in the birth rate. If there is a strong pressure of population in country B with an even distribution of income, the marginal productivity of labor will be low and that of capital high. If A does not suffer from such a strong pressure of population, capital will probably flow from A to B. This factor movement in its turn will influence the growth of the population: the influx of capital will raise the standard of living in B; however, it will soon fall again to the physical minimum of subsistence as a result of the pressure of population. The only effect will ultimately be that a larger population lives in poverty in country B.

This result stands under the assumption of labor immobility. However, if country A opened its territory to the inhabitants of country B, this would result in an increase of the population of country B and thereby increase the distress in the entire world—consisting, in our example, of A and B. Nevertheless, the original inhabitants of A could be favored by a redistributive fiscal policy: if A does not include the immigrants from B in such a policy, the original inhabitants of A could gain from the immigration of citizens of B and the population originating in B could not grow either in A or in B to the extent that it would if A included all inhabitants in its redistributive system. However, the distinction between two classes of population in A—one of which would consist of well-to-do, old-time inhabitants of A, and the other of destitute immigrants from the poor country, B—would pose serious problems of a non-economic character. Only when the number of people in both countries is kept within certain limits will free labor mobility from the country with lower productivity to the country with higher productivity necessarily lead to a rise in the average standard of living.

Finally, changes in international economic policy will also affect the supply of capital. For instance, let us assume that an obstacle to commodity trade or to factor movement between countries A and B is removed. This will normally lead to an increase in productivity. The general real-income level in the world (consisting of the two countries) will rise and savings will perhaps increase as a result. The extent to which savings will rise depends not only on the absolute height of real income, but also on its distribution between and inside the countries. The more the change in commercial policy affects the terms of trade in favor of B, the greater the share of the increase in world income that will accrue to the inhabitants of B. Now, if real income per capita is lower in B than in A, the share of savings in the increase of world income will be smaller, since the marginal propensity to save will be smaller in B than in A as a result of B's lower income. It is even possible that there will be an absolute decline in total savings if the terms of trade change so much in favor of B that a drop occurs in the real income per capita in A, in which the marginal propensity to save is high. Similar results are obtained from an examination of the distribution of income inside the two countries.

Our treatise applied thus far only to the world level of savings. This procedure is legitimate if no natural or artificial obstacles discriminate against the transfer of capital between A and B. If this capital movement entails costs, the volume of savings in A and B have to be examined separately: the accumulation of capital could be more productive in B than in A, and consequently saving in B more desirable than in A.

The volume of savings is not only a function of income and its distribution, but also perhaps of the interest rate. However, since the latter functional relationship cannot be established unambiguously, we abstract from the impact of economic political measures on the interest rate.

251

CONCLUDING REMARKS

THE BOOK PRESENTED HERE was written in 1957. Hence the elaboration of some theoretical aspects of economic integration occurred in a period in which the object of this theoretical examination became a political reality. At that time, only the European Coal and Steel Community served the authors as an empirical example of Continental unification. Now, at the beginning of 1958, the treaty for the European Economic Union has become effective. The six signatories of the Schuman Treaty thereby set out on the road from partial to overall integration, to the Common Market which includes all sectors. The *dynamisme interne,* in the effectiveness of which the founders of the Coal and Steel Community put their confidence, has brought us definitely closer to the goal of European unity.

It is therefore not due to the merit of the authors that several sections of the expositions given above have at the moment particular relevance. Many problems facing the executive organs of the European Economic Union have already been dealt with theoretically in the latest economic literature. However, when one takes into account the precarious situation in which the Common Market had to be established, it becomes clear that most of the theoretical solutions were based on political assumptions which deviated considerably from reality. The Treaty of Rome did not resolve all the difficulties involved.

In the first place, a serious obstacle to the liberalization of commercial and payments transactions in Little Europe must be mentioned: the currency reserves of some member countries have dropped to a critical minimum or even hover in the neighborhood of zero. The failure of all-round economic stabilization even led to new import restrictions on the eve of the ratification of the Common Market treaty. The cause of this backward move and of numerous other disintegrative measures lay in balance-of-payments deficits. Each new request to live up to the principles of free trade will be doomed so long as trade between the European countries is not in equilibrium. If sporadic recourse to restrictions is to be eliminated, the trade partners must be willing to coordinate their economic policies.

This crux of integration was recognized in the Treaty of Rome only as a general directive. But since the unification of Little Europe follows the institutional method, according to the treaty, it can be expected that the organs of the European Economic Union will be forced to take steps toward the coordination of their monetary, fiscal, wage, and price policies.

Coordination is the *conditio sine qua non* for a permanent recovery of trade inside Europe. We must reconcile ourselves to the fact that free trade no longer permits unrestricted national sovereignty. But once the economic policies of the partner countries are in line, the framework for a Continental market is present and the condition for an increase in European welfare has been fulfilled.

Integration, in the sense of the institutional method, means in the European Economic Union, among other things, that all the necessary institutions of a new state are already present in rudimentary form: the *Council*, which represents the governments of the member countries and must strive to coordinate their economic policies; the *Assembly*, the members of which are selected by the parliaments of the partner countries and which is granted certain control powers; the *Court*, which has to decide on the interpretation of the treaty and other constitutional questions concerning it; and, finally, the *Commission* of nine members, which as an actual supranational authority must watch over the fulfillment of the stipulations in the agreement and place proposals before the Council and the Assembly. The provision to have Council resolutions passed by a qualified majority as a rule and gradually to remove the right of veto, retained initially for various questions, as well as the strong position granted both the Commission and the Assembly, shows a disposition to provide the Community with more and more authority and with increasing decision-making powers.

This divergence between the goal of a complete economic union and the rudimentary supranational powers needed for the pursuit of a common economic policy makes it seem likely that the development of the Economic Union will follow a course similar to that of the national integration of feudalist economies in the nineteenth century. For instance, the general directions for the coordination of internal and external stabilization incorporated in the treaty do not provide the supranational authority with the power to force the national governments to take uniform action. For example, it is said of the policy of combating depression: "The member countries consider this policy . . . as a matter of common interest. They will try to come to an understanding with each other and with the Commission about the steps which have to be taken under the circumstances of the moment" (Art. 103, Section 1). A similar arrangement has been made for the adjustment of the national balances of payments and for exchange rate policy. The vagueness in these regulations could not be avoided at the time when the Treaty of Rome was formulated. However, it will become more and more clear in the future that the common interests of the partners compel harmonization and synchronization despite insufficient legal foundations.

The provision for majority decisions and the unlimited duration of the treaty guarantee that the economic objectives of a unified Europe will be attained earlier in the European Economic Union than in a Free Trade Area. To be sure, a Free Trade Area of all the OEEC countries together would have the advantage, compared with the Common Market of the six states, of comprising a larger economic area, so that the trade-diverting forces would be less effective; moreover, the discrimination resulting from uniform tariffs for countries outside the Common Market would be eliminated, for the other OEEC countries, by the formation of a Free Trade Area. But this does not mean that the Free Trade Area as such does not carry the stigma of discrimination. In reality, the expansion of exchange in the Free Trade Area would be achieved partly at the cost of a contraction in trade with the outside world; the disadvantages of discrimination are therefore also in this case shifted to the non-member states. Logically, the advocates of universal trade should therefore be as skeptical about the Free Trade Area as about the Common Market. Since they are not, one might suspect that the Free Trade Area, despite its possible justification as a transitional mechanism, represents a proposal made for defensive purposes only and was not aimed at sabotaging the Common Market.

Apart from the advantage of a larger geographic extent, the Free Trade Area suffers from all the shortcomings of the Treaty of Rome, without guaranteeing even one of that treaty's advantages. First of all, the aim of those who advocate the Free Trade Area is purely commercial and hence corresponds in that respect to functional integration. All attempts at coordination that go further than that are blocked from the very beginning, as a result of the intention to adhere to the principle of unanimity, preserved in the OEEC. The potential member countries are therefore not prepared to give up any essential national powers whatsoever. But the experience of the postwar period clearly indicates that permanent free trade cannot be attained without the transfer of powers to supranational authorities.

The members of the Free Trade Area give up only part of even their commercial sovereignty, for national duties continue to be effective for the rest of the world. From this results a special difficulty: the necessity of certificates of origin. The liberal character that is often ascribed to the Free Trade Area could therefore prove to be illusive; first, because certificates of origin require continued control of commodities and services at the border; and, second, controlling the origin of imports entails an administrative protectionism which can disturb international trade as much as, or more than, taxation by way of duties.

Hardly ever in the course of history have attempts at integration been based so little on feelings and so much on reason as in the case of uniting Western Europe. Thus far, emotional forces have always proved to be the most powerful motive powers of national unification, though one should not forget that the German Customs Union was brought into being by the bureaucracies of various countries after the emotional advocates for unification like Friedrich List had been stigmatized and forced into exile. A feeling of solidarity strong enough to hasten Continental unification to the extent required by the world situation is lacking in any case in Europe today. Hence, if the Continent wishes to prevent its decline at this critical point in its history, the great mass of the people must for once be brought to the point where they do not follow irrational passions but bow to the laws of logic that guide the architects of the European Economic Union.

INDEX

functional method, 84-87; institutional method, 87-98; liberalization of trade, 99-100; national, 91-95; period of transition, 105-10; political, 43f., 252-56

International Labor Office, 90, 107, 109, 215, 226, 227

International Monetary Fund, 41, 126, 142, 153f., 177

intervention, government: commercial controls, 35-37; financial controls, 31-35

investments, 15, 239f.; of Coal and Steel Community, 100f.

iron and steel industry, 5-9, 99f. *See also* European Coal and Steel Community

Isard, W., 100

Italian economy, 89f.

Johnson, H. G., 15

Johnston, B., 15

Jürgensen, H., 22

Kahn, R. F., 215

Kaldor, N., 121

Keiser, G., 76, 81

Keynes, J. M., 3, 42, 111, 133, 141, 146

Kindleberger, C., 40

Kravis, G. B., 11, 16

Kuenne, R. E., 100

Laursen, S., 123, 141, 231

Leontief, W., 19

Lerner, A. P., 116, 231

liberalization of trade, 88, 99-100

Lipsey, R. G., 46

List, F., 27, 256

Lutz, F., 163

Maddison, A., 11, 14

Makower, H., 46

Malthus, T. R., 250

Marshall, A., 116

maximization, of production, 23f., 190f., 230; of welfare, 20, 24, 43, 69-71, 190f., 230f.

Meade, J. E., 21, 28, 32, 40, 42, 46, 59, 71, 73, 97, 113, 115, 116, 122, 124, 137, 160, 163, 167,

177, 182, 184, 185, 215, 233, 246, 249

Mendershausen, H., 82, 201, 218

Metzler, L. A., 123, 141

migration of labor, 224-29, 240f.; causes, 240f.; in Benelux, 225f.; in Coal and Steel Community, 226; in Scandinavia, 227; obstacles, 227f.

Mill, J. S., 26

mobility of commodities, 231-35

mobility of productive factors, 89, 155-59, 190, 225-28, 237-51; capital, 156f., 229f., 241; controls, 246-51; in Europe, 224-30; labor, 158f., 224-29, 240f.

Modigliani, F., 19

money, quantity of, 136-37, 143f.

Morton, G., 46

Mundell, R. A., 231

Myrdal, G., 88, 91, 96, 224, 225

Neumark, F., 215

Ohlin, B., 90, 231

Ohlin-Heckscher theorem, 231-33

Orcutt, G. H., 123

Organization for European Economic Cooperation (OEEC), 10, 41, 77f., 80, 81, 86f., 199, 225

origin principle of taxation, 200-13

Paris Club, 176

Parker, W. N., 100

Parrish, J. B., 5, 8, 100

payments controls, 168-73

Pearce, J. F., 231

Perroux, F., 84

production maximization, 23f., 190f., 230

protectionism, methods, 31-37; motives, 24-31. *See also* free trade, deviations from

Pounds, N. J. G., 100

redistribution policy, 94f., 246-48

Regul, R., 216

restrictions of imports, quantitative, 35-37, 66-68, 73-76, 117, 145f.; import licenses, 73f.

Reuter, P., 4, 105, 110

GPSR Authorized Representative: Easy Access System Europe - Mustamäe tee
50, 10621 Tallinn, Estonia, gpsr.requests@easproject.com

www.ingramcontent.com/pod-product-compliance
Lightning Source LLC
Chambersburg PA
CBHW050411280326
41932CB00013BA/1812